D0988642

People Movements
in
the Punjab

Andrew Gordon, first United Presbyterian missionary
to the Punjab.

from OUR INDIA MISSION

People Movements
in
the Punjab

with special reference to
the united presbyterian church

frederick and
margaret stock

William Carey Library

SOUTH PASADENA, CALIF.

In accord with some of the most recent thinking in the academic press, the William Carey Library is pleased to present
this scholarly book which has been prepared from an author-
edited and author-prepared camera-ready manuscript.

Library of Congress Cataloging in Publication Data

Stock, Frederick, 1929-
    People movements in the Punjab.

    Bibliography: p.
    1. Presbyterian Church in Punjab, Pakistan
(Province) 2. Missions--Punjab, Pakistan (Province)
3. Sects--Pakistan--Punjab (Province) I. Stock,
Margaret, 1929-   joint author. II. Title.
BX9151.P18S76   266'.51'54914   74-18408
ISBN 0-87808-417-7

Published by the William Carey Library
533 Hermosa Street
South Pasadena, Calif. 91030
Telephone 213-799-4559

PRINTED IN THE UNITED STATES OF AMERICA

We lovingly dedicate this book to
Mom and Dad (Mr. and Mrs. F. J. Stock)
who patiently did our housework,
carefully proof-read our manuscript and
lovingly cared for our five children
to make this book possible.

Contents

APPENDIX

A BRIEF COMPARATIVE STUDY OF OTHER CHURCHES IN PAKISTAN

Contents

Figures

Foreword

I. In 1974, at least nineteen-twentieths of the members
of the Church in Pakistan--Presbyterian, Methodist,
Anglican, Baptist, Roman Catholic and Salvation Army--
are descendants of men and women who were born Hindus
and became Christians in Chuhra people movements from
1880 to 1930. The remaining twentieth is composed of
descendants of individual converts from the Muslim, caste
Hindu, and European communities.

During the last hundred years a Christian population of about 900,000 has been built up. Its top
echelons are filled with able men and women--holding
positions of responsibility. The middle ranks are composed of peasant farmers of small holdings, mechanics,
artizans, petty clerks, servants, and respectable lower
class Pakistani citizens. The bottom ranks are made up
of Christian sweepers and landless labor, living under
difficult conditions. L. Vemmelund's study of the 15,607
Christians in the Northwest Frontier Province sets forth
the conditions of these last in distressing detail.

How did this great movement to the Christian
faith take place? It was one part of the surging movement out of the Chuhra prison house which took about equal
numbers into Islam and into Christianity and a sizeable
number into the Sikh faith. But how did the *Christian*
movement develop? This is the story ably told in the
following pages.

Some Missions cooperated with the Chuhra people movement. Other Missions resisted, reluctant to include the Chuhras for fear of the effect this might have on the other castes. They felt called to educational work and evangelism among high caste Hindus and Muslims. Partly because of the slowness of the Churches to enter fully into the people movement, more than half the Chuhras ended up in some non-Christian faith. Today, few of the remaining million Depressed Class Hindus have become Christian as yet--though much evidence exists that they are friendly to the idea.

Under these circumstances, it is imperative that the Churches and Missions in Pakistan study carefully the mighty act of God through which nineteen-twentieths of the existing Church has come to be, and apply the lessons learned through that experience to the present situation among the Depressed Classes.

II. The Stocks' brilliant book, *People Movements in the Punjab*, is essential reading for Christian leaders concerned for world evangelism. It should be taught in all Christian colleges and seminaries on the Indian subcontinent, as well as in courses on Missions in the homeland. Such authentic church history has great relevance for the Church and her leaders today.

Here for the first time is an accurate analysis of what really happened in the Punjab. The Stocks have studied the records to good effect. Their story is carefully documented and well told. They portray the sociological and ethnographic background soundly and clearly. Many charts and maps aid understanding. Many myths and rationalizations as to how the Church came into being, vanish into thin air. A clear understandable picture remains.

Moderators, District Superintendents, Bishops, Pastors, Seminary Professors, and Lay Leaders--both men and women--together with the whole missionary contingent on the subcontinent should study this book carefully.

Future ecclesiastical and evangelistic policies should be determined in the light of what God has done during the past hundred years and the desperate need of the multitudes He is now calling to discipleship.

The book describes chiefly the growth and development of the United Presbyterian Church, but let this fact deter no one in other Churches from reading it. The development of most other Churches in the Punjab (indeed, in many other parts of the subcontinent as well) is very like that portrayed in this book. Factual data about other Churches is given in the Appendix. As other denominations read *People Movements in the Punjab,* they will see their own Church long before they come to the Appendix. The book is correctly named, for it was exactly this kind of movement from this same Chuhra people which created the major denominations throughout the Punjab. Christians of any variety can read this book with profit.

III. Readers will develop a new awareness of the winnability of about a million Pakistani citizens of the Depressed Classes who are yet "not Christians". This prophetic book illuminates both past and future. The oppressed are still looking for release. God still says:

> I have seen the affliction of my people ...
> and have heard their cry because of their
> taskmasters; I know their sufferings. I
> have come down to deliver them ... and to
> bring them up out of that land to a good
> and broad land ... flowing with milk and
> honey. (Exodus 3:7-8)

God sends His Churches and His missionaries:

> ... to preach good news to the poor ...
> release to the captives, recovery of
> sight to the blind, to set at liberty
> those who are oppressed, and to proclaim
> the acceptable year of the Lord. (Luke 4:18)

Like all good church history, *People Movements in the Punjab* speaks to the contemporary People of God. His voice sounds forth on every page.

Donald McGavran
The School of World Mission
Fuller Theological Seminary
Pasadena, California, USA

Preface

In 1956 we went to Pakistan as evangelistic missionaries
full of zeal and enthusiasum to take part in the work of
the Lord. Eleven years later, returning for furlough
after two terms of working with the Christian Church in
Pakistan, we were perplexed and torn, wondering what the
future held for Missions in that country.

We loved the land and the people, had many close
friends among them, and saw a multitude of needs in the
Church that we could fulfill. Yet we were dismayed by
the results of our ministry. The Church was becoming
increasingly ingrown and torn by factionalism. No
significant church growth or effective outreach to non-
Christians was apparent. We had often heard of the
"mass movement" that had brought thousands of "outcastes"
into the Christian Church near the turn of the century.
Their 3rd and 4th generation descendants made up the
bulk of the Church with whom we were working. The
multitude of problems we were facing must have had their
roots in the mistakes of the past.

Convinced that our missionary predecessors had thoroughly bungled the job, and wondering if the time had
not come when we had "worked ourselves out of a job" and
should gracefully step out of the picture, we arrived
at the School of World Mission and Church Growth at
Fuller Theological Seminary in the Fall of 1967. That
year of study revolutionized our ministry.

The School of World Mission faculty immediately confronted us with questions that led us into fascinating
and productive research:

1) What caused the Church in the Punjab to grow at the
   turn of the century?

2) Which missionary methods were effective; which
   ineffective?

3) What segments of society proved responsive?

4) Are any of these factors part of the present-day
   scene?

As the past opened up before our eyes, a profound respect
was born in our hearts for those who had gone before.
The insights and dedication, the tireless efforts and
prayerful lives of both missionary and national leaders
shone clearly through the pages of history. The vigorous
self-supporting Church of the 1920's that operated its
own Home Mission program was testimony to the fact that
present-day problems could not be blamed on the origin
of the Church. We began to put our finger on the root
of the problem and solutions started to emerge.

Gradually we found our eyes lifted from the struggles
and tensions of the 1.4 per cent in Pakistan who already
bear the name of Christ, and focused upon the 98.6 per
cent who as yet do not give Him allegiance. More
specifically our attention was drawn to the "whitened
fields"--those ready for harvest now, the Scheduled
Castes.

How can we speak of "working ourselves out of a job"
when the vast majority of Asia is still without a Savior,
and millions are literally knocking at the doors asking
for teaching? What an opportunity for the national
Church to become involved in a constructive program of
outreach to responsive people! God grant that the
scales may fall from our eyes so we will see the exciting
possibilities in Mission today.

Primary sources of information for this study have
been church and mission records for the various groups
working in Pakistan. Books written about the Churches,
and biographies of missionaries and national leaders
have also been used. Particular attention has been
given to the excellent analyses of the early days of the
United Presbyterian Mission given by Andrew Gordon in
his enthralling account, *Our India Mission,* and by
Robert Stewart's more scholarly approach in *Life and
Work in India.* Census Reports for 1891, 1901, 1911, 1921,
and 1931 have proved invaluable sources of information
and have been used extensively in this study. Interviews
with missionaries and elderly Pakistanis have provided
much first-hand information. Many of the principles
discovered in this study have been tested on the field
since 1968 and have proved applicable to the present
church situation in the subcontinent.

Although this book is limited to a study of the growth
of the Church in that part of undivided India that
became West Pakistan after the partition of India in
1947, the pattern of development and the church growth
principles involved apply to scores of areas on the
India subcontinent and can be applied with profit to
work today. We will compare the individual approach to
evangelism with the group-movement approach, and will
examine two people movements in detail: 1) a small
arrested movement among the Megs; and 2) a large well-
developed movement among the Chuhras. Our purpose is
to analyze the many factors involved in these movements
in order to form more realistic and productive plans
for future evangelism. We pray that the principles
emerging from this analysis will open our eyes to the
"whitened fields" and serve as guidelines for reaping a
bountiful harvest.

We wish to acknowledge our deep indebtedness to all
of the faculty of the School of World Mission and Church
Growth at Fuller Seminary for the wealth of research
and experience they have shared with us. These have
expanded our horizons, clarified our vision, and equipped
us with practical tools essential on the mission field
today. Special gratitude goes to Dr. D. A. McGavran
whose deep insights into church growth principles

coupled with his many years of experience on the Indian
subcontinent were invaluable to us in our study. We
are also grateful to our colleagues in many denominations
who have made their records available to us and encouraged
us in our research. Thanks to Dr. J. D. Brown, Miss
Marian Peterson, and Mrs. E. H. Llewellyn who took time
to read the rough draft and contributed valuable
corrections and suggestions.

Frederick and Margaret Stock

Introduction

*"It is a light thing that thou shouldst
raise up the tribes of Jacob and restore
the remnant of Israel. I will give you
as a light to the Gentiles that my salvation may reach to the ends of the
earth."*
                              --Isaiah 49:6

In May 1853 the Associate Presbyterian Synod of North
America meeting in Pittsburgh resolved to establish a
Mission in India. After prayer for guidance, they
nominated ten men in the hope that some of them would
be willing to accept appointments as missionaries.
Not one of the ten was willing.

In June of the following year Synod was held in
Albany, New York. Andrew Gordon, a young unordained
graduate of theological school, dropped in on the
meeting as an observer. Sitting in the farthest cor-
ner of the church he listened with interest to a heated
debate on the subject of how to obtain missionaries.

"Call for volunteers. Don't appoint a man until you
know he is willing to go. One volunteer is worth two
of those who go because it is required of them," argued
some.

"No. Choose men truly qualified. If they refuse to go, the responsibility is theirs. Our Scottish forefathers _suspended_ young preachers for refusing to go where they were sent," was the emphatic response from others.

This latter opinion met with general favor and was accepted as the basis for an election held that same afternoon. Two young men were chosen who had forcibly advocated this principle in the morning. Considerably subdued and downcast they rose to decline the appointment.

Andrew Gordon left for home convinced that the matter would be shelved for another year. Two days later a friend gently broke the news that before adjourning the Synod had once more brought up the subject of foreign missions and had elected Andrew Gordon and an older more experienced pastor to be missionaries to India. The other man refused.

Andrew Gordon had never seriously considered missionary service, for he did not enjoy robust health. Yet this appointment, completely unsought and unexpected, came with the force and authority of a clear call from God. Later when misgivings arose he was reassured by the knowledge that he had not chosen this life but had been *sent* by the Church as were Paul and Barnabas.

His wife, Rebecca, retiring by nature and an ardent lover of home, struggled for weeks before she was able to give her consent. One evening after their decision had been announced, a respected friend in a tone of deep concern said to Rebecca, "Do you intend to take your little girl with you to India? Don't you realize that she will be exposed to diseases and evil influences that could destroy both body and soul?"

All the pent up grief and struggle of the past weeks burst forth as Rebecca rushed from the room tearfully exclaiming, "It is too much! I cannot go!"

Next morning her parents, Mr. and Mrs. Smith, torn between their Christian convictions and their sorrow at the coming separation, said to Andrew and Rebecca, "We'll take the little girl riding while you pray over this matter and come to a final decision." Earnestly they searched the Scriptures and prayed, but the Smith's return found them still confused and uncertain.

Rushing in excitedly, Mrs. Smith displayed a bloody wound in her arm. "A bullet from a careless hunter's gun passed within a fraction of the girl's head and lodged here in my arm!" she exclaimed. "It was a mercy she wasn't killed!"

Sudden assurance came to Rebecca. "Undoubtedly, this was sent to teach us that our daughter is no safer at home than in a foreign land," she said with quiet conviction. "If God is calling, we must trust Him with our loved ones."

As further confirmation of God's leading, Andrew's sister, Miss Elizabeth Gordon, offered to accompany them as a co-worker for Andrew and companion for Rebecca. On September 28th, 1854 they sailed from New York on the *Sabine,* rounded the Cape of Good Hope, and arrived in Calcutta February 13th, 1855, four and a half weary months later. The final 1,100 miles to their destination, the Punjab, took twenty days' travel in wooden carts drawn by coolies.

To what kind of a land had they come and what is it like today?

Geographical Background

The Punjab means "five waters," referring to the five rivers that divide it--the Chenab, Jhelum, Ravi, Sutlej, and Beas that later flow into the Indus River near the south-western end of the province. From 1865 to 1920 the British engineered an intricate network of canals stemming from these rivers and irrigating large tracts of arid land. As these areas developed, thousands of people migrated to them from the central and eatern portions of the Punjab to seek new homesteads and better jobs. This migration influenced the pattern of church growth as we shall see.

The geographical area covered by this study is that portion of north-western India that became West Pakistan in 1947, with particular emphasis on the western sector of the Punjab Province, the original home of most of the Christians found in Pakistan today. (See Figure 1.)

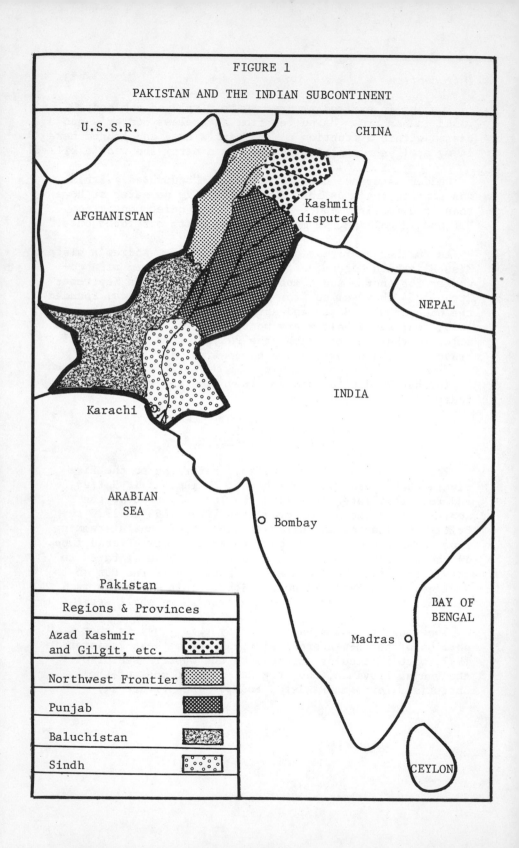

FIGURE 1

PAKISTAN AND THE INDIAN SUBCONTINENT

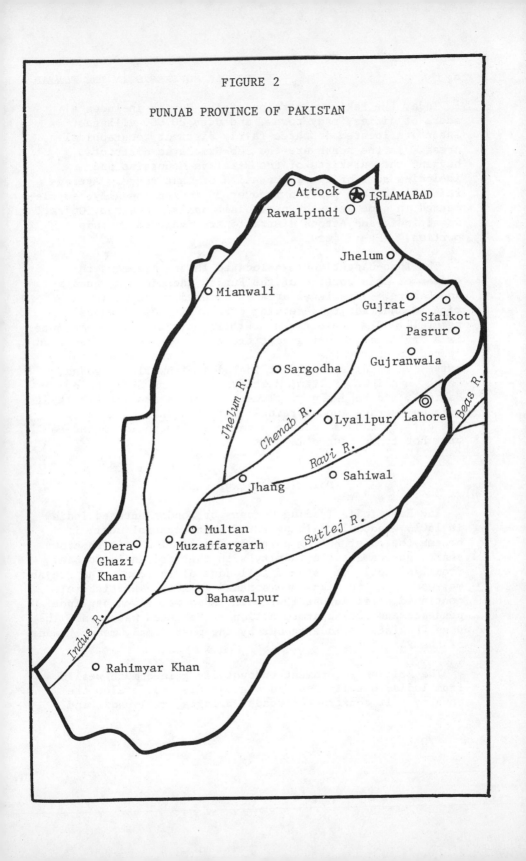

FIGURE 2

PUNJAB PROVINCE OF PAKISTAN

Today the Pakistan portion of the Punjab includes a
score of cities, many towns, and over 20,000 villages.
These are located in three fairly distinct geographical
areas. In the north are the sub-Himalayan districts,
hugging the outskirts of the Himalaya Mountains and
including some of the lower hills of that range. Average
rainfall in this portion is over 30 inches annually, supplemented in some areas by perennial canals. Sialkot, Gujrat,
Rawalpindi, and Attock districts are included in this
portion. (See Figure 2.)

The Indo-Gangetic Plain located in the mid-eastern
sector of this portion of the Punjab includes Gujranwala
and Lahore. This level area is watered by canal irrigation in addition to receiving over 20 inches of annual
rainfall. The western and southern portion of the province
is a dry area including vast tracts of previously arid land
opened to cultivation since the turn of the century by the
extensive canal system. It includes Mianwali, Sargodha,
Jhang, Lyallpur, Multan, Muzaffargarh, Dera Ghazi Khan,
Sahiwal, and Bahawalpur. These districts are largely level
with an average annual rainfall of less than 15 inches.
The climate ranges from an occasional freeze in winter to
very hot temperatures in June.

Political Background

The East India Trading Company of London entered India
in 1601, gradually gaining territorial control until it
became the chief ruling power in India. The British crown
shared governmental authority with the East India Company
from 1784 until it assumed full control in 1858. The Punjab
was won from the Sikhs and annexed in 1849. British rule
continued until August 1947 when India was given her independence and the separate nation of Pakistan was born. The
name "Pakistan," made famous by the poet Iqbal, means "Land
of the Pure."

The British government undoubtedly gained much wealth
from India, but it also did a great deal to develop the
country. It constructed roads, bridges, railroads, and

canals; planted trees; established schools; provided tele-
graphic and postal arrangements; and unified the land under
one central government. It also proved of great benefit to
mission efforts in a number of ways. Robert Stewart in his
book, *Life and Work in India,* mentions some of them:

> ... British rule is in many ways helpful to
> mission work in India. It secures almost
> perfect safety for the missionary wherever he
> may go throughout the length and breadth of
> the land ... It secures to every individual
> the right to worship God according to the
> dictates of his own conscience--criminal acts
> excepted--and hence reduces religious perse-
> cution for Christian profession to the smallest
> possible degree. It abolishes, or condemns,
> from time to time, old laws and practices,
> even if they are based on Hindu *Shastras,*
> which are opposed to human rights and
> Christian morals ... It exhibits in its
> administration a remarkable degree of
> fairness, impartiality and justice. (1896:
> 35)

Since foreign missionaries were members of the ruling
race, they were treated with respect and given places of
prestige in the community. The British policy was to give
aid impartially to all faiths in proportion to the number
of their adherents. Since the majority communities were
non-Christian, they received a much greater proportion of
financial help and government support. Nevertheless, the
government sold ample property for mission compounds in
major cities at nominal cost, and gave financial aid to
schools, hospitals, and orphanages run for benevolent
purposes. Some British officers, deeply concerned for the
salvation of India, proved tireless in their evangelistic
efforts and generous in their support.

British rule was not always advantageous to missionary
effort, however. Stewart points out two major drawbacks:

> The very fact that Christianity in a general
> sense is the religion of the governing power
> and receives civil protection and commendation

> gives it a prestige with some aspiring people
> that works unfavorably in the production of
> false and insincere converts; while on the
> other hand this same fact brings the Gospel
> into bad odor with a different class of
> persons (those who hate the government) and
> prejudices them against it.   (1896:37)

Many British civil and military personnel, not being
committed Christians, gave Indians a false impression of
the faith. The latter, assuming that all Westerners are
Christians, failed to distinguish between nominal and
genuine Christianity.

In 1947 when Pakistan was separated from India by
partition, the scene changed in many significant ways.
Until 1947 Muslims comprised over one half of the population
of the Punjab and nearly three-fourths of western Punjab.
With Partition came a massive shift of populations. Hindus
and Sikhs moved out of Pakistan and millions of Muslim
refugees poured in from India. Since then the population
of West Pakistan has been approximately 97 per cent Muslim.

The Christians and Scheduled Castes became the only
sizable minority communities in this overwhelmingly Muslim
land. The constitution of Pakistan guarantees Christians
freedom to practice and to propagate their faith. Under
the first constitution minority seats were reserved for
them in the legislature. These were later cancelled, making
it almost impossible for a Christian to gain an elected
position in the government.

The formation of Pakistan was accompanied by a surge of
nationalistic spirit, coupled with dislike of anything
associated with former British domination. Missionaries
no longer enjoy as elevated a status, but often find themselves objects of resentment and suspicion. In October 1972
the government took control of most private schools and
colleges including Christian institutions. This loss was
deeply felt by the Christian community, but has awakened
the Church to a fresh realization of her crucial role in
making Christ known and loved in Pakistan.

Linguistic Background

The Urdu language originated in the 11th century in the camps of the Muslim conquerors of India. It is based on Hindi grammar but contains many Persian and Arabic words. It became the written language most used in government affairs in the Punjab. Stewart writes:

> It is used largely in schools, is the language of men more than of women, of the bazaar more than of the household, of cities more than of villages, and of Muhammadans more than of Hindus. (1896:85)

At Partition, Urdu and Bengali were declared the national languages of Pakistan. Since the formation of Bangla Desh in 1971, Bengali has been dropped.

Punjabi, a more Indian tongue built on a Sanskritic base, is the mother tongue of the Punjab. The 80 per cent of the people who are illiterate and rural speak Punjabi and have only limited understanding and use of Urdu. Even highly educated families speak Punjabi in the home and on informal occasions.

Although English is taught in the schools and used in government offices, less than five per cent of the population can understand it well enough to comprehend spiritual truths adequately through this medium. Urdu or a local dialect such as Punjabi, Pushto, or Sindhi, must be used in reaching the masses of Pakistan for Christ.

Religio-Cultural Background

To understand church growth in the Punjab, one must be aware of the basic religio-cultural sub-divisions that were present in north-western India at the time of the formation of the Church, as well as the changed situation since Partition in 1947. The major groups were as follows:

Caste Hindus

Hinduism is the oldest major religion in India. Two-fifths of the people of the Punjab in 1855 were Hindus, but only a tiny minority of .48 per cent remained at the formation of Pakistan. Hinduism is so varied and complex that it defies definition. Stewart says concerning it:

> Theoretically it is pantheistic, but practically polytheistic. Accepting three original and supreme manifestations of the eternal spirit-- Brahma, Vishnu and Siva (the Trimurti)--it has admitted into its pantheon a multitude of gods either related to them by marriage, descent or service, or identified with them through the principle of incarnation or special embodiment. These are presented to the eye in the form of idols, pictures, persons, animals, tombs or natural objects ... Hindus of the Punjab, as a general thing, neglect the worship of the great and confine their attention to local deities, or those benevolent or malevolent beings which are supposed to affect their daily life. (1896:111)

Salvation is variously defined by different sects of Hinduism. For some it is the giving of themselves in devotion to Krishna to find release from self. Others obtain release from worldly thoughts and desires through the discipline of Yoga. Ultimate salvation is to escape from the cycle of continual reincarnation, and to be absorbed into Brahma. The highest goal in life is to lose all desire. This has given rise to extreme forms of asceticism such as the *fakirs* who lie on nails, hold their arms above their heads until they wither, or follow some other path of self-inflicted torture.

In order for ordinary people to find salvation and still enable society to function, the New Brahmanical Tradition came into dominance about A.D. 1000. It offered hope for a better future through the performance of *Dharma,* that is, to accept one's caste position and fulfill faithfully all caste responsibilities and obligations. This does not result in social equality in this life, but makes possible

reincarnation in higher forms that can ultimately lead to
release from the reincarnation cycle. In this way cosmic
justice is meted out to those who faithfully live out their
caste role in life. Hopkins sums up the system by saying:

> Caste values and duties were in this way
> internalized and reinforced, making present
> conformity not only bearable but desirable.
> (1971:85)

One of the most important characteristics of Hindu
society is its complex caste system. Lewis defines a caste
as:

> ... an endogamous social unity, membership
> in which is determined by birth; it is often
> associated with a particular occupation and
> with restrictions about the acceptance of
> food and water from other caste groups.
> Castes tend to be ranked, with the Brahmins
> being traditionally assigned the highest
> status and "untouchable" castes like the
> Bhangi [sweeper] the lowest. (1958:55)

The caste system is basically an inter-related labor
structure whereby a village is assured of maintaining its
basic technical and labor requirements. This is called the
Jajmani system. The lower castes have traditional occupations and a family relationship of service with some land-
lord. The carpenter, washerman, blacksmith, sweeper and
field laborer each performs his function for the village
throughout the year and is paid in kind at harvest time.
Before a family may migrate from a village, they must provide a replacement (usually from their own relatives) to
carry on the work. The landlords of each village are
careful to maintain this delicate balance of interdependence
so that all the necessary services are available.

Many scholars have attempted to delineate the factors
that have led to the formation of the caste system.
Undoubtedly many factors have contributed to it, including
the following:

(1) geographical isolation
(2) doctrine of reincarnation
(3) hereditary occupations, trades, and crafts
(4) antagonistic cultures
(5) a succession of conquering races
(6) religious differences
(7) political differences

Most Indians accept the explanation of the origin of
the caste system as given in the "Laws of Manu" in the
Rig-Veda (x.90.11-14) of about the second century A.D.
This story notes that the four basic social caste categories,
called *varnas*, came into being from the body of primeval
man:

> From his mouth issued the Brahmins, who became
> priests and scholars. From his arms came the
> Kshatriyas, warriors and rulers; from his thighs
> came the Vaishyas, tradesmen; and from his feet
> rose the Shudras, cultivators. (Mandelbaum 1970:
> Vol. I, 22-23)

Dr. Mandelbaum points out several weak features of this
scheme: (1) There is no place for the numerous "untouchable"
castes. These are essential for maintaining traditional
village society. (2) All castes are not represented
throughout India. (3) There is no universal system for
ranking the castes. This varies somewhat from place to
place. Nevertheless, this scheme enables the ordinary
villager to sort out his relationships and responsibilities
to some of the more than 3000 castes present in India.

Hinduism tends to be syncretistic. It is ready to add
Christ to its pantheon of gods and to incorporate many of
the precepts of Jesus into its teachings. Hindus are
impatient with the Christian claim to uniqueness. Although
seemingly open-minded, they form a close-knit caste
community that wields tremendous social pressure on each
individual. A caste Hindu who becomes a Christian is
usually ostracized by his family and friends.

Muslims

Ninety-seven per cent of the present population of
Pakistan are Muslims. (See Figure 3.) They worship one
God--supreme, remote, unknowable, who must never be
represented by an idol or a picture. They honor Mohammad
as the last and final prophet, whose ministry made the
message of all previous prophets obsolete. They believe
Mohammad supercedes Christ, the Qur'an replaces the Bible,
and Christians are polytheists worshipping three gods--
Father, Son, and Virgin Mary. They interpret the cruci-
fixion as the triumph of evil over God, and therefore
unthinkable. They believe Jesus was rescued by angels and
taken alive into heaven, while Judas was mistakenly
crucified in His place.

In addition to these theological barriers, there are
powerful social factors that make it difficult for an
individual to become a Christian. Muslim family structure
is so cohesive that for anyone to make a major decision
apart from his family is interpreted as rebellion--a
great dishonor to the family. A convert is under such
pressure to conform to the values of his family group, that
he either submits or has to break family ties. At times
he may even be in danger of his life.

Muslims in other lands pride themselves on their lack
of class consciousness. In India, however, the Hindu
caste system has influenced the Muslims to make certain
caste distinctions among themselves, and to relegate
Christians to an inferior status. Even Scheduled Caste
people who have embraced Islam are designated as *Musallis,
Dindars,* or *Shiekhs* and not allowed full social equality
in the Muslim community. Grave worship, visitation of
shrines, and reverence for *fakirs* or "holy men" are common
Hindu or animistic aspects in popular Islam.

Sikhs

The Sikh faith was founded by a religious leader of the
15th century named Guru Nanak who revolted against idolatry
and caste. He was greatly influenced by the poet Kabir

who sought to combine the teachings of Hinduism and Islam.
According to C.H. Loehlin in his booklet, *The Christian
Approach to the Sikh,* Sikhs believe the following about
God:

> God is one, his name is truth, he is omnipo-
> tent and merciful (immortal, fearless, and
> without enmity). This is ethical monotheism;
> and in spite of a tinge of Hindu pantheism
> and Muslim arbitrary absoluteness, this is
> the general tenor of the *Granth.* *(1966:47)*

Sikhism has not been able to break the caste system, but
they are much less rigid in their observance of it. Only
scattered individuals have become Christians from this
religious group. At Partition the Sikhs migrated to India,
so do not constitute a factor in the present religious
situation in Pakistan.

Scheduled Castes

The Scheduled Castes or "Depressed Classes" (sometimes
mistakenly termed "outcastes") can be said to be a product
of the Hindu caste system, although strictly speaking they
were not counted as Hindus until the 1930's when they
became politically important. Stewart says:

> It is probable that they represent what is
> left of the aborigines of the country, re-
> inforced from time to time by the addition
> of persons who, for some reason, lost caste
> and were excluded from the so-called higher
> classes. (1896:119)

The Scheduled Castes were despised by Hindus, Sikhs, and
Muslims alike. In 1855 they comprised about one-eighth of
the population of the Punjab and were practically destitute
of social, political, and legal rights. In 1886 Andrew
Gordon in his book, *Our India Mission,* says concerning
them:

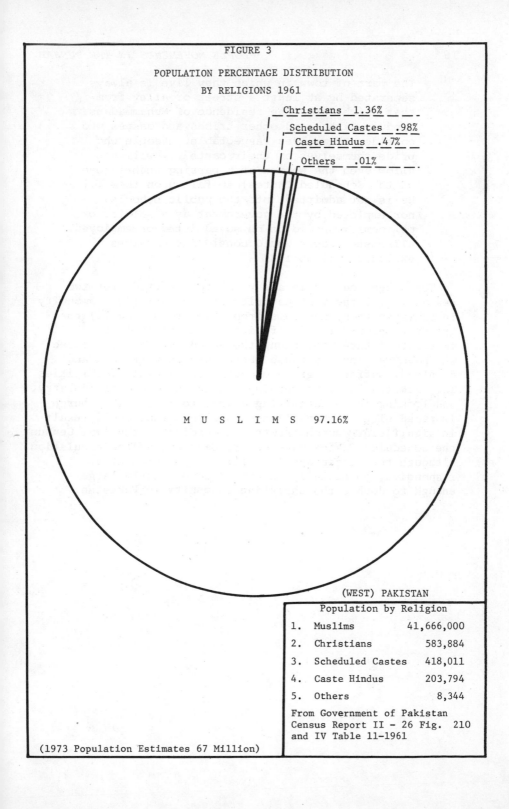

FIGURE 3

POPULATION PERCENTAGE DISTRIBUTION

BY RELIGIONS 1961

Christians 1.36%

Scheduled Castes .98%

Caste Hindus .47%

Others .01%

M U S L I M S   97.16%

(WEST) PAKISTAN

Population by Religion	
1. Muslims	41,666,000
2. Christians	583,884
3. Scheduled Castes	418,011
4. Caste Hindus	203,794
5. Others	8,344

From Government of Pakistan
Census Report II − 26 Fig. 210
and IV Table 11−1961

(1973 Population Estimates 67 Million)

The part of town in which they live is always
separated by at least a street or alley from
that which forms the residence of Muhammadans,
Hindus, Sikhs, and other tribes and castes who
consider themselves respectable. People who
pride themselves on their caste ... will not
allow even the shadow of a passing Chuhra [one
of the Scheduled Castes] to fall upon them ...
He is not admitted into the public schools,
nor employed by the government as a soldier or
policeman; should he be so admitted or employed,
all caste people would consider themselves
excluded. (1886:174)

The Scheduled Castes are vital to our study for two
reasons: (1) the vast majority of the Christian community
in Pakistan today has come from this group; and (2) the
greatest opportunity for fruitful evangelism in the
immediate future lies among the Scheduled Castes. Those
who have remained in these castes are down-trodden and
despised, suffering grave economic and social disabilities.
They are restless, increasingly disenchanted with idolatry,
and looking for a satisfying answer to life. The Church
is faced with an evangelistic challenge that could result
in significant church growth. According to the 1961 Census,
the Scheduled Castes make up .98 per cent of the population.
Although the percentage is small, they represent a
responsive, potentially winnable group, nearly large
enough to double the Christian community in Pakistan.

1
Pioneer Period (1855-1872)

The Associate Presbyterian Church of North America began
mission work in the Punjab of North India with the arrival
of Andrew Gordon, his wife, their young daughter and his
sister, Miss Elizabeth Gordon in 1855. Three years later,
in 1858, this Church merged with the Associate Reformed
Presbyterian Church to form the United Presbyterian Church
of North America (hereafter designated as the U.P. Church).
Andrew Gordon and his party first traveled to Saharanpur
to consult with other missionaries concerning the field
where they should begin their labors. The area of the
Punjab around Sialkot was selected because it was least
occupied, having been recently annexed by Britain. (See
Figure 4.) Here work could be initiated and even extended
with least danger of infringing upon missionary societies
already established.

Preparation

During his stay in Saharanpur, Andrew Gordon, in addition
to doing language study, learned as much as possible about
different types of missionary effort. Not content to rely
on trial and error, he carefully studied the merits and
weaknesses of various current missionary methods and made
a conscious effort to evaluate them so as to use those
most effective. He observed experienced workers witnessing
and distributing literature at a two-week fair, the famous
Hardwar Mela. He also attended the annual meeting of the

Ludhiana Mission of the American Presbyterian Church and
learned much that determined the character of the early
years of the U.P. Mission. From the start a good spirit of
cooperation existed between the American Presbyterian
Mission and the U.P.'s.

In August 1855, Andrew Gordon went to Sialkot visiting
various mission stations on the way. Friends among the
British officers encouraged him to buy property and build
a suitable residence. When money from America was delayed,
they demonstrated their support by collecting money to
begin the project. Two more ordained men and their wives
joined the original missionaries in 1856. This meant
constructing more houses and introducing the new missionaries to language study, consequently delaying the start
of evangelistic work.

Evangelism

Andrew Gordon and his colleagues were faced with a
bewildering variety of people to evangelize. There were
the three major religious groups--the Hindus, Sikhs, and
Muslims. Then there were the caste stratifications, with
each caste unwilling to mix socially with those considered
lower than themselves; and a great gulf fixed between the
upper castes and the Scheduled Castes. It was difficult
to know where to start.

Stress on High Castes

Taking their cue from Missions established before them,
the U.P.'s began with bazaar preaching in the city,
accompanied by the distribution of tracts. Preaching was
in Urdu, the literary language spoken by the educated and
those who had business dealings in the city. Their purpose
was to win anyone whose heart was open to God's Word.
However, their methods were such that they reached a select
few. City preaching gave them access to the urban population. The use of Urdu limited it to higher class people.
Tracts were effective only among the one per cent who were
educated coming from respected Hindu, Sikh or Muslim
families. Few women frequented the bazaars in those days,
nor did they understand Urdu, or feel free to stand in a

FIGURE 4

PAKISTAN
SHOWING THE UNITED PRESBYTERIAN MISSION AREA

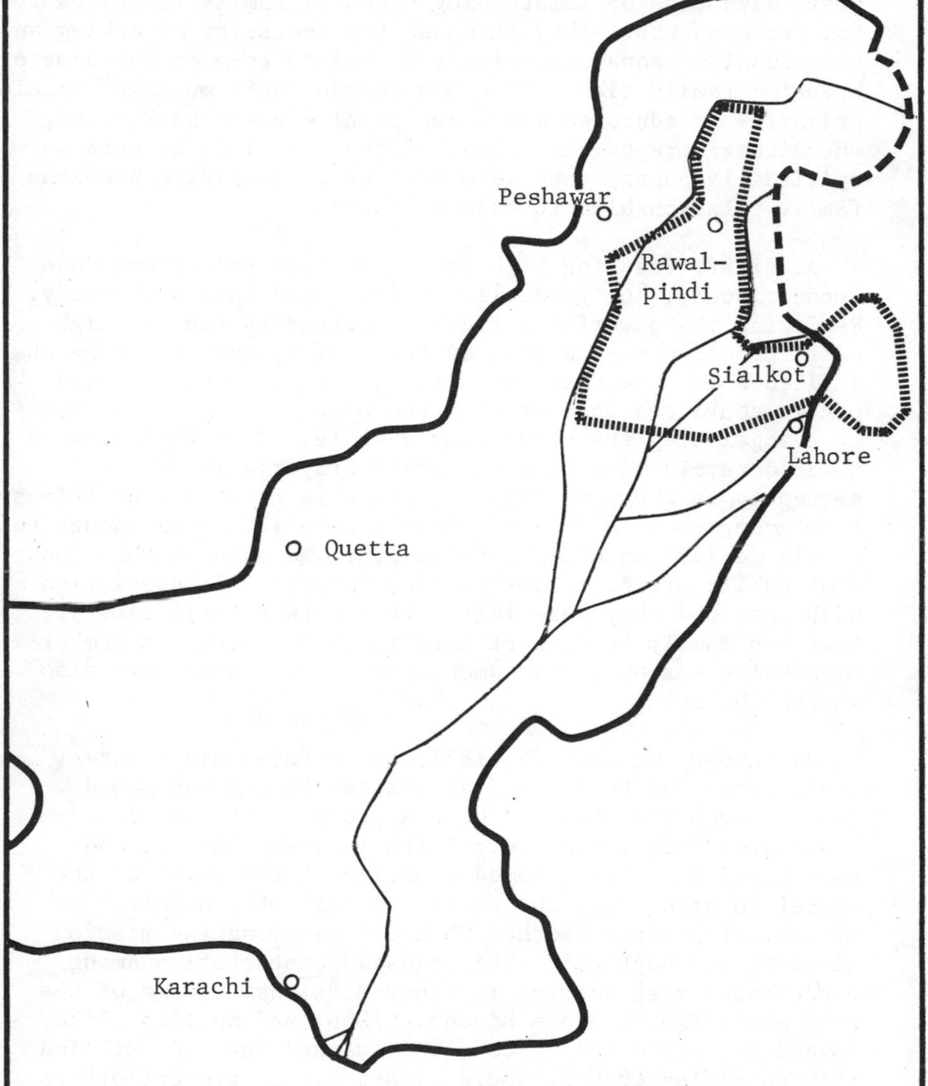

Peshawar

Rawal-
pindi

Sialkot

Lahore

Quetta

Karachi

U.P. Mission area

0   50   100 150
         Miles

crowd to listen; so only men were attracted, not whole families. The missionaries, coming from Western society where individuals are encouraged to make their own personal decisions in religious matters, failed to understand the great advantage of maintaining cohesive family relationships for new converts. They stressed the necessity of making an individual personal decision for Christ, even at the cost of breaking family ties. For this reason their message appealed primarily to educated urban men of high caste background, who either were on the fringe of their society or were so spiritually hungry they were willing to sacrifice previous family relationships to gain salvation.

At first, reaching high caste educated people was done unconsciously, but gradually it developed into a strategy. Realizing the powerful influence exerted by the few high caste people upon the rest of the nation, and conveting that influence for the cause of Christ, the missionaries soon became convinced that winning the high castes was the key to evangelizing the country as a whole. This strengthened their determination to concentrate prayerfully and earnestly on the conversion of those in strategic positions. From among these a few individuals were attracted enough to openly declare themselves believers. As soon as they took that public stand, their families cut off all association with them and they were left without the natural ties of home and family to support them in their faith. A number of mission servants from among the lower castes were also won to Christ.

On Sunday, October 25, 1857, an educated high-caste Hindu named Ram Bhajan and an illiterate old man named Jauhari from the despised Chuhra group of so-called "outcastes," declared their faith in Jesus Christ, and were baptized. This seemed symbolic of the power of the Gospel to bring down the proud and exalt the humble. Shortly afterwards another Chuhra from among the mission servants was baptized. This caused consternation among experienced missionaries in other Missions. Aware of the deep prejudice of caste Hindus, Sikhs, and Muslims alike toward the Scheduled Castes, they warned the U.P. Mission that receiving Chuhras would almost surely prevent others from becoming Christians. Gordon answered, "If the honorable, the wise, and the great should be deterred from coming to Christ, the sin would lie in their pride, and not in our receiving the lowly." (1886:178)

The fear expressed was not realized, for three weeks after the baptism of this second Chuhra, a respectable Muslim came forward and was publicly baptized as the fourth convert. Within the following year nine more were received, all of whom were either respectable Muslims or high-caste Hindus. One of them was the first woman convert.

During the next fifteen years a large number of Indians from all classes were taught as inquirers, but only a few had the couage to be baptized. Gordon spent ten years in Gurdaspur concentrating his efforts on winning men of the top castes of society. He found they listened to his carefully prepared logical lectures on Christian evidences with great attention and appreciation. Some of the men acknowledged privately that they believed the Bible was the Word of God, and that Jesus was the Son of God and the Savior of sinners, but few of them were willing to confess Him publicly. At one time there were 50 sincere, well-educated, wealthy inquirers with whom he spent many hours of counselling, and for whom much prayer was offered. Only seven of the fifty were baptized; four of them later apostatized.

It is significant that many high-caste people were theologically convinced of the truth of the Gospel, but the barrier to their becoming Christians was the cultural unit of which they were a part. They were unable to face the opposition and ostracism of their relatives and friends. One wonders what might have happened in those early years right after the annexation of the Punjab when British prestige was high, if a deliberate attempt had been made to induce a wide-spread movement to Christ in some respectable caste. Many of the educated were searching for truth and might have responded had they been able to do so within the context of their social unit.

Care of Converts

In the first twenty years of mission work in the Punjab, the problem of caring for converts became increasingly acute. The difficulty arose because of the intense hostility of all castes and religious groups to the conversion of any of their members to Christianity. A baptized believer was immediately under pressure from his

family and caste members to recant or suffer the
consequences. Attempts to poison or murder converts were
common in high-caste Hindu and Muslim families, who sought
in this way to obliterate from their family the disgrace
he embodied. Sincere converts and even inquirers had to
flee their homes and friends to save their lives.

What should a Mission do in such a situation? The most
logical and loving solution appeared to be for the
missionaries to provide housing and financial help to such
converts at least on a temporary basis. In this way the
mission station became the center for the new band of
believers.

The philosophy of this approach is very reasonable.
Inquirers and converts need instruction. If they remain
scattered, without fellowship with other Christians, they
have little spiritual support to enable them to meet
persecution. Many may fall away and return to their former
faith. Therefore, they should be provided with food and
lodging where they can be tested as to sincerity, be
protected from persecution, and be taught more of Christ
until they can obtain employment elsewhere. The mission
station is the logical center for such an operation.

The mission station approach, however, had many weaknesses and produced unfortunate results. It encouraged
insincere inquirers who were more interested in the free
room and board than in the claims of Christ. The Mission
found themselves flooded with "converts" given to idle
habits. Gordon writes:

> When they found they could not eat without
> working in one Mission, they would go to
> another ... in the hope of finding somewhere
> a kind-hearted Padri Sahib with plenty of
> money, who assuming the loving relation of
> *ma-bap* (parents) to them, would tenderly and
> indulgently nourish and cherish them just as
> a loving Christian parent should. (1886:265)

The mission station approach created an artificial world
of almost total dependence upon the missionaries. Not only
did converts need food, shelter, and employment, but the
Mission had to take over the parental responsibility of

providing wives for many. Fifteen girls from the mission
orphanage eventually became the wives of converts. Such
dependence hindered sincere converts from developing an
independent spirit so necessary to self respect and
spiritual growth. It encouraged a love of money and often
caused jealousy among those living on the mission station.

Of the 43 adult baptisms from non-Christians performed
from 1855 to 1872, one was a Sikh, 9 were Muslims, 28 were
Hindus and 5 were Scheduled Caste people. These had little
in common other than their newly-found faith. Only 5 of
the 43 were women, so most of the men were without their
families. To unite individuals from such a wide variety of
backgrounds into a warm supportive fellowship was next to
impossible. Cut off from the stabilizing influence of home
and family, many converts fell into bad habits. The first
Session Book of the Sialkot congregation reveals that 20
of these 43 converts (nearly half of them) had to be
suspended on serious moral charges within a few months of
their baptism.

The most unfortunate result of the separation of converts from their families was that this blocked the most
effective channel for evangelism (i.e. clan ties) and
resulted in the Christian message reaching only a limited
section of society. Bishop J.W. Pickett in his book,
Christian Mass Movements in India, comments on this as
follows:

> More effective in closing the hearts of
> Hindus and Moslems against Christianity than
> the conversion of the lowly Chuhras was the
> break in social relations that followed the
> baptism of converts from their own groups.
> Living in the mission compounds to be
> indoctrinated and protected against tempta-
> tions, the new converts were too much
> separated from their people. The effects
> of this separation were perhaps equally bad
> on the converts and in turn on the attitude
> of their relatives, friends and neighbors
> towards Christianity. (1933:43)

Converts, cut off from their friends and relatives
among whom they could have witnessed more effectively, soon
lost their interest in trying to win others. The resulting
Church became increasingly ingrown and self-centered. The
mission station approach was obviously not a satisfactory
answer to the problem of the care of converts.

An industrial school was started for the purpose of
furnishing training and employment to new Christians. It
was to provide a definite solution for idleness, leave the
lazy with no excuse, and establish the principle, "If any
man would not work, neither shall he eat." Difficulties
soon arose.

It is a prevailing sentiment in India that to be truly
religious a man must live by begging and not engage in any
form of industry. High caste converts regarded manual labor
as degrading. Gordon writes:

> We soon found that a vigorous and persevering
> effort was necessary on our part to prevent this
> false idea of work from gaining a place in our
> young Christian community, and spreading like
> some deadly plague. To devise work for our
> converts was difficult. To induce them to take
> hold industriously and do with their might what-
> soever their hands found to do, was ten-fold
> more so. But the most difficult task of all was
> to prevent, or to remedy, the many evils which
> were naturally resulting from idleness, and
> threatening our whole work with utter ruin.
> (1886:181)

Missionaries interpreted the reluctance of converts to
perform various tasks as simple laziness as in come cases
it was. They failed however to recognize the effect of
caste on Indian thinking. Hindus are convinced that God
has entrusted certain types of work exclusively to certain
castes. It was utterly foreign to their concept of fitness
for a man to engage in work other than that of his
particular caste. To find a means of employment suitable
to all the early converts with their variety of religious
and caste backgrounds would have been impossible. The
project finally had to be abandoned.

The Rev. George Washington Scott   The Rev. Elisha P. Swift

The first two national workers. *--from OUR INDIA MISSION*

Evangelists and Pastors in the 1880's, including three early Chuhra converts: Ditt (seated on the floor in front); Prem Masih and Chaughatta (two men standing on the right); and the Rev. I.D. Shahbaz who paraphrased the Psalms into Punjabi verse (seated at the right).

--from OUR INDIA MISSION

HOUSES
of
WORSHIP
in
INDIA

Moslem Mosque

Sweepers Shrine
called Bala Shah

The Christian Church
in their midst

Hindu Temple

"Golden Temple"
of the Sikhs

A Balmiki leader seated by his Bala Shah Shrine

In 1867 Mr. Martin and Mr. Scott, seeking to solve the difficult question of temporal support for converts, procured about 200 acres of land on which they settled seven Christian families. This colony was named Scottgarh. (See Figure 6.) The colonists were given some money to see them through the first year, and although they had a good crop, five of the seven farmers showed little inclination to work. They depended upon the small capital given them to begin with, and looked for more when that was exhausted. Within three years all seven families had deserted the project.

The failure of this experiment led the missionaries to question the wisdom of their whole approach to evangelism. Converts who had been won individually were dislocated from their own society and formed a dependent Church, sealed off from natural channels of outreach and growth. This perplexing problem was foremost in their concern and prayers when God sent an unexpected solution in the form of the group movement among the Chuhras that will be discussed in detail later.

Education

A Church Missionary Society representative, Mr. T.H. Fitzpatrick, had started a school for non-Christian boys in Sialkot. He offered it to Andrew Gordon shortly after he arrived in 1855, but Gordon, having determined not to undertake school work, declined to take it over. Mr. Stevenson who arrived in March 1856 did not agree with Gordon's position. This sparked the first controversy in the Mission. Reading between the lines of Gordon's account, one can easily imagine that this issue was heatedly debated.

> He and I discussed fully the question of carry-
> ing on schools as a method of evangelizing the
> heathen. He was decidedly in favor of such
> schools, and quoted in support of his position
> the example of the Apostle Paul, who labored for
> two years in the school of one Tyrannus. I said
> I was willing to do what Paul did--go into a
> school and preach--if we could find a man who,
> like Tyrannus, would carry it on and at the same
> time allow us the privilege of preaching to his

> scholars; but I could not undertake to be both
> Paul and Tyrannus. Brother Stevenson declared
> his willingness to undertake the work of both
> Paul and Tyrannus until the Church should send
> out teachers for the special purpose of carry-
> ing on educational work. We agreed to differ
> without opposing one another. (1886:117)

From then on schools for non-Christians were a regular part
of the U.P. mission work.

Evangelistic Purpose

The motivation for establishing schools for high-caste
non-Christians was the conviction that this would prove
the prime strategy for winning India as a whole to Christ.
Alexander Duff who came to India in 1830 maintained that
education was by far the best tool for spreading the Gospel
and attracking Hinduism at its heart. He believed that the
influence of Western science and philosophy would soon
destroy the pseudo-science of Hinduism, and the whole
system would crumble to dust. The conversion of Brahmans,
the recognized leaders of Hindu life would be speedily
followed by the conversion of the whole nation.

Since the motivating force behind educational work was
a sincere desire to win non-Christians to the Lord, the
study of the Bible was central to the curriculum. All
students were required to take Bible courses and attend
daily chapel services. Every opportunity was taken to make
the Gospel clear and meaningful to the students. Yet, as
the years went by, it became more and more apparent that
the high caste students were not being won in any numbers
through mission schools. When an occasional conversion
took place, it usually caused such violent demonstrations
of opposition that the school involved had to close down
for a time.

Nevertheless, educationalists were convinced that in
the long run this work would be abundantly rewarded. They
had a captive audience for Bible teaching. They believed
firmly that even if the present students were unable to
openly acknowledge themselves as Christians due to their
youth and lack of status in the power structure of their

society, they became well acquainted with Christianity and
its claims. Their prejudices would be broken down and
they would not oppose the spread of Christianity or object
if their children embraced the new faith. In a generation
or two all of India would be won to Christ in this way.

Andrew Gordon opposed the above strategy. He felt that
education either as a short range or a long range method of
evangelism was not effective. Note his keen pragmatic
analysis of the situation:

> First, viewing the subject practically, we
> find that scarcely any souls have been con-
> verted as the result of this method, whereas
> many are being converted by the direct preach-
> ing of the Word. It is therefore better to
> work by the method which receives the bless-
> ing--to cast in our nets where the fish are
> likely to be caught.
>
> Second, looking at it from a military stand-
> point, the educating of men is like the
> drilling of soldiers. If a British officer
> should enter Russian territory, there to
> drill an army of Russians, in the hope that
> some of them would enlist and fight loyally
> for the Queen of England, we would all pro-
> nounce his course unwise, and say that he
> had better enlist them first and drill them
> afterwards. So men should be first enlisted
> under Christ's banner, and then trained up
> to power and efficiency in our institutions
> of learning. (1886:469)

From the standpoint of historical perspective, we can
judge which of these views has proved to be the more
accurate in the Punjab. Little of the hoped-for result has
come out of the school method. It may even be said that
non-Christian youth have become inoculated against the
Gospel by going through Christian schools, learning biblical
truths but withstanding the urgings of the Spirit. Non-
Christian religions have undergone reform movements
from within, often led by those who have imbibed

Christian ethics at mission schools but lack the dynamic of
lives changed by the Holy Spirit. Far from being more
receptive, reformed Hinduism and Islam have shown a greater
resistance to Christianity.

Reasons for Ineffectiveness

Why have schools proved so ineffective as evangelizing
agents among non-Christians? At the start their evangelistic purpose was kept uppermost and every effort was
bent to win the students to Christ. Preoccupation with
teaching secular subjects sometimes crowded out prayerful,
persistent efforts to witness. The riots and unpleasant
publicity that resulted when a student was converted discouraged administrators from urging anyone to a definite
commitment. The teaching of Bible as an academic subject
often robs it of its power, for it is studied objectively
as history or literature without the aid of the Holy Spirit
to prepare the heart to believe and obey. All these reasons
only partially explain why evangelism through education has
proved unfruitful.

Probably the most basic factor causing ineffectiveness is
that schools reach young people at an age when they have
little or no influence upon their society. Many students
are responsive and seemingly have a sincere faith during
their school days, but apostatize shortly after leaving
school. They are accused of feigning faith in order to
receive financial assistance in their education. This may
be true of some, but most students who are won to Christ
genuinely believe, but lack the maturity to stand up against
the power structure of their own society once they leave
school. Not having sufficient influence to persuade their
parents and non-Christian relatives to their new viewpoint,
they find themselves under great social pressure to recant.
Their future employment and marriage arrangements are at
stake. This is more than most can endure. Having denied
their faith, many react to guilt feelings by becoming
actively anti-Christian. For these reasons schools have
proved ineffective in making permanent disciples of Jesus
Christ.

Care of Orphans

In 1857 Miss Elizabeth Gordon started an orphanage in
Sialkot. Andrew Gordon approved of this, for he felt the
care of orphans was a truly charitable work, and the children were under Christain influence all day, not just part
time as in day schools. These children could be trained
to be useful Christian workers and homemakers. The first
catechists employed by the U.P. Mission were two Indians
from the Presbyterian orphanage at Ludhiana, George
Washington Scott and Elisha P. Swift. They proved to be
faithful workers and contributed greatly to the witness of
the Mission in the early days. The first Indian professor
in the Theological Seminary, G.L. Thakur Das, was one of the
orphans from Miss Gordon's home. Later the boys were moved
to the Boys' Industrial Home in Gujranwala where they were
taught simple trades. Of the twelve orphan boys two became
ordained ministers, one was an unordained evangelistic worker,
seven were fine Christian laymen, and only two were not
committed Christians.

Some of the girls were brought to the orphanage by
Christian British officials who had rescued them from being
sold into prostitution. Of the seventeen girls brought up
in the orphanage in those early years, only three remained
unconverted, while the others proved to be helpful Christian homemakers. As mentioned earlier, many wives for
converts were provided from the girls at the orphanage.
This fulfilled a real need for the men who were converted
apart from their families. This ministry was phased out as
it gradually developed into the Girls' Boarding School at
Hajipur, Sialkot.

In 1900 the Mission was unexpectedly plunged into
orphanage work once again because of a severe famine in
Central India. Miss Emma Dean Anderson was commissioned by
the Mission to rescue orphans of famine victims. It took
five days by train just to reach the area. She found
cholera rampant in the refugee camps. One day ten dead
bodies were discovered just outside the mission compound
where she stayed. She and her helpers brought 165 boys and
girls between the ages of four and fourteen on a thousand
mile train trip to Pasrur. Missionaries along the way
provided food for the party; nevertheless twelve children

died before they arrived at their destination. Two years
later she gathered up two train carloads from another
famine area north of Bombay. These included sixteen babies
under three years of age. The boys were taught trades at
the Boys' Industrial Home in Gujranwala, and the girls were
divided up among several of the Girls' Boarding Schools
then in operation. Nearly all of them later confessed
Christ as Savior and became helpful members of the Church.
In this way orphanage work was used to build up the Church,
but it never became a major emphasis in the U.P. Mission.

Summary

The pioneer period from 1855 to 1872 was a time of slow
beginnings, not so much because the work was new, but
because the wrong strategy was adopted. Evangelism through
bazaar preaching and the distribution of Gospels and tracts
won a few educated urban men from high caste Hindu and
respectable Sikh and Muslim families. A total of 43 adults
from non-Christian backgrounds were baptized, but twenty
of these were later disciplined for serious offenses, and
a number of them apostatized.

The total communicant membership of the Church was only
71 by 1872. (See Figure 5.) This included the families
of the evangelists and missionaries, as well as older
orphans. Converts dislocated from their society were taught
and cared for in dependent communities centered around
mission stations. The difficulty of providing them with
food, shelter, and employment had reached major proportions
by 1872, and was threatening to demoralize the Mission.
The strategy of winning converts one-by-one from the high
castes proved unrewarding and produced an unhealthy
dependent Church. School work was growing but was also
unfruitful in terms of conversions. This was the situation
on the threshold of the Chuhra group movement that began
in 1873, and in the gracious providence of God transformed
this weak static Church into a vigorously growing one.

The tragedy is that this same faulty strategy was current
in every Mission in the Punjab and in many others throughout
India. Most of the Missions persisted in concentrating on

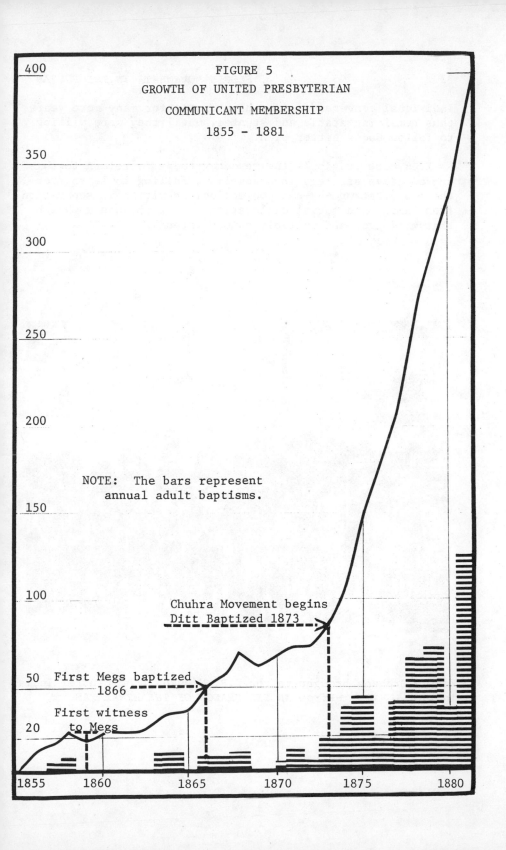

FIGURE 5
GROWTH OF UNITED PRESBYTERIAN
COMMUNICANT MEMBERSHIP
1855 - 1881

NOTE: The bars represent
annual adult baptisms.

Chuhra Movement begins
Ditt Baptized 1873

First Megs baptized
1866

First witness
to Megs

individual conversions from high castes for many more years,
thus remaining static and stunted, until they were willing
to follow God's better plan.

Even more tragic is the tendency today to return to this
unproductive strategy in evangelism, failing to learn from
the past that one-by-one conversions resulting in separation
from family and social dislocation cannot produce a Church
that will grow and multiply as God intends.

Famine Orphans brought to the U.P. Mission from Central India
in 1901.   *--from IN THE SHADOW OF THE HIMALAYAS*

2

The Group Movement Among the Megs

Although the movement among the Megs, starting in 1859, is part of the pioneer period already covered, it provides so many important lessons in church growth principles, that we will study it separately in some detail. It is an illustration of an arrested group movement, all too common in India and elsewhere, and provides a striking contrast to the well developed people movement that followed it among the Chuhras.

The Megs (sometimes written Megh, Mihngh, or Meng) are a caste of the depressed classes who in 1855 lived in the foothills of the Jammu mountains mainly in the Sialkot, Gurdaspur and Gujrat districts. Since they were weavers by caste, though some were field laborers and grass cutters, they were classed above the Chuhras who were largely sweepers, scavengers and field laborers. Weavers were despised and relegated to a low caste largely because the indigenous handloom necessitated work with the lower half of the body in a pit. This accounts for the weaver being described as having "half the body in the grave and the other half in life."

The Megs shared two objectionable habits with other depressed groups: (1) they ate the flesh of dead animals; and (2) they ate the leavings of Muslims and high-caste Hindus. In 1879 they were persuaded by a *guru* or religious leader to pledge themselves to total abstinence from the flesh of dead animals. Then in March 1900 at a mass meeting of all the Megs they unanimously resolved never to eat the leavings of others. At the time they were first contacted for Christ, however, these objectionable habits were still common among them.

A Group Movement Begins

The movement among the Megs evidences the unique way the Holy Spirit prepares the hearts of men for the seed of the Word. The twenty-five families of Megs living in the village of Jhandran near Zafarwal in Sialkot district (See Figure 6.) had lost their attachment to idols and were searching for something better. An educated man, Mastan Singh, who had rejected formal religion and held rationalistic views, applied to these people to become their spiritual teacher or *guru*. He demanded that they provide him with a personal servant and supply all his needs for food, lodging, clothing and tobacco, promising in return to give daily religious instruction. So great was the spiritual hunger of the Megs that they willingly took on this financial burden, faithfully attended daily classes, and memorized countless religious lessons.

Mastan Singh proceeded to tear down Hinduism and Islam. After 18 months he cautiously revealed his own rationalistic views, declaring that there is no being greater than man, and no reward or punishment at the end of this life. The Megs were shocked and bitterly disappointed. Unable to accept his teaching, they ran him out of their village, but were left with an even greater thirst for truth.

Four months later a newly employed, poorly educated catechist, Jawahar Masih, stopped at a sugar mill just outside of Jhandran and began to read the Gospel of Mark to a group of men loading sugar cane. Their initial curiosity soon gave place to genuine interest. At their urgent request Jawahar Masih stayed for three days giving intensive teaching. Gordon says:

> ... interest deepened and extended, until it pervaded almost the entire Meg community of Jhandran to such a degree that for three days and nights they scarcely took time to eat or sleep. So intent, indeed, were they upon hearing the precious "old, old story" of Jesus, the Son of God, the Savior of sinners, that they seemed no longer to care for anything else. (1886:199)

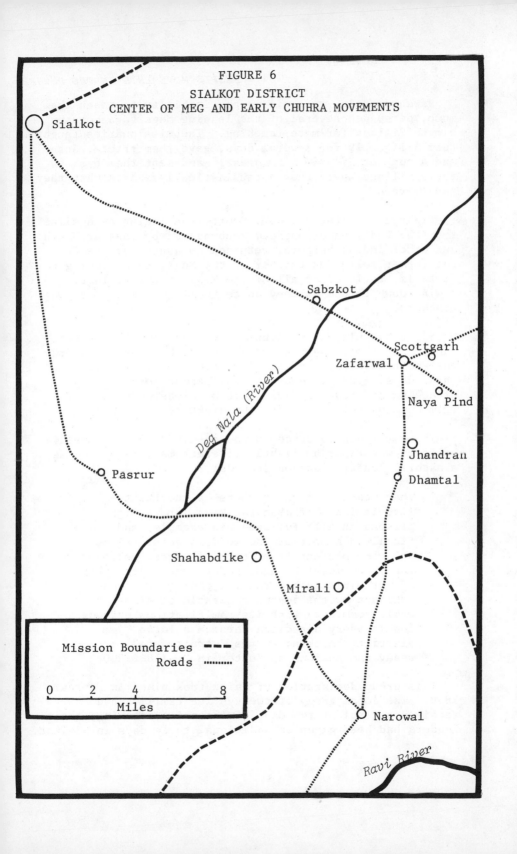

FIGURE 6
SIALKOT DISTRICT
CENTER OF MEG AND EARLY CHUHRA MOVEMENTS

Jawahar Masih, recognizing his inability to teach them
much, persuaded several of the leading Megs to accompany
him to Sialkot for more teaching. The missionaries taught
them diligently for several days, gave them tracts, Gospels,
and a copy of *Pilgrim's Progress,* and sent them back to
their village where they enthusiastically shared what they
had learned.

Eight days later Mr. G.W. Scott, the Indian evangelist
from the Ludhiana orphanage, accompanied by Jawahar Masih
and other Indian helpers, returned to Jhandran. Fakira,
the former religious teacher of the Megs, came running to
meet him, followed by all of the Megs of the village,
bowing down to him as they do to their own religious
teachers.

Scott and his party spent a week teaching this eager
band. While they were there about 300 Megs gathered from
the entire district to attend wedding ceremonies lasting
three days. They evidenced such intense interest that
preaching and teaching were kept up almost continuously
from morning until far into the night.

The first man to stand up and openly declare himself a
believer was Pipo, a slightly literate man, respected as
a natural leader. Gordon records:

> Then nearly all the members of the twenty-
> five families of Jhandran Megs (about eighty
> persons in all) followed his example; and
> finally a number of the wedding guests also,
> who were present from other villages, believed.
> Thus, our mission band, before the fourth year
> of our ministry had run its course, was made
> jubilant by the joyful spectacle of almost a
> whole community with its ramifications extend-
> ing in every direction through a large
> district, knocking at the "strait gate",
> ready and anxious to "enter in." (1886:200)

This group declaration of faith took place in February
1859. The local group of twenty-five families had
received a total of ten days of intensive teaching; their
leaders had been given an additional three days in Sialkot.

Nevertheless, Mr. Scott left without baptizing anyone, for current mission policy demanded several <u>months</u> of preparatory instruction preceding baptism.

Opposition Arises

As Scott left Jhandran, two young lads, Bhajna and Magana, secretly followed, determined to accompany him in his travels. He refused to take them with him, but allowed them to run along beside his pony for a while as they talked of spiritual matters. Unconsciously they went farther than intended and were twelve miles down the road when angry relatives caught up with them. It undoubtedly appeared to the upset families that Scott had deliberately encouraged the boys to leave home without parental permission. This was used by the adversary to crystalize the antagonism already in the heart of Magana's father, Diyala.

Opposition arose within ten days of the February 1859 visit. Initially it came from Diyala, a bigoted idolater who was one of the headmen (*nambardars*) of the Meg community. Realizing that Christianity posed a threat to his idolatrous faith, and more important, to his position of leadership in the community, he actively stirred up opposition both from within and without the Meg caste.

Opposition from among the Megs themselves centered on social rather than religious issues. Parents who had already made marriage arrangements for their children feared these would be cancelled if they became Christians. Their strong sense of caste identity made them shrink from any move that would cause division.

Muslim landlords in the area, hearing that their Meg workers were considering a change in faith, determined to prevent it. Gordon says they feared that Christians would refuse to work on the Sabbath. It is more likely that, in addition to their traditional antagonism to Christianity, they anticipated that this adoption by the Megs of the religion of the rulers of India would lift them from their depressed status and render them less vulnerable to exploitation.

After a brief absence, G.W. Scott returned and ptiched
his tent on the outskirts of the village, anticipating
another fruitful time of teaching. He found organized
resistance. The opposition, led by local Muslims and
Diyala, forced the timid group of eighty Megs to declare
their readiness to receive baptism only on the following
conditions:

> First, that they be allowed to limit their
> marriages to families of their own caste,
> and to have their marriage ceremonies per-
> formed according to their old religion, which
> would involve them in the observance of
> certain idolatrous rites.

> Second, that they should be allowed to work
> on the Sabbath.

> Third, that they should be permitted to
> acknowledge their own religious teachers
> and gods equally with Jesus Christ. (Gordon
> 1886:203-204)

Rather than considering each point individually and
attempting to come to an agreement which would calm their
fears without compromising on essential Christian doctrines,
the Indian evangelist, Mr. G.W. Scott, flatly refused the
conditions with the statement: "No man can cross a river
on two **boats**. You must forsake all for Christ, or you will
not be counted worthy of Him." (Gordon 1886:204)

This crucial confrontation caused a charp division among
the Megs. Most of the inquirers turned away from Christ
in order to placate their Muslim masters and avoid persecution. Only a few, with Pipo as their leader, declared
themselves willing to forsake all for Christ. Had the
group maintained its solidarity, a growing movement would
probably have resulted. This division, however, seriously
weakened the position of the few loyal believers.

The full force of persecution was then directed at these
few believers. They were forbidden to draw water from the
village wells, to smoke the pipe with old friends, or to
take part in village activities. They were beaten so
severely that their leader, Pipo, was bedridden for six

months and nearly died. The opposition group planned to
drive the families from their homes if they did not renounce
these Christian ideas. For one whole year the small band
of believers held out, encouraged by more than a dozen
visits by members of the Mission. Then all but Pipo
succumbed, paid a fine, and put on a feast for the Megs
of the area to celebrate their re-instatement in the
community. They returned all Christian books to the
missionaries, and ceased to communicate with them. Only
Pipo and his family stood firm, secretly visited with the
evangelists and missionaries, and kept reading the New
Testament. Pipo was never baptized, but Gordon says:

> He had come to love Jesus with a love so
> strong that he could not yield. He kept the
> Holy Book lying open before him on his loom,
> and continued for years to weave and read
> and meditate, telling the good news to all
> comers as he had opportunity. (1886:205-206)

In 1862 a Meg from a village six miles from Jhandran
requested literature from the missionaries and revealed
a considerable understanding of Christian truth. He and
ten others in his village had been taught by Pipo.

During the summer of 1866 Pipo became ill. Realizing
that he did not have long to live, he called together all
his near relatives and friends, some of whom were not
sympathetic to Christianity. After urging the whole
company to believe in Jesus and follow Him, he turned to
his younger brother Bhajna, and said gently, "I confidently
believe that Jesus Christ will cause us to meet again, and
we shall dwell together in one place." (Gordon 1886:215)

Baptism of Kanaya and Bhajna

Pipo's younger brother, Bhajna, and his friend, Kanaya,
were deeply affected by Pipo's life and witness. Four
others also had their interest rekindled by Pipo's death-
bed scene. They began to meet secretly at night in a
secluded garden where Bhajna read God's Word to them. This
was short lived because 18 families including Bhajna and
Kanaya moved to a new village, Naya Pind, three miles from
Jhandran, causing the little band of believers to be divided.
(See Figure 6.)

When Scott camped a few miles away, Bhajna visited him at night and promised to come to Sialkot for baptism after sowing his grain. A month later he fulfilled his promise by walking 26 miles to Sialkot only to discover that Scott was camping six miles away. Scott greeted him warmly when he arrived tired and hungry, but advised him to delay his baptism until he could get his new bride from her parents' home, as they might refuse to send her to him after his baptism. He decided to try to get her, but promised to return for baptism in ten days' time.

Returning home, Bhajna told his parents of his decision to become a Christian. They were displeased. His only supporter was Kanaya who declared himself ready to take the same step in spite of the fact that he had a wife and five children. Bhajna tried to persuade his in-laws to give him his wife, but they delayed beyond the ten day limit he had set with Mr. Scott. Not wanting to break his promise to Scott, Bhajna set out with Kanaya for Sialkot without waiting for his bride to be given to him. They arrived in Sialkot only to learn that Scott was again out on tour.

While in Sialkot that evening a significant event took place. A Christian invited Bhajna and Kanaya to eat supper with him. They hesitated, for eating with Christians meant breaking caste. Should their people learn of their action, they would be forbidden to eat, drink, smoke the *huqqa* or associate with other members of their caste. It was a momentous decision for them. With that meal they took up their cross, determined to follow Him to the end.

The two weary travellers tramped a total of 100 miles in search of Mr. Scott who was on an evangelistic tour. Most of that journey was accomplished without food, for Muslims and Hindus alike refused to feed them when they admitted to being Christians. Great was their joy when at last they arrived at Scott's tent and announced their intention of being baptized.

Incredibly, after such a demonstration of earnest faith and determination, they still were not baptized, but simply taken into a class of inquirers to be more fully taught! Relatives sought them out with the sole purpose of persuading them to renounce this new faith and return home.

They used humble entreaty, tears, and threats—all to no
avail. The two young disciples remained firm. After a
few days they again begged for baptism. Gordon writes:

> A convenient day in November 1866 was set,
> when Kanaya, Bhajna, Abdullah and three
> others were formally and solemnly received
> into the Church; and we can well appreciate
> their feelings on this joyful occasion, as
> expressed by Bhajna, who had loved Jesus for
> seven long years.* He said, "The great desire
> of our hearts is at last fulfilled; we have
> now given ourselves up to Jesus Christ."
> (1886:230)

Note on Figure 5 the time lapse between the original contact
with the Megs and the first baptisms.

Reconciliation Attempts

When Bhajna and Kanaya came to Sialkot, they expected to
be baptized almost immediately and then released to return
home. This, however, was not mission policy. Even after
baptism they were detained for further teaching. Gordon
writes:

> After the new converts had been taught and
> confirmed by the brethren in Sialkot for a
> period of three months,* Mr. Scott and
> Mr. Clement, accompanied by Kanaya and Bhajna
> and other Christians, went to Zafarwal and
> pitched their tent outside of the town.
> (1886:231)

Imagine the psychological effect those three months of
separation must have had on the families and relatives of
the new converts. Kanaya's wife and five children justi-
fiably resented this seeming desertion by their bread-
winner. Bhajna was the only living son and therefore the
sole support of his parents. To show such indifference

---

* Underlining by author

toward one's family and to forsake one's responsibilities
just for the sake of some new religious teaching was
incomprehensible. It is most unlikely that Kanaya and
Bhajna would have chosen this long separation had it been
left up to them. They were forced by mission policy to
take a course they must have known would be misinterpreted
by their people.

When they did return after three months to camp near
their village, the men visited their homes and repeatedly
asserted their eagerness to live with their families and
assume their normal responsibilities, on condition they be
allowed to do so as Christians. On Several occasions
Kanaya said to his wife:

> "You must not imagine that I wish to be
> separated from you all. It is my wish and
> intention to live in my own village, in my
> own house, and with my own wife and children
> whom I dearly love ... I will do for your
> support and comfort as much as I ever did,
> and care for you as affectionately; but I
> will do it all as a Christian, and will
> remain a Christian. (Gordon 1886:234-245)

Once while Kanaya was talking to his wife, Diyala and others
rushed in and severely beat him and Bhajna, forbidding them
ever again to come into the village. When Mr. Scott
reported this attack to the government, they took action
against the offenders. Through fear of the law opposition
temporarily lessened, permitting Kanaya and Bhajna again
to visit their homes in the hope of affecting a reconciliation. Soon a group of 25 villagers set a watch day and
night with the intent of capturing them and having them
imprisoned on the false accusation of thievery. Warned
of this plot, the converts reluctantly ceased all attempts
to contact their families in their home village of Naya
Pind.

We must not think that the three months' instruction at
the mission station caused the caste to reject the converts.
It simply aggravated the basic grievance they had against
them--that of having broken caste by eating with Christians
who were outsiders. This was considered the unforgivable
sin. This is illustrated by another significant event that

took place soon after at a wedding feast held in a Meg
village not far away. Kanaya and Bhajna attended with
Mr. Scott, again hoping to be reconciled to their families.
Bhajna's relatives were divided into two parties--those
personally fond of him, who saw some good in Christianity;
and those strongly opposed. His mother-in-law who loved
him dearly was convinced the kindness would win him back.
After asking Mr. Scott to leave, she urged Bhajna and
Kanaya to eat the feast with the family. In their eyes this
meant reinstatement into the caste, for only caste members
may eat together. They were convinced that once caste ties
were re-established, religious differences would soon
disappear. The converts were delighted with this turn of
events, still firm in their determination to be Christians
within their caste structure. However, when the opposing
party caught sight of the group about to dine together,
they shouted:

> NO! NO! If these *Kiranis* [a term of reproach
> used for Christians] are permitted to eat with
> us, our caste too will be broken; we will be
> polluted, and left without a religion.
> (Gordon 1886:242)

This caused such a furor that a *Panchayat* (clan court) was
called to decide the issue. The party favorable to Bhajna
was severely rebuked and the two converts were ejected
from the festivities. The sympathetic party followed them
out, still entreating them to reconsider. Bhajna's mother-
in-law expressed her bitterness of soul by saying:

> "Why do you thus dishonor us? You have
> embraced a religion which separates father
> and son, mother and daughter, husband and
> wife, and sunders all the sweet ties of
> love and friendship. What profit have you
> found in such a religion? Better, far
> better, had it been if you had died with
> your brother, Pipo, for then we could have
> borne your loss with resignation, as we
> have borne his. But now, living, you load
> us with an infamy that is insupportable.
> To endure it and live is impossible. Death
> only can end it." (Gordon 1886:243)

Note that she mentioned no doctrinal issue in her
denunciation of Christianity. She was horrified, not by
Christian teaching, but by the rift that had been created
in the family through that teaching. Social, not
theological, barriers proved the most difficult to overcome.

With the conversion of Kanaya and Bhajna hope revived
in the Mission that a group movement among the Megs would
develop. However, opposition continued to be so powerful
it was impossible for them to live in their homes. Bhajna's
wife was remarried to another, and Kanaya was reunited with
his family only after long months of arduous effort and
thrilling experiences told in detail by Gordon in *Our India
Mission*.

The Meg Movement Arrested

The Meg movement developed slowly for a few more years.
A chronological list of the principal Megs who became
Christians, their names, and the dates of baptism, based
on the account by Gordon, is shown in Figure 7. Note that
after the baptism of Kanaya and Bhajna, the next baptism
was of Kanaya's wife five years later. Again a lapse of
six years occurs before Kanaya's father was baptized in 1877.
After that one or two baptisms took place each year. The
largest group recorded for any one year was 14 in 1881.

Early converts were able to win some of their near
relatives. Gordon reports that the number of communicants
from the Megs by the end of 1884 was 59. Figure 8 reveals
the way the people responded who were close relatives of
early converts. Note that Bhajna and Kanaya and their
families make up 13 members. They with two other families,
those of Faklia and Jassu, total 30 members. Thus 50 per
cent of the communicant members were from these four family
units and were located in four villages--Jhandran, Naya
Pind, and Scottgarh being within a three mile radius of
Zafarwal, while Sukho Chak was ten miles away. (See Figure
6.) From this we see that the Meg movement affected only
a few families and was confined to a limited geographical
area.

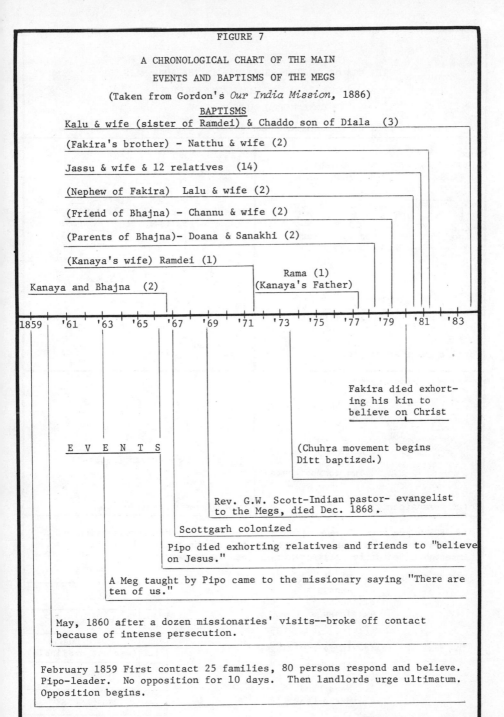

FIGURE 7

A CHRONOLOGICAL CHART OF THE MAIN
EVENTS AND BAPTISMS OF THE MEGS

(Taken from Gordon's *Our India Mission*, 1886)

BAPTISMS

Kalu & wife (sister of Ramdei) & Chaddo son of Diala   (3)

(Fakira's brother) - Natthu & wife (2)

Jassu & wife & 12 relatives   (14)

(Nephew of Fakira) Lalu & wife (2)

(Friend of Bhajna) - Channu & wife (2)

(Parents of Bhajna)- Doana & Sanakhi (2)

(Kanaya's wife) Ramdei (1)

Kanaya and Bhajna   (2)

Rama (1)
(Kanaya's Father)

1859   '61   '63   '65   '67   '69   '71   '73   '75   '77   '79   '81   '83

Fakira died exhort-
ing his kin to
believe on Christ

E V E N T S

(Chuhra movement begins
Ditt baptized.)

Rev. G.W. Scott-Indian pastor- evangelist
to the Megs, died Dec. 1868.

Scottgarh colonized

Pipo died exhorting relatives and friends to "believe
on Jesus."

A Meg taught by Pipo came to the missionary saying "There are
ten of us."

May, 1860 after a dozen missionaries' visits--broke off contact
because of intense persecution.

February 1859 First contact 25 families, 80 persons respond and believe.
Pipo-leader. No opposition for 10 days. Then landlords urge ultimatum.
Opposition begins.

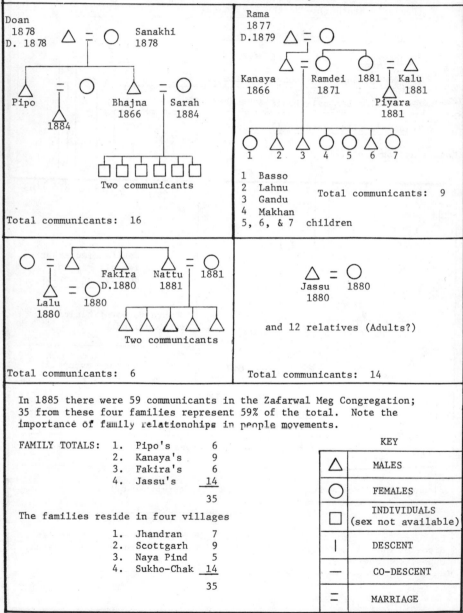

FIGURE 8

THE WEB OF KINSHIP RELATIONS IN THE FOUR MAIN
FAMILIES OF THE MEG CONGREGATION
OF ZAFARWAL AREA IN 1885

Showing number of communicants and dates of baptism under each name.

Doan
1878
D. 1878   Sanakhi
               1878

Pipo   Bhajna   Sarah
            1866   1884
    1884

Two communicants

Total communicants: 16

Rama
1877
D.1879

Kanaya   Ramdei   1881   Kalu
1866   1871   1881
                     Piyara
                     1881

1 Basso
2 Lahnu
3 Gandu   Total communicants: 9
4 Makhan
5, 6, & 7 children

Fakira   Nattu   1881
D.1880   1881

Lalu   1880
1880

Two communicants

Total communicants: 6

Jassu   1880
1880

and 12 relatives (Adults?)

Total communicants: 14

In 1885 there were 59 communicants in the Zafarwal Meg Congregation;
35 from these four families represent 59% of the total. Note the
importance of family relationships in people movements.

FAMILY TOTALS: 1. Pipo's   6
                 2. Kanaya's   9
                 3. Fakira's   6
                 4. Jassu's   _14_
                                 35

The families reside in four villages

                 1. Jhandran   7
                 2. Scottgarh   9
                 3. Naya Pind   5
                 4. Sukho-Chak _14_
                                  35

KEY	
△	MALES
○	FEMALES
□	INDIVIDUALS (sex not available)
│	DESCENT
—	CO-DESCENT
=	MARRIAGE

After 1884 the movement among the Megs stopped growing. The Zafarwal congregation, organized of Meg converts in 1874, shows the following membership over the next twenty years:

1885 -- 72 members	1900 -- 60 members
1890 -- 68 members	1905 -- 65 members
1895 -- 85 members	

It is assumed that the above members were mostly Megs, as the Chuhra movement developed in another area.

In the *Triennial Report on the Foreign Mission of the U.P. Church of North America 1919-1921* is found the following statement concerning the outcome of the Meg movement:

> It is not cheering to have to say that the movement among the Meghs of Jandran, related by Dr. Gordon did not continue until it embraced the most of that class. The enmity shown against Kanaya's family did not grow less, and only eight or ten families eventually became Christians. The descendants of these people are now quite numerous and many of them are engaged in the work of the Mission. The majority of the Meghs have now been affiliated with the Arya Samaj [a Hindu reform movement]. (197)

The report goes on to make an interesting prediction:

> It seems certain, however, that they will not long be held by that loose bond [with the Arya Samaj], since they are ineligible for final induction into Hinduism, and while they practice many Hindu rites, are still of necessity to some degree reckoned as untouchable by Hindus of higher caste. (197)

It is significant to note that although the Megs were declared "cleansed" by the Arya Samaj, they were in actuality still given an inferior status, and in spite of verbal promises, were never allowed the full rights of a caste Hindu group. Nevertheless, they have continued to the present to be Hindus. Once the group decision against

Christianity had been made, it was never reversed. The golden opportunity had been lost.

Why the Movement Was Arrested

The Meg movement had convinced leaders in Pipo, Kanaya and Bhajna. It took place in a dissatisfied population who were seeking the truth and eager for change when first contacted in 1859. Even as late as 1908 a leader of the Meg community openly advised his people to enter other communities, he himself favoring the Christian religion. That same year 22,115 out of the 40,000 Megs joined the Arya Samaj. This provides ample evidence that they were restless and searching in those years. Why then was the movement arrested when it had all the ingredients of becoming a sweeping movement, bringing in most or all of this caste?

On the surface it appears that one of the major reasons for the Meg movement being arrested in its growth was extreme persecution that developed both from within the group and from the surrounding Muslims. Traditionally Islam has shown active antagonism to Christianity, so the Megs found themselves pressured and intimidated by their Muslim landlords. As avowed converts were severely beaten and threatened, fear gripped the inquirers who had not yet taken an open stand for Christ. To escape persecution they actively joined the opposition.

What factors were key in producing such deep seated antagonism? Was this fierce opposition inevitable? Was it all due to the natural offense of the Gospel, or could the whole situation have been handled in such a way that opposition would not have developed to such a detrimental extent? The following factors all contributed to fan the flames.

Delayed Baptism

A major reason for arrested growth was that interested inquirers were not baptized at the most opportune time. The Megs of Jhandran had sought a new religion, had received and then rejected a *guru*, so that when Jawahar Masih came

to them and began teaching them from the Scriptures, he
found them unusually prepared in heart. Twenty-five families
received a total of ten days' intensive teaching and their
leaders had an additional three days. This teaching resulted in 80 persons publicly declaring their faith in Jesus
Christ in front of about 300 Megs gathered at a wedding
feast in February 1859. Was that not an indication of
genuine faith sufficient for baptism? Yet not one of them
was baptized! Why?

Evidently Scott, well indoctrinated with current mission
policy, felt that much more preliminary teaching was
necessary before baptism could be administered. To baptize
too quickly was considered unscriptural. Yet, what is the
New Testament pattern for baptism? Is a long period of
preparatory teaching essential? In Acts 2:38 Luke records
Peter's sermon to the Jews on the day of Pentecost in which
he says:

> "Repent and be baptized every one of you in
> the name of Jesus Christ for the forgiveness
> of your sins; and you shall receive the gift
> of the Holy Spirit." ... so those who received
> his word were baptized, and there were added
> that day* about three thousand souls.
> (Acts 2:38,41)

At Pentecost believers were baptized the first day they
heard the message. Teaching followed, as stated in verse 42:

> And they devoted themselves to the apostles'
> teaching and fellowship, to the breaking of
> bread and prayers.

True, these people being Jews had much background preparation. However, the same pattern is seen in Samaria
where Philip preached. No extended time of teaching is
mentioned. Luke records:

> But when they believed Philip as he preached
> good news about the kingdom of God and the
> name of Jesus Christ, they were baptized,
> both men and women. (Acts 8:12)

---

* Underlining by author

The Ethiopian eunuch, having a divinely prepared heart with
some knowledge of the Old Testament was baptized by Philip
on confession of faith after possibly only an hour or two
of instruction. The Philippian jailor and his family,
presumably from a completely pagan background, still were
baptized by Paul after only a couple of hours of teaching.

It is important to note that although this group of 80
Meg believers were a minority of only a fourth of those
present at the wedding, no antagonism was expressed then.
It took several days for opposition to crystalize. Had this
large group been baptized immediately, they would have taken
a definite public stand difficult to renounce with honor.
They formed a large enough unit that social pressure could
not be exerted upon them with the devastating effect it had
later on the few lone believers who remained faithful. This
illustrates a biblical principle seen in operation in Acts.
Large enough numbers of men and women became Christians at
one time that outsiders were more or less helpless to apply
severe social pressures to make them recant. At Pentecost,
when 3,000 became Christians, there was no active opposition
from the Jewish rulers. As Dr. D.M. McGavran points out
in his book, *The Bridges of God:*

> ... this was not because the rulers felt
> kindly toward the Christians. It was because
> so many had become Christians that ostracism
> was impossible. (1955:18)

If these eighty Megs had been baptized on their confession
of faith after ten days of teaching, they would have
presented a solid block of 25 families or more who could
not have been easily splintered, pressured, and drawn back
into unbelief. They would form a social unit large enough
to give one another moral support, provide needed Christian
fellowship, and even attract others to join them.

In summarizing this principle, McGavran says:

> Christian movements against which ostracism
> can be used grow slowly if at all. Christian
> movements against which ostracism cannot be
> used are able to grow rapidly. (1955:20)

Seven years after the above event, Kanaya and Bhajna
promised Mr. G.W. Scott that they would openly declare their
faith in Christ and be baptized. They had been secret
believers for some years. In order to carry out this
promise, they made a 100-mile trek in the early fall of 1866
in search of Scott, who was on tour. This was ample
evidence of their sincerity. Nevertheless, in accordance
with mission policy, their baptisms were delayed until
November 1866. Here is a gap of seven years between that
spontaneous responsiveness shown in 1859 and the first
baptisms in 1866. How many Christians would there be in
the world if all believers had to go through so many
difficulties just to be baptized? This faulty mission
policy was partially responsible for lack of growth among
the Megs.

Broken Caste Ties

The powerful effect of caste must not be underestimated.
Had the missionaries fully understood the importance of
caste as a channel for the spread of the Gospel rather than
a barrier to it, the end result among the Megs might have
been different. To all people of Hindu origin it is
unthinkable to eat with members of another caste. When
a Christian offered food to Kanaya and Bhajna out of
simple courtesy, that signified to them a complete break
of caste. It is significant that immediately after that
meal they traveled nearly 70 miles in search of Mr. Scott,
and were unable to get food. Gordon writes:

> In the evening hunger began to remind them
> that they had not tasted food since they
> had broken caste by eating at Sialkot on the
> previous evening ... "Who are you?" was
> everywhere the first question asked; and the
> villagers on learning that they were weavers,
> sent them to weavers of the Muhammadan faith;
> these again questioned them sharply and sent
> them elsewhere. They were once asked whether
> they were Hindu weavers, and on answering that
> they were not [because of having broken caste
> the day before], were sent away very rudely.
> (1886:226-227)

The enforced time of instruction on the mission compound confirmed this break of caste. Later at the wedding
when they were about to eat with relatives as a sign of
reinstatement into their caste, the opposition swayed
opinion against them by saying, "If these are permitted to
eat with us, our caste too will be broken; we will be
polluted and left without a religion." Gordon adds:
"Nothing will rouse a Hindu community like a question of
eating, drinking, and such other acts as affect their
caste." (1886:242)

Had the missionaries fully realized how much of a
barrier would be raised by this matter of eating with others,
they could have taken a different approach. Suppose they
had said, "We will not allow you to break caste at this
time by eating with us. Christians do all eat together.
We believe that all men are brothers and equally precious
in God's sight. Eating together is one of the special
characteristics of the Christian community. But we know
that if you eat with us now, your caste fellows will not
accept you and even your families will be forced to
ostracize you. We feel it is important for you to remain
in your homes, witnessing to your friends and relatives
about your new faith. Therefore, we will not allow you to
create such a barrier over a point that is not essential
to salvation. When there are a large number of believers
from your caste, then we will be happy to have you join in
eating with us."

By taking such an approach, the missionaries would have
risked misunderstanding by the new converts. They might
have interpreted this as another way of keeping them in a
lower status, just as other faiths did. It would probably
have aroused criticism from Westerners as well, as being
a denial of the Christian doctrine of the brotherhood of
man. Nevertheless, it might have enabled the converts to
remain in their normal status in society where they could
witness to their own people.

It is possible that even without breaking caste,
the converts would not have been accepted in their village.
But at least one less superficial barrier would have been
raised between them and their non-Christian neighbors.
History has proved that new believers are most effective in
winning their own relatives and those of the same clan or

class. In this way caste becomes a channel for growth. If
this natural means of outreach is blocked, church growth is
bound to be seriously retarded.

We must not be too critical of our pioneer missionaries,
for it is much easier to exercise hindsight than foresight,
and to understand afterwards what could or should have been
done. They had amazing insight into many aspects of the
work. Andrew Gordon in particular reveals in his book
an astonishing discernment of the cultural and psychological
factors involved. He was far ahead of most in anthropological
understanding and in grasping church growth principles that
have gained acceptance only in recent years.

Stress on Non-Essentials

Lacking clarity of insight into what consitutes the
kernel of the Gospel and what aspects are cultural husks,
church leaders often stress non-essentials. This is most
clearly illustrated by the way the compromise proposal
presented by the 80 believers in Jhandran was handled. Had
the believers been baptized immediately, and figuratively
burned their bridges behind them, these compromise conditions
would never have been prepared--the ideal situation. However, even after they were presented, if the issues had
been handled with more understanding and tact, the result
could have been vastly different.

The first proposal was that they be allowed to limit
their marriages to families of their own caste and have
their marriage ceremonies performed according to their old
customs which included certain idolatrous rites. There is
nothing non-Christian about marrying within one's caste,
and no set marriage ceremony is prescibed in Scripture.
The major part of this proposal could have been accepted.
It probably would not have caused permanent damage to
allow the old wedding ceremony to continue in use
temporarily. This usually happens in newly emergin,
Churches. Eventually as the Christian community grew,
changes could be made. This approach would have calmed
their fears, proving that all ties with previous traditions
were not being cut, and would have enabled non-Christians to
honor previously arranged marriage alliances without undue
apprehension. Such mixed marriages in a responsive

community can prove a means of spreading the Gospel more
rapidly. Later among the Chuhras this is what did happen.
More than thirty years after the start of the Chuhra
movement, the Annual Meeting Minutes for 1909 expressed
satisfaction that an increasing number of Christian marriage
ceremonies were being performed. This implies that up to
that time the majority of the Chuhra weddings were done
Hindu style.

A better solution would have been to accept the Hindu
traditional wedding ceremony in outline, but by means of
open discussion enable the Megs to distinguish the elements
that were idolatrous and to create Christian functional
substitutes for them. In this way the believer could be
true to his convictions and not have to worship idols as
part of the wedding ceremony, yet the basic traditional
pattern would remain the same, as reassurance to those not
yet Christian.

The second compromise proposal concerned working on the
Sabbath. The United Presbyterians were at that time
extremely strict in their observance of the Sabbath. Gordon
states that the Muslim landlords were incited to oppose the
Meg movement to Christianity on hearing that the new
Christians would refuse to work on the Sabbath. Had the
converts been instructed to time their worship services
to Friday afternoons when the Muslims had theirs, this might
not have developed into a bone of contention. It could
have resulted, however, in the missionary being recalled
to the homeland post-haste for suggesting such a heresy!

The third compormise condition was that the Megs be
permitted to acknowledge their own religious teachers and
gods equally with Jesus Christ. This, of course, touches
on the kernel of the Gospel and could not be tolerated.
However, if through discussion they were tactfully led to
admit that their old religious teachers and gods had not
brought them salvation or peace of heart, as they had
already experienced with their previous *guru*, they might
possibly have dropped this matter. It is unlikely that
this theological point was foremost in their concern.
Most religious controversy arises from social and cultural,
not theological, issues.

Instead of dealing with each item individually with understanding and tact, Mr. Scott demanded complete separation from the past with his statement, "No man can cross a river on two boats." This resulted in immediate and deep-seated division. How important it is to stand fast on essentials, and to be flexible in devising half-way measures in dealing with non-essentials.

Caste Consciousness

Although the Megs were restless and seeking, it appears that they still had a strong sense of caste consciousness. They identified closely with one another and were anxious to maintain their unity and integrity as a group. When they did change their religious status by joining the Arya Samaj, they did it as a large group of over 22,000 in 1908. The *Census Report of 1911* states: "Meghs are practically all Hindus, there being only 639 Sikhs and 37 Muhammadans." (Kaul, Part I, p.468). Only one and a half per cent of the whole Meg community adopted other religious faiths rather than identifying with their caste in joining the Arya Samaj.

Western stress on the importance of an individual decision for Christ blinded the eyes of the Mission to the possibility that a group decision could be authentic. The caste consciousness that worked against a decision for Christ could have sparked a people movement of the whole caste to Christ. By allowing and even encouraging a few stronger individuals to make their separate declarations of faith, the Mission created the impression that it was not important to remain part of the group. This resulted in such deep alienation that the Megs as a whole looked elsewhere for spiritual help.

Caste consciousness also played a large part in the reaction of the Megs to the Chuhra movement. As that movement gained momentum in the 1880's, Meg baptisms fell off. Note on Figure 7 that only three Meg baptisms are recorded after 1881. Megs considered themselves a superior caste to the Chuhras. As a large influx of Chuhras came into the Church, the Megs who were still hesitating on the brink of decision were no doubt repelled. Word soon spread that to become a Christian one must associate closely

with those lower on the social scale. This was a serious
deterrent. Had the missionaries fully understood what an
obstacle this was to the Megs, they could have established
a completely separate Church just for Megs at this early
stage, and such alienation might well have been avoided.

Hindu Pressure

    Another reason the movement among the Megs did not grow
was because of a renewed effort on the part of caste Hindus
to strengthen ties with the Scheduled Castes and make them
more solidly Hindu in orientation. Anderson speaks of
this as follows:

> To counteract the influence of Christianity,
> the non-Christian Megs sent over into Kashmir
> territory for a noted *guru* among them, and had
> meetings whose object was to enforce a strict
> adherence to their Hindu customs. (1909:217)

This effort culminated in the group movement to Arya Samaj
in 1908.

    It is true that a trickle of Meg converts continued for
several years, but the Christian movement among the Megs
did not expand and develop as it could have. The greatest
tragedy is that this is just one example of <u>hundreds</u> of
similar arrested people movements throughout the Indian
sub-continent.

Early Christian Workers --*from OUR INDIA MISSION*

3
The Chuhras

The Chuhras, the largest of the depressed classes in the
Punjab were considered the very lowest and most despised
of all groups. Many rural Chuhras worked as landless
laborers, but others performed those duties and jobs which
Hindus and Muslims consider to be most defiling, such as
(a) removing dead cows and other animals from fields and
premises; (b) skinning these animals; (c) removing bodies
of the dead who have no relatives to take care of them;
(d) executing criminals condemned by government order; and
(e) cleaning up and removing excreta from latrines and
public comfort areas.

In addition to their despised occupations, they defiled
themselves by eating the flesh of animals that had died of
natural causes, and by eating leftover food from the tables
of others. Rural Chuhras were paid only at harvest time,
receiving a small percentage of the wheat, rice, cotton,
sugar cane or other crop. The rest of the year they were
expected to subsist on daily handouts of food from their
landlords. Usually these were leftovers. The city sweepers
were also given cooked food not needed by their employers,
as a supplement to their meager salaries. Briggs remarks:

> There is nothing more degrading in the eyes
> of Hindu society than the eating of mixed
> leavings of the food of others. (1953:39)

One legend on the origin of the name "Chuhra" stresses this
point as H.A. Rose writes in his book, *A Glossary of the
Tribes and Castes of the Punjab*:

> Once Balmik, the founder of the caste, arrived
> late at a feast given by a Bhagat and found
> only fragments of it left. These he devoured
> and earned the name of Chuhra or "one who eats
> leavings." (1911:182)

Originally Chuhras lived outside the village limits in
houses constructed of bones and hides. A drum beat
indicated that an animal had died and they were to come
and remove it. They would take the hide and to satisfy
their perennial hunger they would eat the flesh of the
animal. At the time of the burial of Hindus they would
be given the funeral shroud.

Origin

Such a variety of traditions exist as to the origin of
the Chuhras that it is impossible to gain a clear picture
of where they originated or what caused them to fall so
low in the caste structure. Nearly all traditions concur
on one point:

> ... all claim to be "Disciples of Balmik"
> (who is considered progenitor or at least
> patron saint of the caste) or of Lal Beg
> (his adopted son). (Rose 1911:183)

Balmik was called Bala Shah by some groups of Chuhras.
This name is thought to be a Muslim name for the Hindu
saint, for its use originated about the time of the Muslim
conquest of India.

One of the more logical legends of their origin is
described by W.P. Hares in his article, "The Call From the
Land of the Five Rivers," and has an interesting bearing
on the people movement among them.

> There were four brothers, Brahmins, who
> lived together. One day one of their cows
> died, and after some disputation as to who
> should remove the carcass, the younger
> brother undertook to do it on the under-
> standing that he should not be outcasted as
> a result. He removed the carcass, but when

he returned to the house his three brothers
refused to receive him, as through contact
with the dead body he had become unclean.
They promised, however, to receive him on the
fourth day, but when the time arrived they
postponed his reception to the fourth week,
then to the fourth month, again to the fourth
year, and finally promised to receive him
back on the fourth *Jug* (age). The present
era, according to Hindu reckoning, is the
fourth *Jug*, and the Chuhras say that the
time of their restoration has now come.
(1927:5)

Other legends are common among groups in different areas.
Some believe the Chuhras are descendants of Dravidian
people conquered by the Aryan invasions. It may be that
the Chuhras have, in fact, a variety of origins.

Social Structure

Hindus considered Chuhras to be "untouchables." They
had to live in separate sections on the outskirts of the
village or in a separate part of the town, with at least
one street between their residences and those of higher
castes. In many places they were restricted from using
certain roads, schools, and temples so as not to "pollute"
them. A Chuhra was so despised that even his shadow was
carefully avoided lest a higher caste man be defiled by it.

The Chuhras lived in a joint or extended family system,
patriarchally controlled. The sons brought their wives
home to become part of the family unit. Polygamy was
allowed but practiced by only a few. If a young man died,
his brother was obligated to take the widow as one of his
wives. A barren woman was considered under a curse and her
husband usually took a second wife. The birth of a son
was proclaimed by a string of acacia leaves hung across the
door, calling for a great celebration. When a girl was
born, neighbors delivered appropriate words of consolation.

A collection of families, known as a *biradari*, were
governed by a group of men chosen by common agreement of
the people. This was call the *Panchayat* (literally "the
five member group.") These representatives chose their
own permanent leader known as the *Pir Panch*. All disputes
within the caste were brought before this group; their
decisions were considered final.

Religion

As with the other aspects of Chuhra life, their religious
beliefs seem to vary from place to place. The main tenets
of their faith were as follows:

1.   Sin is a reality.
2.   There is one God.
3.   Bala is a mediator.
4.   Sacrifices and offerings should be given at
     times. These include animals, corn, raw
     sugar and *ghi* [clarified butter].
5.   The spirit returns to God at death.
6.   There will be a resurrection of the body.
7.   There will be a judgment.
8.   There are angels.
9.   There are good and evil spirits.
     (Rose   1911:204)

The Chuhras had a priesthood, and considered Bala Shah
to be their High Priest-Mediator. They had no temples,
but made dome-shaped mounds of earth facing east, dedicated
to Bala Shah, with niches for lamps. They frequently lit
oil lamps at the graves of "holy men." Congregational
worship was conducted on Thursday and led by the priest.
It consisted of sacrifices, offerings, and chants of Psalm-
like hymns in praise of God and Bala Shah. John W. Youngson,
writing in *The Encyclopedia of Religion and Ethics* gives
the following translation of a chant:

        O God!   O God!
        God's will be done!
        May the gift of Thy hand avert evil!
        May He have mercy on all!
        We call on the One True Name,
        The great Shah Bala.
        At Thy door there is supply for all.
             (1930: Vol. III, 616)

After each chant the congregation would respond with "Amen."

Although the Chuhras are considered to be basically Hindu in orientation, the tenets mentioned above indicate a strong Islamic influence on their religion. Rose quotes translations of hymns in which the name of Mohammad is mentioned. The powerful monotheism of Islam eroded their belief in a multitude of deities, yet they were conscious of the reality of sin and their need of a mediator.

Many elements of Chuhra belief prepared them to accept Jesus Christ as High Priest-Mediator and to understand other aspects of the Christian fatih. Denzil Ibbetson writes in his book, *Outlines of Punjab Ethnography:* "They ... have a curious religion which in its doctrine resembles Christianity more than anything else we have in India." (1881: Vol. I, 154) This was one of the factors that encouraged a large movement to Christ among the Chuhras.

At the time of the Chuhra movement, however, their religious convictions were at low ebb. Gordon writes in 1886, "They ... tell us plainly that they have no religion." (175) Stewart nearly ten years later stated that their minds were nearly a blank on the subject of religion. Superstition, fetishism and ancestor sorship were common. Spirits were believed to be everywhere who had to be placated so as not to haunt or harm man. A Chuhra's primary concern in life was to maintain a safe and proper relationship to them. Fear and dread prevailed. Therefore, it appears that the bridge formed by their religious beliefs was less significant than the vacuum formed by the break-down of those beliefs.

Relationship to Others

According to the 1881 Census Report, there were 1,078,739 Chuhras in the Punjab, centered mostly in the central districts of the province. Stewart indicated that the Chuhras, although previously numbering about one-eighth of the population of the Punjab, were by 1896 rapidly joining other communities because of their restlessness and desire to improve their position. He breaks it down, as follows:

(1) Those who associate themselves with
    Hinduism (not necessarily being
    received by them)   -- 75%

(2) Those associated with Islam   -- 19%

(3) Those associated with Sikhism   -- 6%

This was not a new trend among the Chuhras; they had been
attempting for many years to raise their social status by
aligning with various religious groups.

In 1675, after Aurangzeb had executed Tegh Bahadur, the
ninth *guru* of the Sikhs, a group of Chuhras was sent to
bring back the limbs of the great leader. As a reward for
the great difficulties they had endured, a few were allowed
to become Sikhs. The Sikh leader, Gobind, who had said
that the lowly should be raised and live next to him, performed the ceremony of *Pahul* or initiation by sprinkling
sugar water on five men, three of whom were "outcastes."
Later larger numbers of Chuhras were taken into the Sikh
fold as a means of swelling their ranks in fighting the
Muslims.

Cunningham mentions this:

> These Sikhs, the descendants of converts from
> the despised Sweeper caste, were welcomed by
> the Khalsa at a time when they were engaged
> in a desperate struggle with the forces of
> Islam. But when the Sikhs dominated the Punjab,
> they found that the equality their religion
> promised them existed in theory rather than in
> fact   (1918:71-72)

In practice the Chuhras were never given equal status
but relegated to an inferior group called the *Mazhabi* Sikhs
or Sikhs "by religion." Hutton states:

> ... when he (a Chuhra) turns Sikh he becomes
> a Mazhabi, and the taint of his origin prevents
> his ever being admitted to full social equality
> with the Sikh of *Rajput* or *Jat* origin, despite
> the Sikh repudiation of caste. (1963:38-39)

The Muslims also did not accept them fully but called them *Musallis* (in some areas *Dindars*, *Sheikhs*, or *Kutanas*) treating them with a measure of distain.

After a sizable number of the Scheduled Castes had become Christians, the Arya Samaj and other Hindu reform movements put forth special efforts to keep them in the Hindu fold. They were afraid of losing the Scheduled Castes who were vital to the structure of the caste system because they performed the essential "unclean" jobs for the community. They foresaw the possibility that Christianity could gradually undermine the caste system. To counteract this they performed a special ceremony of purification (*Shuddhi*) that was supposed to remove the stigma of "untouchability" and raise the depressed classes to the level of recognized castes. In spite of all efforts, they were unable to overcome public prejudice and give the Chuhras full rights as a caste group. Hutton states:

> ... these persons without exception are not
> allowed to drink from wells belonging to real
> Hindus, Muslims, or Sikhs, and are not permitted
> to enter into their places of worship. (1963:219)

So we see the Chuhras, a people pressured and cajoled, increasingly eager to rise to better social standing, anxious to have more opportunities in life on an equal footing with their neighbors. Being under heavier economic and social pressure than the Megs, they were more ready to align themselves with other religions. For this reason, of all the groups in the Punjab, the Chuhras were the most potentially winnable and responsive. The ground was prepared by God for the seed of the Word. What a tragedy that so much effort had been expended on "hard ground" yielding little fruit! So many years had passed without recognition of this prepared field which was to yield so abundantly. Had all the Missions in the area mobilized a concentrated effort upon the depressed classes from the outset (particularly upon the Chuhras), instead of awakening to the realization of their responsiveness after 20, 30 or 40 years, surely a much larger Church would have developed.

4

The Chuhra Movement Begins
(1873-1880)

Ditt's Conversion

The Chuhra movement began in a seemingly insignificant way
in 1873. Nattu, a young Hindu convert of the *Jat* caste,
who himself proved to be a weak brother, witnessed to an
acquaintance named Ditt, a member of the despised Chuhra
caste. Ditt lived in Shahabdike, three miles south of
Mirali in Sialkot district. (See Figures 6.) Gordon
describes him as:

> ... a dark little man, lame of one leg, quiet
> and modest in his manner, with sincerity and
> earnestness well expressed in his face, and at
> that time about thirty years of age. (1886:422)

Ditt doubted at first that the message of God's love
through Jesus Christ could be for "outcastes." Being
reassured on this point, he gave his heart to Christ and
wished to be baptized. In June, 1873, Ditt accompanied
Nattu on the thirty mile hike to Sialkot with the request
that he be baptized immediately. Mr. Samuel Martin felt
hesitant to baptize this poorly taught man without an
opportunity for giving him instruction and testing his
sincerity. He repeatedly urged Ditt to stay a few weeks
on the mission compound for further teaching. Ditt insisted
he had to return to his job and family at once but did not
want to go without fulfilling his desire to publicly take
a stand for Christ. Martin, much perplexed, did what most
men do in such circumstances--talked it over with his wife!
As they prayed together they were reminded of scriptural

precedents in the Ethiopian eunuch and the **Philippian**
jailor, both of whom were baptized immediately on request.
So with Mrs. Martin's encouragement, Martin:

> ... finally decided to baptize Ditt, not
> because he saw his way decidedly clear to
> do so, but rather because he could see no
> Scriptural ground for refusing. (Gordon
> 1886:422)

Immediately after receiving baptism, Ditt asked permission to return to his home. Martin was reluctant to
allow this. It had become mission policy to keep new
converts at the mission station for a period of teaching
and testing both before and after baptism. Gordon expresses
the logic behind this course of action, especially in the
case of a man like Ditt:

> Did he not need a course of instruction before
> going back to live among heathen opposers? How
> could he, a poor illiterate man, answer their
> arguments? How could he hold out and stand
> firm in the face of opposition? How could he
> even subsist in the midst of persecuting foes?
> (1886:422-423)

It was not a new thing to have Chuhras come to Christ
and join the Church. One of the first two converts in
1857 was a Chuhra, evidently from the city of Sialkot.
One or two others are mentioned in the records, as if God
were giving a hint of what was to come. Those, however,
were probably rebellious individuals, on the fringe of
their society, eager to leave the rigid restrictions of
caste, who saw in Christianity a way of escape. At least
they did not win others from among their caste. Ditt was
a man in good relation with his family and clan, anxious
to return and live among them as a Christian.

With considerable misgivings Martin allowed Ditt to
return to his home and his despised work of buying and
selling hides. Martin doubted that he would ever see him
again. He feared that persecution and the lack of fellowship and teaching would quickly quench the spark of faith
he had seen in this weak, illiterate child of God.

When Ditt arrived home declaring himself a Christian,
his relatives began a concerted program of opposition. In
special protest meetings they taunted him with having high
aspirations for social advancement--"hob-nobbing with
foreigners." Probably the greatest sin in their minds was
that Ditt had acted individually without consulting his
caste fellows. His sister-in-law expressed this:

> Alas, my brother! You have changed your
> religion without even asking our counsel;
> our relationship with you is at an end.
> Henceforth you shall neither eat, drink,
> nor in any way associate with us. One of
> your legs is broken already; so may it be
> with the other! (Gordon 1886:424)

In by-passing his people's counsel, Ditt appeared to be
denying his relationship to them. They reacted by cutting
him off; barring him from eating, drinking and smoking
the *huqqa* pipe with them--in fact excommunicating him from
their society. He was outcaste from the "outcastes."
Where could he go?

One of the most amazing factors in this whole incident
is that Ditt did not run back to the missionaries. He
lived at home quietly; bore the social pressure, reproach,
and ostracism patiently; drank from the river; and
steadily witnessed to his immediate relatives.

No reference is made to outside opposition from Muslim,
Hindu, or Sikh landlords such as the Megs experienced.
Probably since this was the conversion of a lone individual
and there had been no visits from missionaries or evangelists to the village, the matter seemed unimportant to the
higher castes, who in his village of Shahabdeke were largely
Sikhs.

Two months later, in August of 1873, Ditt had the
pleasure of walking the thirty miles back to Sialkot with
his wife, a daughter, and two of his near neighbors, all
of whom he had won to Christ. Mr. Martin was amazed to see
Ditt, having had grave doubts that he could remain true so
far from Christian fellowship. On questioning Ditt's
converts, he was pleased to find that they gave satisfactory

evidence of faith in Christ as Savior and were firm in
their desire to follow His teachings. After Mr. Martin
baptized them, they too immediately returned to their
village homes to witness to others.

It took longer for Ditt to win his next converts. Not
until February 1874 did he return to Sialkot with Kaka,
his uncle, the first male convert from his own family, and
three other men. Ditt had an extended family of over
sixty relatives as well as numerous business contacts from
buying and selling hides. As he went from village to
village doing his work, he shared his faith with all who
would listen. Gradually the little group of Chuhra
believers grew, reinforced largely from Ditt's relatives
and friends living in the Mirali area.

Other Chuhra Conversions

It is interesting to note that in 1873 another Chuhra
man, Karim Bakhsh, was baptized by Mr. J.P. McKee forty
miles from Mirali in the Dogra section of Gujranwala.
Shortly afterwards two Chuhras, Chaughatta and Prem Masih,
became believers in the Gurdaspur area. As far as we know
they had had no previous communication with Ditt. Gordon
comments:

> A widespread and earnest spirit of inquiry has
> been found among these poor people simultane-
> ously, in districts which were separated by
> considerable distance, and by bridgeless rivers.
> (1886:428)

From 1873 to 1881 through the witness of Ditt and his
family in the Sialkot area; Karim Bakhsh and his fellows
in Gujranwala; and Chaughatta and Prem Masih in Gurdaspur,
the Chuhra movement began to accelerate. After initial
difficulties they found many of their caste responsive to
the message of Christ. (Note the sharp rise in baptisms
from 1873 to 1881 shown on Figure 5.) In this quiet
unspectacular way, through the instrumentality of unletter-
ed men, despised in the eyes of the world, the Holy Spirit
began a work that was to sweep thousands into the Christian
Church, many of whom came to know and love Jesus Christ in
a deep personal way.

5
Amazing Growth (1881-1891)

The decade from 1881 to 1891 was a time of incredible
reaping among the Chuhras. Missionaries received far more
invitations to teach than they had the time or strength to
fulfill. In these ten years the U.P. Christian community
rose from 660 to 10,165; the communicant membership grew
from 400 to 6,900. (See Figure 9.)

A comparison of the statistics of the various Missions
working in the Punjab during this decade is most revealing.
The Protestant Indian Christian community in the Punjab in
1881 was 4,762; in 1891 it was 20,729. While nearly 9,000
people became Christians in the U.P. area, only 6,000 were
added to all the other Churches put together.

What was the reason for such disparity? Did the U.P.'s
have far more missionaries and national workers than other
groups? Only 12 of the 91 ordained missionaries; 24 of
the 126 women missionaries; and 10 out of a total of 50
ordained Indian ministers in the Punjab were working with
the U.P. Mission at that time. The unusual movement in the
U.P. area obviously was not dependent upon the number of
workers.

Was the difference due to superior methods used by the
U.P.'s, or to a system of church government more suitable
to Indian indigenous structure? If so, one would expect
all of the U.P. area to be equally fruitful. In actuality,
results within the U.P. area varied greatly from place to
place. Christians were not scattered uniformly over the
whole mission area, but were concentrated in the Sialkot,
Pasrur, Zafarwal, and East Gujranwala mission districts
as shown in the table below:

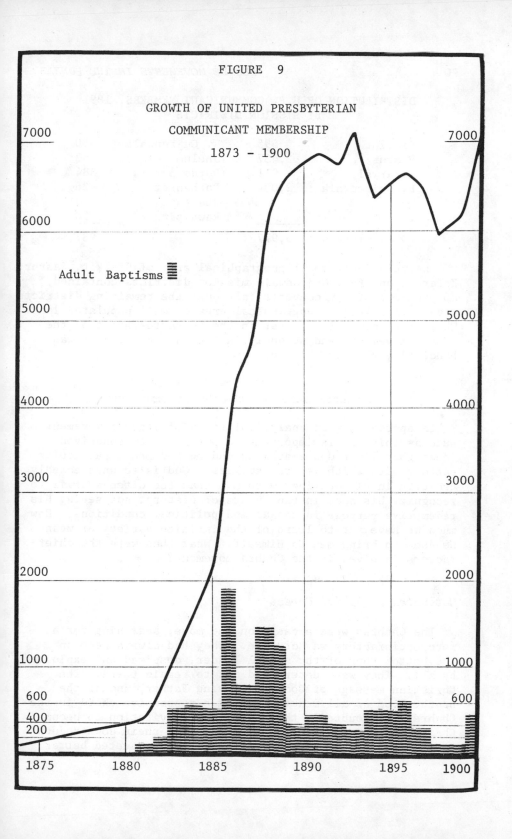

FIGURE 9

GROWTH OF UNITED PRESBYTERIAN
COMMUNICANT MEMBERSHIP

1873 – 1900

Adult Baptisms

DISTRIBUTION OF U.P. COMMUNICANT MEMBERS, 1891
BY MISSION DISTRICTS

Sialkot	595	W. Gujranwala	450
Pasrur	2,437	Jhelum	53
Zafarwal	911	Gurdaspur	384
E. Gujranwala	2,034	Pathankot	26
		Jhang	4
		Rawalpindi	20
Totals:	5,977		937

The relatively small geographical area of Sialkot, Pasrur,
Zafarwal and East Gujranwala mission districts contained
86 per cent of the converts, although the remaining districts
cover a far larger geographical area of well populated land.
Why? The answer lies first in the characteristics of the
Chuhra movement, and secondly in the way in which it was
handled by the U.P. Mission.

Characteristics of the Chuhra Movement

In approaching an analytical study of a group movement
such as this, it is important to put aside preconceived
ideas that limit God's actions and methods to a particular
pattern with which we are familiar. God is so unexpectedly
creative in His dealings with man that too often we fail to
recognize His hand in the events of history, not seeing His
redemptive purpose in social and political conditions. How
much we have yet to learn of the infinite variety of means
He uses to bring men to Himself. What then were the chief
factors involved in the Chuhra movement?

Motivated by Social Unrest

The Chuhras were a caste on the move, searching for a
more satisfactory way of life. They had always been on
the bottom rung of the social ladder, despised and exploited
by all. They were determined not to remain there. The
Christian message of God, the loving Father, and of the
brotherhood of all mankind struck a responsive chord in the
Chuhras. Undoubtedly they saw in the invitation to become
Christians an opportunity to escape from their downtrodden
position and become people of worth. They coveted better

jobs for themselves and their children. They needed help
and protection from the oppression of their landlords which
the influence of foreign friends could often obtain. Many
simply "followed the crowd" when friends and relatives
decided for Christ. They had much to gain and little to
lose by becoming Christians. As Stewart says:

> ... it was doubtless felt by many poor people
> that the change from an outcaste condition to
> that of brotherhood in religion with the ruling
> race was a distinct rise in civil and social
> standing. (1896:202)

We immediately tend to repudiate such motivation as
unworthy and "worldly." J.W. Pickett made a thorough study
of the correlation between the motives given by group
movement Christians and the quality of Christian life they
evidenced some years later. He details this in his book,
Christian Mass Movements in India. Out of 3,947 Christians
studied, 34.8 per cent claimed spiritual motives for
becoming a Christian, such as "seeking salvation," "to find
peace," etc. The others admitted secular motives as
dominant at the beginning. All had received follow-up
teaching. Pickett summarized his conclusions as follows:

> The smallness of the margin between Groups 1
> and 2, we venture to say, will surprise many
> of our readers who have not supposed that a
> purely secular motive, such as the desire for
> help against oppression, may lead to conversions
> and a wholesome, productive religious experience
> ... God uses social forces to bring men under
> the influence of the gospel.
>
> We find that 70 per cent of the men who say
> they became Christians for some motive not
> accounted as spiritual, and 75 per cent of
> those who declare that they became Christians
> because others of their family or caste did
> so, have become regular attendants at church
> services. We also find that the homes of 93.2
> per cent of the former and 94.8 per cent of
> latter are free from all signs of idolatry;
> that 90.5 per cent of the former and 91.4 per
> cent of the latter contribute to the church;

that 86.8 per cent of the former and 84.1 per
cent of the latter regularly confess themselves
as Christians to their non-Christian neighbors
and in such official records as the census,
despite many inducements to refrain from doing
so.   (1933:167-168)

Pickett concludes that the motivation behind the decision
to become a Christian is not as important as the quality
and promptness of the teaching which follows this initial
commitment.

One Homogeneous Unit

The movement to Christ which was gaining such momentum
in the 1880's was mistakenly thought to be a movement of
the "poor" or the "depressed classes" in general. This
was not true. The primary reason for phenomenal church
growth in one section of the U.P. mission area as over
against theothers is that it was not the "poor" who were
responding. Every district abounded in poor people. It
was not all the depressed classes, for each district had
plenty of them. It was specifically the Chuhra caste.
These lived in great numbers in Sialkot and Gujranwala
civil districts. At that time only a few of them had
migrated to districts farther west or north.

This movement provides evidence that caste structure can
be an effective channel for the Gospel. The cohesiveness
of the caste encouraged the rapid spread of Christian truth.
As some caste members became Christians, others were drawn
not just by spiritual hunger, but by their desire to maintain unity within the caste. Mr. J.A. McConnelee speaks
of this in his address, "The Movement Among the Chuhras
of the Punjab" delivered at the North India Conference of
Christian Workers in 1909:

... after the Gospel had once gained an entrance,
one of the most effective aids to its propagation
was the family and tribal spirit and cohesion
among this people. The Chuhras are a clannish
people and their family and tribal ties are
strong ... in the early days of the work in the

Punjab, it was very manifest how this family
cohesion worked to the spread of the Gospel.
(*Mass Movements in Indian Evangelization*
1909:57)

God used these cultural factors to draw more men to Himself.

The homogeneous character of the movement attracted others
of the same caste, but deterred or repelled interested
members of other castes. The Chuhras were not the only
depressed class seeking for a better way of life. Converts
in small numbers were won from the Megs, Doms, Chamars,
Batwals, Sansis and others. Missionaries contacting these
other castes recognized their potential responsiveness and
expected a movement to develop among them. Instead, in
1908, 22,000 Megs became Arya Samaj; and in 1912 a large
group of Doms did likewise. Others became *Musalli* Muslims
or *Mazhabi* Sikhs. Their adoption of another faith is proof
of their openness to evangelism, but they were not prepared
to integrate into a predominately Chuhra Church. They
needed to be discipled in separate homogeneous units.

The careful study of group movements in India made by
J.W. Pickett reveals the significant fact that no Church
has been successful in winning large numbers of two
different castes in the same area at the same time. Caste
barriers are too strong. The responsiveness of one caste
will repel the others, for traditionally they have had no
dealings with one another. As was pointed out previously,
baptisms among the Megs were negligible after the Chuhra
movement became well established.

On the other hand, on several occasions another Church
has moved into the same geographical area and begun work
among the "less responsive" caste, reaping a large harvest.
Pickett writes:

In several areas where only one church is at
work the mass movement has advanced rapidly
in one of these castes and very slowly in the
other ... In parts of the Telugu country two
or more Protestant churches have been
established in the same areas, and even in
the same villages. Yet those churches have
not often engaged in the kind of competition
that has created ... distressing situations ...

> The mass movement among the Madigas began
> under Baptist influence, and in areas where
> the Baptist and other churches are found in
> the same territory the Baptist converts are,
> for the most part, Madigas, and those of the
> other churches Malas ... a senior Baptist
> missionary declared that while his church
> alone was working in the district in which he
> was stationed, the Malas could not be reached,
> but when the Lutherans came, a Mala movement
> began.   (1933:326-327)

The second group responded because they could become
Christians within their caste structure as a homogeneous
unit, without closely associating with members of a
different caste.

Is it not contrary to Christian teaching and principles
to encourage this type of segregation? It is significant
that as the two sister Churches, among the Madigas and
Malas mentioned above, grew and developed separately side
by side, the Holy Spirit gradually broke down caste
barriers and united them in Christ. Pickett writes:

> Non-Christian Malas and Madigas have engaged
> in a feud for hundreds of years. Where they
> have become Christians the hostile feeling
> between them has perceptibly lessened.
> Denominationalism does not in this case
> divide a previously united people ... but,
> on the contrary, seems in some cases to draw
> groups from the two previously hostile castes
> together. (1933:327)

Too often missionaries, running ahead of the Lord, have
sought to break down caste barriers by forcing integration
at the beginning of a group movement, not realizing that
this erects formidable barriers to winning the remainder
of the caste. We must bring as many as possible to the
Savior using the dynamic of caste consciousness and
cohesion, trusting Him to transform their deeply ingrained
prejudices and unite them in spirit with other castes in
His good time. Tragically, many potential group movements
have been blocked or stunted by ignoring the importance of
homogeneous units.

It is stimulating to conjecture what might have happened
in the Punjab if the various Missions interested in the
Chuhras had made comity divisions among themselves not on
the basis of geography, but on the basis of the various
castes that were evidencing a responsive spirit. If the
U.P.'s had pastored the Chuhras, the Church of Scotland
taken the Megs, the C.M.S. the Doms, etc., it is possible
that a group movement could have developed in each of
these castes.

Multi-Individual Decisions

Having no standing in the caste structure, the Chuhras
were much freer from the restraining rules and harsh
customs that prevented the spread of the Gospel in higher
castes. Dissatisfied with their position, with a lesser
degree of pride, they did not ostracize Christians as
rigidly as the caste Hindus or Muslims. They allowed the
early converts to remain at home where they were able to
witness to their relatives most effectively. Prejudices
were gradually overcome and after careful consultation and
deliberation, whole family units chose to become Christians.
This was not a "mass" movement in the sense that hordes
of untaught masses blindly made a decision for Christ with
little understanding of the step they were taking. Nor
were there large ingatherings through mass meetings or
Pentecostal-type demonstrations of the Spirit. Most converts
were influenced by the social pressure of their relatives
and friends to take Christianity seriously as an option
and to investigate its superiority over their old faith.
Group discussions on these matters led to individual
decisions for Christ, strongly influenced no doubt by the
response of friends and neighbors, but nevertheless genuine
and personal. The closely knit social structure did not
encourage individuals to make a decision independent of
the extended family group. Only a few had the courage to
do so. When by common consent a whole family unit decided
for Christ, then the individuals in it found a supportive
fellowship in which to grow in faith. Converts remained
a part of the social structure to which they were accustomed. Unlike the individuals who had been expelled from
their high caste homes, the Chuhras by remaining part of
their society were far more stable morally. Stewart
writes concerning the general standard of Christian life
among the Chuhra converts:

... the standard of morality and good conduct
among our people is higher than it is among the
classes from which they have sprung. Cases
of discipline, scandalous sin, and apostasy
do indeed sometimes arise; but they are rare--
rarer, too, among lowcaste converts than among
others. (1896:252)

Rural

Although some Chuhras were in urban centers, most of the
Chuhras becoming Christian lived in villages. Stewart
says:

The proportion of village to city Christians
may be inferred from the number of points
where they reside (557 in all) and the fact
that we have at most only a few places
altogether within the limits of our field
that may be called cities or even towns.
Probably nineteen-twentieths of our people
live in villages of less than 800 inhabi-
tants. (1896:243)

Evangelism Led by Chuhras

At the start evangelism among the Chuhras was not spearheaded by missionaries or trained national workers of
higher castes, but by earnest Chuhra leaders like Ditt,
Chughatta, and Prem Masih. Though economically poor and
practically illiterate, they went from house to house and
village to village telling the story of Jesus to friends
and relatives. Gordon speaks of these workers in the
highest terms:

Those whom God uses to convert sinners are
often the humblest of laymen, unlearned and
ignorant, filled with the Spirit. Such men
seem well adapted to the work--so far as it
depends upon their efforts. The most
illiterate believer can tell unbelievers
the story of the Gospel, which, accompanied

> by the Spirit of God, leads them to the Savior;
> whilst the learned preacher, approaching them
> 'with excellency of speech or of wisdom' may
> and often does fail. (1886:463)

These Chuhra leaders thoroughly understood their own
culture and ways of thinking. Although their knowledge of
Scripture was limited, they could adapt their message to
the understanding of their hearers and speak with authority.
Such leaders had no formal training. Nevertheless, they
taught many to know and love the Lord.

Changes in Mission Policy and Methods

In light of the growing Chuhra movement, some striking
changes took place in mission policy and methods. Prior
to the Chuhra movement efforts were directed largely
toward educated individuals of any caste who responded to
the Gospel. Language study, sermon preparation, the
widespread use of tracts and books, and the stress on
education were all geared to converting the intellectual
people of the land. In spite of the best efforts of the
missionaries, these people had not responded in any
numbers to the invitation of Christ. Instead, the despised
Chuhra caste became the ones whom God had chosen. Gordon
writes:

> ... that wonderful passage in I Cor. 1:26-29
> began to shine with a new light ["... not
> many wise ... not many mighty, not many noble,
> are called: but God hath chosen the foolish
> things of the world to confound the wise; and
> God hath chosen the weak things of the world
> to confound the things which are mighty; and
> base things of the world, and things which are
> despised, hath God chosen ... that no flesh
> should glory in his presence."] .. its Divine
> philosophy began to be understood, at least
> by some of us, as never before. (1886:428)

These then, the "foolish things," the "weak things," the
"things which are despised" were the ones whom God had
chosen.

Attention Concentrated on Chuhras

In the annual mission meeting of 1877 a new step was
taken:

> ... we all with one accord resolved to go home
> to our several districts, and in our evange-
> listic labors give "special attention to the
> poor," by which was meant that we would take
> pains to reach the despised Chuhras,* making
> them understand clearly that the Gospel was
> for them no less than for the rich, the
> educated and the powerful. (Gordon 1886:429)

This was a dramatic moment. The Mission could have
decided not to encourage the Chuhras for fear their inclusion
might hinder the conversion of the higher castes. But under
the guidance of the Holy Spirit, the U.P. missionaries
realized that God had prepared the hearts of these people
in an unusual way. Special effort must be put forth to
reach them. Gordon mentions that the national workers,
impregnated from childhood with caste prejudice, were
with difficulty reconciled to this new approach. Yet as
they humbled themselves to work among the Chuhras, and
experienced their eager responsiveness, most national
workers too became convinced that this was God's will.

Itineration

Initially it was hoped that the Gospel would spread from
city centers to the surrounding district. Much effort
was expended on urban evangelism in principal cities, and
relatively little time given to rural itineration. Now,
Chuhra converts were living in their own homes in villages
scattered many miles from mission stations. The importance
of city centers diminished and the villages became the
focus of concern. Leaving their urban work which had
proved so unproductive, missionaries and national workers
began to itinerate in the villages for weeks at a time--
instructing, examining and baptizing converts, organizing
churches and Sabbath-schools, and establishing village

---

* Underlining by author

schools. Itineration became the peculiar characteristic of
the U.P. Mission. By 1884 the term "principal station" was
dropped altogether and the whole field was divided into
"mission districts." Notes from the diary of Mr. Lytle
while on itineration reveal the kind of response they found
even as early as 1883:

> Nov. 21st, (1883) Back to Chauwinda again.
> Christians here glad to see us. Public worship
> at 7 p.m. Baptized five men and nine women ...
>
> Dec. 8th. Encamped at Mahanwala ... Christians
> glad to see us. Divine service held at night;
> the tent full, and audience attentive ... Walked
> over to Dhilli and held public service during
> the daytime, baptizing four men, four women and
> seven children, all belonging to one household.
> Same Sabbath at 4 p.m. in Bath ... baptized
> three men, four women and six children ...
>
> Dec. 15th. Arrived at Dhoda ... Baptized two
> men, one woman and five children. These,
> added to the number of Christians already
> here, make fifty-four. (Gordon 1886:457-459)

In 1886 Mr. Gordon looking upon the situation in retro-
spect was able to write:

> We have in this way, not through our own
> wisdom by any means, but through the wise
> and gracious leadings of our Divine Master,
> corrected some fundamental mistakes, and
> got down to the level on which He himself
> labored. Instead of beginning at the top,
> with our large cities, principal stations
> and better classes of people, as we did at
> first, we have got down to the Chuhras and
> are beginning to build upwards; and, to
> return to our old ideas, would undoubtedly
> be equivalent to going a full generation
> backwards in the great work. (432)

Paid Chuhra Workers

As early as May 1857 the U.P. Mission hired two Indian evangelists, G.W. Scott and E.P. Swift, orphans educated by the Presbyterian Mission (U.S.A.) at Ludhiana. Although they lacked formal theological training, they were ordained by the U.P. Mission in 1859 and remained the only ordained pastors until Scott's death in 1868. That year one other was ordained bringing the number back up to two. No others were ordained until 1886.

In 1877 a Theological Seminary was started in Sialkot under the auspices of Sialkot Presbytery, with Dr. J.S. Barr as principal, assisted by Andrew Gordon and G.L. Thakur Das, an orphan educated by the Mission. Nine students with the equivalent of an eighth grade education were started on a five year course including Hebrew, Greek, Theology, Church History, Apologetics, Homiletics, Hermaneutics, etc.-- patterned directly on Western seminary courses. Between terms of study at the Seminary the students had practical pastoral experience in a congregation. Four students graduated in 1882 and became licentiates, but were not ordained until 1886. The next year the total of ordained ministers was twelve, but from 1888 to 1900 the number fluctuated between 7 and 11. Due to their specialized training they were paid by the Mission a salary considerably above that earned by the average Chuhra family.

When the Chuhra movement began, it was discovered that simple Chuhra leaders were more effective in winning their caste than these more highly trained men. At first Chuhra laymen witnessed and taught voluntarily, but as some evidenced a gift for evangelism they were given a nominal salary. Gordon writes concerning Ditt:

> ... he never asked for any support from the
> Mission. Many long journeys were performed
> by him on foot for the love he cherished to
> this good work, which grew upon him until at
> the end of seven years from his conversion
> [in 1880] it was observed that he had scarcely
> any time left for his own business, and
> consequently nothing to live upon. Even
> then he did not ask for money; but six or
> seven rupees a month, enough to support him

in the humble way these people live, were
given him as his right, thus enabling him
to devote his whole time to this grand--
this glorious work. (1886:427)

By 1882 there were 54 Christian helpers and teachers listed
in the annual records in addition to the ordained ministers.
Thirty-one of these were evangelistic workers laboring
primarily in rural areas, and six were rural school teachers. Two years later (1884) there were 79 Christian
helpers and teachers, 49 of whom were evangelistic workers.
By 1886 the number of Christian helpers had risen to 136,
the great majority being rural workers. (See Figure 10.)
By the close of the decade (1889) there were a total of
179.

The rural evangelists were selected from among the
Chuhras. They were chosen for their spiritual insight,
natural leadership ability, and willingness to serve.
Since the Chuhras were all illiterate at the beginning of
the movement, these men had no more than the equivalent
of a second or third grade education at the most. Several
of them, including Ditt, never mastered the art of reading.
Others learned to read as adults following baptism. Their
knowledge of the Bible and of spiritual truths was minimal.
However, they knew some Bible passages and basic doctrine,
understood their people, and had the patience to teach
them "line upon line and precept upon precept." None of
them was ordained or could perform the sacraments of the
Church. They received just enough salary to enable them
to give most of their time to evangelistic work and
continue to live in the village at the economic level of
their Chuhra neighbors. Their function was to locate
serious inquirers, teach them what they could, and inform
the missionaries so they could plan to visit those most
ready for baptism.

Stewart describes as follows the normal evangelistic
procedure followed by itinerating missionaries when a
number of persons in a village or in several neighboring
villages had been baptized:

... the first thing usually done afterward
is to put a Christian helper there to act as
an underworker. He goes from house to house,
gets acquainted with the peculiarities of

each individual, corrects any wrong impress-
ions which the people may have had respecting
Christianity, confirms their opposition to the
false religion which they have abandoned,
teaches them as fast as he can passages of
Scripture, a Bible Catechism, the Ten Commandments, the Lord's Prayer and the fundamental
principles of our holy faith, urges them to
abandon every form of sin, and exhorts them
to commence family and secret prayer. He also
meets with them as often as he can--perhaps
every day--for public worship, and on the
Sabbath is expected, not only to conduct a
regular religious service and preach, but
also to hold a Sabbath School and catche-
tically instruct all, old and young, in regard
to divine things .   (1896:262-263)

This describes the ideal. Few of those early workers
had the training, ability, or industry to accomplish it all.
Nevertheless, these men laid the foundation upon which the
Church grew. Missionaries and ordained pastors did not
have time to teach illiterate believers individually, or
to discover those areas where non-Christian beliefs and
practices still governed their lives. They had their hands
full examining candidates prepared by the "underworkers"
for baptism or communicant membership. Had these simple
evangelistic workers failed to fulfill their function,
the Church could not have grown nearly as rapidly as it
did during this period.

There was controversy in the Mission over hiring men
to do the evangelistic work. Since many Missions and
missionaries today strongly advocate the policy of not
employing Christian workers paid by foreign funds, it is
important to consider this matter carefully. Several
alternatives were suggested at that time.

Volunteer Workers: A number of missionaries believed
that evangelistic work should continue to be on a purely
voluntary basis. Early growth had come as converts
witnessed to relatives and friends. Why not trust this to

Motor truck driven by Dr. David Gordon (son of Andrew
Gordon) with J.A. McConnelee and the Rev. Mallu Chand,
first pastor to go on self-support.
        --from U.P. MISSION ANNUAL REPORT, 1913

Preparing Inquirers for Baptism   *--from AFTER SIXTY YEARS*

Moving Camp--the old way   --from *AFTER SIXTY YEARS*

Moving Camp--the "modern way"
--from *FOREIGN MISSIONS HANDBOOK, 1922*

Large family tent is to the right; tent in center is for the
Missahiba; workers' tents clustered around. "In Camp"
--from *AFTER SIXTY YEARS*

continue? Would it not be sufficient? If certain members
were paid to witness, would this not have a deterring
effect on the others and in the long run prove a hindrance?*

In considering this argument it is important to dis-
tinquish between "witnessing" and "teaching." All believers
are called upon to be witnesses. This can be done at work,
at social functions, and during informal "bull sessions"
in leisure hours. Most of the Chuhras were encouraged to
take the initial step of faith in leaving idolatry and
giving full allegiance to Jesus Christ through just such
times of witness and discussion. Not only were unpaid
workers able to accomplish this, usually they were more
effective than employees of the Mission, for their motives
were not suspect and they naturally sought out those with
whom they had the closest association and greatest influence.

After this initial step of faith has taken place,
however, it is essential that more teaching follow quickly.
New converts are excited about the stand they have taken.
They are eager to learn more of their new faith. If much
time elapses before they are given further teaching, their
enthusiasm wanes and is difficult to rekindle. Also their
lives are permeated with non-Christian beliefs and practices.
These must be recognized and rooted out. If instruction
is delayed, these non-Christian ways become interwoven
with their new faith. The shot of Christian teaching
they have received, mixed with the germs of their old
false concepts, acts as an inoculation immunizing them
against accepting true teaching later. The writer has
observed this hardening effect on several occasions in
villages where follow-up teaching was neglected.

Only a few Chuhra converts had the status, ability, and
willingness to give the teaching needed by people newly
emerged from idolatry. These, being scarcely literate
themselves, had to be given training in elementary biblical
truths, not just once, but each month. They in turn had
to spend long hours of patient effort instructing other new

_____

*It is interesting to note that John L. Nevius was experi-
menting successfully with this approach in China at about
the same time. His method later became famous and calls for
volunteer local workers overseen by a limited number of
well qualified paid supervisors.

converts. The Chuhras, being a depressed class, worked
under the jurisdiction of others. Their time was not their
own. During busy agricultural seasons they worked twelve
to sixteen hours a day. Even in slack seasons they had to
be available to do whatever their landlords demanded. None
were wealthy enough to neglect their daily jobs to be
trained themselves and then to teach others on a volunteer
basis. Had the Mission depended on the job being done this
way, the Chuhra movement would have been short-lived,
reaching only a few, and resulting in syncretism or serious
misunderstandings of the Gospel.

Workers Supported by the People. Some missionaries advocated
that each national worker be encouraged to rely solely on
the financial support provided by the people he serves.
They pointed out that Muslims and Hindus support their
religious leaders; why not the Christians? This would
produce a self-supporting Church from the start and avoid
the trap of becoming dependent upon foreign funds.

It is significant to note that dissatisfaction with the
policy of paid workers was not expressed in the early
stages of accelerated growth among the Chuhras. The
missionaries were so overwhelmed by the task of evangelism
and follow-up teaching they were desperate for the service
the evangelistic helpers provided and were happy to pay
for it.

As the movement grew to 6,691 communicant members by
1892, the number of helpers increased to 220. These
workers were concentrated in Gujranwala, Pasrur, Zafarwal
and Sialkot districts, because less than 500 communicant
members lived outside of those areas. Each missionary in
charge of those districts, therefore, had 15 to 30
workers responsible to him. The one ordained missionary
in Pasrur had 40 helpers. Lacking adequate education and
training, these helpers required a great deal of teaching
and supervision. Some no doubt proved lazy, dishonest,
or immoral and had to be dismissed. Others were plagued
with personal or family illness. All their lives they had
been dependent upon the village landlords whom they served.
In sickness, in times of financial distress or family
emergency, they were in the habit of turning to them for
help. This dependent attitude was readily transferred to
the missionary in charge of the district, with the result

that an increasing amount of his time was taken up in
caring for the personal needs and problems of his workers.
By 1892 this was increasingly frustrating. Missionaries
were seeking some other solution to their problems.

In addition, the financial burden of supporting 220
helpers was undoubtedly beginning to weigh heavily upon
the Mission. Even if each helper received only Rs. 7 or 8
a month, that would total approximately Rs. 20,000 or
$6,200 annually. It is probable that the Board in the
U.S.A. was questioning the validity of such a large
expenditure.

It is not surprising then that Samuel Martin in his
report to the Decennial Missionary Conference in 1892
argued that the mission policy of hiring workers hindered
church growth by setting up a system that could not be
perpetuated indefinitely, due to the lack of funds. This
was true, but on the other hand, the early extensive
growth would probably have not taken place without such
paid workers. Stewart forcefully argues that the most
practical solution to the problem is to put on paid
workers temporarily so that self-support can be feasible
as larger concentrations of believers are formed. He
wrote in 1896:

> ... the work of evangelism should be continued
> with energy and zeal. The idea of waiting
> until our present congregations are drilled
> up to a high point of liberality and Christian
> grace before advancing much further effort to
> convert sinners, is, in the writer's opinion,
> detrimental to the speedy attainment of a
> condition of pecuniary self-support on the
> part of the native church ... The larger the
> subscription list, the greater the aggregate
> sum of contributions obtained as a general
> rule. (1896:330)

Stewart obviously envisions this as a _temporary_ measure,
to be discarded as soon as practicable.

Dr. Donald McGavran in his book, *Understanding Church
Growth*, writes concerning this subject:

> Sometimes direct payment from mission funds is
> necessary. It is no sin. It is not the best
> and most permanent arrangement, but it has
> produced good churches in hundreds of cases ...
> Sometimes at the very beginning priming the
> pump is necessary, but it must never be for-
> gotten that the goal is to get an abundant
> flow without pouring in a stream of subsidy ....
>
> Work constantly for church multiplication.
> When churches grow, subsidy to the pastors
> and workers can be much more readily ended
> or diminished ... Stopping church multipli-
> cation till an indigenous unpaid leadership
> has been created is a counsel of despair.
> (1970:347)

Many Churches established on the basis of aid from
foreign funds have never succeeded in becoming self-supporting. This has convinced many Christian leaders and
mission thinkers today that the whole system is wrong,
even as a temporary step. The United Presbyterian Church
in Pakistan is a happy exception to this common experience.
It later became self-supporting and proved that it is
possible to become independent financially after sufficient
numbers have been won. How this came about will be
detailed later.

Christian Fakirism. For a time the concept of Christian
workers adopting the life style of a *Fakir* (*Sadhu* or "holy
man") was very popular. Hindus, Muslims, Sikhs, and
Buddhists all have such fakirs who wander from village to
village living on the contributions of their followers.
Fakirism was believed to be an indigenous method that would
be easily understood and accepted by all, and would solve
the problem of financial support for Christian workers.

There have been a few examples of successful Christian
Fakirs such as Sadhu Sundar Singh. The Character of their
ministry and the resulting fruit testifies to the reality
of their commitment. These, however, are the exceptions.
Too often other motives underlie a man's adoption of the

Sadhu role--an unhappy marriage or home situation, a dislike for hard work, the inability to get along with people,
or the desire for status and honor. To make this a
standard form of ministry would discourage stable family
men who are natural leaders from becoming pastors, and
would hinder any organized program of follow-up teaching.

None of these alternatives provide a thoroughly satisfactory solution to the problem of support for national
workers. In order to finance evangelistic workers a
Mission must be prepared to channel a considerable share
of its field budget into helpers' salaries, not just for
one or two years, but for one or two decades. A shorter
period would result in instability in the work. During
this time intensive stewardship teaching must be given so
that as foreign funds are phased out, local funds will
increase to fill in the gap. For Missions or missionaries
with sparse or fluctuating financial backing, such a
commitment of funds takes great faith and courage. Can
we not, however, trust the Lord who has caused the harvest
to ripen, to provide the means for its reaping?

Stewart expresses his opinion with force:

> The necessity and the duty of paying mission
> helpers for their services cannot be justly
> denied, and if the people to whom they minister
> cannot, or will not, do so, others who have
> the ability to pay them ought to assume this
> responsibility. Natives have as much right
> to compensation for their work as missionaries
> themselves have. (1896:323)

A dependent Church that is growing and moving toward
self-support is better than a small static Church that
supports its handful of workers. To hinder the sowing
process because of lack of self-supporting workers amounts
to unfaithfulness to Christ's commission to "make disciples
of all nations." The policy of employing evangelistic
workers financed from foreign funds undoubtedly has drawbacks and dangers. The young Church can become too
dependent upon this help, and it is expensive. In the
writer's opinion, however, the alternatives to having a
paid ministry in the early stages of a people movement

present even graver dangers. Baptized believers become
hardened or develop false doctrines due to lack of teaching. Worst of all, prepared hungry hearts are left
unsatisfied, and lost sheep never find the Shepherd.

The U.P. Mission prudently provided funds from foreign
sources for the salaries of evangelistic helpers, keeping
in mind that this should be just a temporary provision,
but prepared to undertake the burden for a couple of
decades.

Medical Work

During this period the Mission established medical
work as a new means of outreach. Daily confronted by
innumerable diseases, every missionary found himself
dabbling in medicine. Interestingly, the first U.P.
Mission hospital was started by two school teachers.
Andrew Gordon's daughter, Euphia, and a dedicated Anglo-
Indian woman, Mrs. Sophia Johnson, repeatedly tried to
open small rural schools for girls. The villagers actively opposed any such innovation, but appreciated any
medical help they were able to give. The ladies found
closed doors soon opened to them when they brought pills
along. Women were rarely allowed to go to a male doctor
for treatment, so turned to charms and amulets or relied
on untrained midwives for their medical needs. Miss
Gordon and Mrs. Johnson were drawn increasingly into dispensary work as a means of bringing the gospel message
to women. In 1880 they opened a small hospital for women
in Gurdaspur. Five years later they temporarily closed
it while both ladies enrolled in Women's Medical College
in Philadelphia to become full-fledged doctors.

In 1888 the first trained doctor, Dr. Maria White,
arrived on the field and established Memorial Hospital
in Sialkot. Within three years the staff were treating
over 24,000 patients annually in the dispensary and performing nearly 500 surgical operations--eloquent proof
of the need for this ministry.

Dr. Sophia Johnson returned in 1890 and opened the
Good Samaritan Hospital in Jhelum and a dispensary in
Bhera. That same year Dr. White started a branch hospital
in Pasrur. The Mary B. Reid Hospital was established in
Sargodha in 1905 by Dr. M.M. Brown, the first male medical
missionary in the U.P. Mission. One outstanding convert
from his ministry was Abdul Haqq who became famous throughout India as an expert Christian apologist. Taxila Christian Hospital was founded in 1921 and has become famous as
a center for eye surgery, treating thousands each year.

What role has medical work had in the growth of the
Church? From the start medicine was intended to be a
means of evangelism. Bible women and evangelists were
part of each hospital staff in order to present the Gospel
to patients and their relatives as they waited their turn
in clinic or spent time in the wards. Through hospitals
Gospels and tracts found their way into countless homes of
every faith and caste. What were the results?

Undoubtedly medicine has a vital function in missionary
service as the practical outworking of Christ's concern for
the whole man. Hospitals are also important in preparing
the soil and sowing the seed as widely as possible. Their
ministry of love and healing, coupled with the gospel
message comes to people at a time of crisis when they are
conscious of their weakness and acutely aware of the power
of death. Nevertheless it is important to recognize that,
contrary to expectation, medical work has proved ineffective
in the Punjab in bringing significant numbers of people to
a saving faith. Stewart writing in 1896, after the U.P.
Mission had been engaged in medical work for more than a
dozen years, makes this statement:

> As for results, two baptisms occurred among
> the patients at Gurdaspur Hospital and one
> notable conversion was reported at the
> beginning of the work in Sialkot ... while
> several instances have been given of persons
> upon whom it is thought a deep religious
> impression was made. (183)

Medical work has had a profound effect on many, but most
of them are individuals isolated from their normal cultural
setting for the moment, and unprepared to make a major

decision apart from their family and clan. When a group
movement is in process, however, medicine becomes another
means of encouraging more rapid growth.

Schools for Christians

    Prior to the Chuhra movement, mission schools were
operated with the primary purpose of evangelizing high
caste Hindus and Muslims by giving them a top-notch education plus Christian teaching. They had proved ineffective
as evangelizing agencies. Unlike medical work that has a
pre-evangelistic function in preparing hearts for the Word,
schools have a post-evangelistic function, effective as a
follow-up measure after a group movement has begun. As the
Chuhra movement accelerated, the Mission recognized the
value of concentrating educational efforts on the children
of Chuhra converts in order to develop and train Christian
leaders. In 1881 they took official action to abolish all
institutions above the primary level that had a purely
evangelistic object, or make them almost exclusively into
schools for Christians, charging only nominal fees and
placing a strong emphasis on teaching the Scriptures.

    The next four years witnessed a dramatic increase
in village schools for Christians. Schools for non-
Christians began to decline, though vested interests and
emotional ties always hinder the closing of work once
established. Note the figures below taken from the
Annual Reports for the years mentioned:

Year	Village Schools for Christians	No. of Pupils	City Schools for Non-Christians	No. of Pupils
1882	6	104	29	1847
1883	20	390	21	1773
1884	37	632	16	1682
1885	53	903	16	1398

In just four years the number of village schools jumped
from 6 to 53, while the non-Christian schools declined
from 29 to 16. (See Figure 10.) The city schools for
non-Christians still used the lion's share of the
educational budget, for they had many pupils and more
highly qualified staff. Village schools had a minimum of
equipment and poorly trained teachers. Many had no school
house at all but were held under a tree or in the courtyard of a private home. To encourage better teaching
and faithful attendance, these schools were frequently

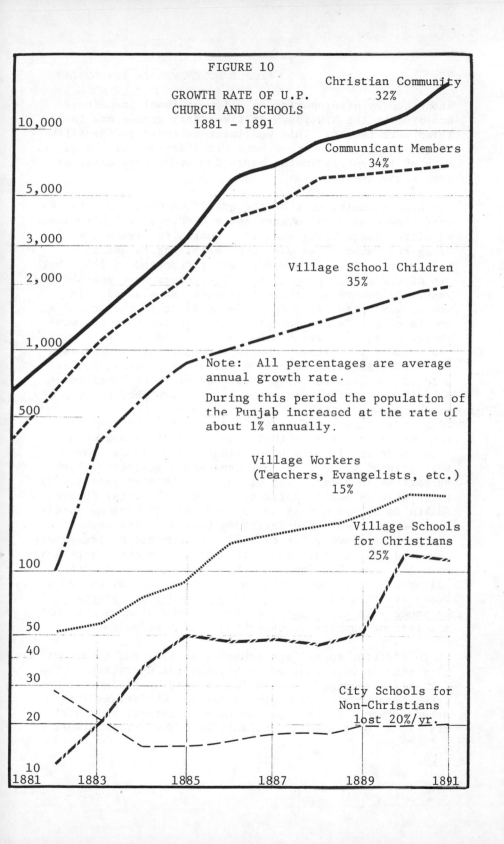

FIGURE 10

GROWTH RATE OF U.P.
CHURCH AND SCHOOLS
1881 - 1891

Christian Community
32%

Communicant Members
34%

Village School Children
35%

Note: All percentages are average
annual growth rate.

During this period the population of
the Punjab increased at the rate of
about 1% annually.

Village Workers
(Teachers, Evangelists, etc.)
15%

Village Schools
for Christians
25%

City Schools for
Non-Christians
lost 20%/yr.

inspected by missionaries or a few national inspectors
employed by the Mission. At first only grades one to
three were taught. This was later extended to the fifth
class so that a primary school certificate could be given.
Many of the pupils in the early days were teen-agers or
even young adults.

Unfortunately, most of the qualified Christian Chuhras
were needed as rural evangelistic workers, and Christians
of higher caste background were loathe to live and work
among the Chuhras, so many non-Christians taught in
village schools. Zafarwal district reported in 1883 that
ten of their twelve rural school teachers were non-Christians. To counteract their influence, an evangelistic
worker was often assigned to teach Bible in the school a
couple of days a week.and to check any tendency the non-
Christian teacher might have to undermine the faith of
the students. Village schools were not established as a
means of evangelism among non-Christian Chuhras, but as
a follow-up measure where believers had been baptized.
Schools were not opened until there was a good nucleus
of Christians in the village.   Then no time was lost.
Qila Didar Singh in Gujranwala district is typical of
many other villages at that time.   In 1882 there were
three baptisms in Qila Didar Singh. A Christian worker
was assigned to work in that area among scattered Chuhra
Christians in neighboring villages. The next year (1883)
there were 29 adult baptisms, bringing the total Christian
adults to 32. A school was opened with 25 boys as pupils.
Some of these were non-Christian Chuhras. The result
was greater growth, for by 1885 the communicant membership
numbered 79. In this sense the schools became evangelizing
agencies among the Chuhras. As a general rule in the
Indian sub-continent, schools have been used by God as a
means of evangelism to a group only after a movement is
in process in that caste. They have not been used to win
significant numbers in the absence of a group movement.

In addition to village schools, in 1881 two important
city schools were started in Sialkot for Christians. The
Christian Training Institute was opened by Sialkot
Presbytery as a preparatory school for Christians interested in becoming village teachers or evangelistic workers. Most of the early students were adults; many were

married. They were given the equivalent of a primary
education as fast as they could learn it. Then most were
employed by the Mission as teachers or evangelists.
Promising ones were admitted into the Theological Seminary
after 1894 when the Seminary agreed to accept primary
school graduates as candidates for the ministry.

The Christian Training Institute gradually developed
into a secondary school preparing students for the matriculation examination following 10th class. It became
noted for outstanding volleyball and basketball teams
that won many championships throughout North India. This
did much to boost the self-image of the Christian students
from depressed class backgrounds.

The Girls' Boarding School at Hajipur in Sialkot
started as an orphanage in 1857 under Miss Elizabeth
Gordon. In 1879 it was expanded to become a small day
school for non-Christian girls. Two years later in 1881
the facilities were converted into a boarding school for
Christian girls. Both the Christian Training Institute
and the Girls' Boarding School were purposely run in
native style, sparsely equipped in keeping with the
village background of the pupils. Students studied on
mats on the floor and took turns cooking their usual diet
of curry and *chapattis* (tortilla-like unleavened wheat
bread). The purpose was to avoid teaching them extrava-
gant city ways that would create discontent with their
village homes, but rather to equip and fit them for
their life work as rural housewives.

In 1891 the American Presbyterian Mission turned over
their work in Rawalpindi to the U.P.'s including a high
school for non-Christian boys. This was raised to college
level that same year and became Gordon College. Although
the great majority of students have always been non-Christians, Gordon College through the years has enabled many
Christians as well to obtain a college education. In
this way it has contributed much to the development of an
educated Christian leadership.

Since 1885, most of the schools under college level
have existed primarily for the education and training of
Christians. They teach the basic subjects in the

vernacular and charge only nominal fees. Christian
leaders of quality, graduated from these schools, are
found in every Church in Pakistan.

Sunday Schools Established

The U.P. Mission, being very strict on Sabbath (Sunday)
observance, was keen to provide a Sunday School program
for Chuhra converts to encourage them to "keep the
Sabbath day holy" and to provide a special time of
instruction. In 1882 the first seven village Sunday
Schools were opened in Gurdaspur and Zafarwal districts.
By 1885 there were 48 Sunday Schools; 37 of them in
Zafarwal district. By 1890 the number had risen to 86.
Zafarwal had one in every congregation. Not just children, but all believers and inquirers gathered to learn
Bible stories and memorize Scripture verses and catechism
questions. This teaching confirmed their faith and
reinforced their committment to Christ during the early
crucial years of accelerated growth. Scripture memorization was continued to be strongly stressed until recent
years. An annual "Synod Bible Course" of twelve memory
passages was prepared in the Punjabi language for use in
local congregations, and memorized by many each year.
Such follow-up measures are essential to healthy church
development. J.W. Pickett in his book, *Mass Movements
in India,* commended the U.P. Mission for having done an
outstanding job in the realm of teaching subsequent to
baptism.

Autocratic Church Discipline

The Presbyterian system of church discipline is based
on democratic procedures. A local congregation elects
elders to make up the ruling body or "session" of that
worshipping group. Each congregation sends a pastor and
a representative elder to the Presbytery which governs
the congregations in a district. Then each Presbytery
chooses representatives to Synod, the church court that
presides over several Presbyteries. The final court of
appeal is the General Assembly, also made up of representatives from each Presbytery. In Pakistan each

congregation may send an elder and pastor to Synod, and
as yet no General Assembly has been formed.

A common criticism leveled at missionaries is that
they transport Western ideas, church structures and
polity *in toto* to an Eastern society and superimpose them
without adaptation to local culture. It is undeniable
that many Western patterns of thinking are so ingrained
in foreign missionaries that subconsciously they affect
their actions and reactions, and are reflected in the
young Church that is established. In reading the records,
however, one cannot help but be impressed with the deep
sensitivity to Indian culture and thinking shown by the
early missionaries. True, the U.P. Mission set up the
Presbyterian structure of church government, in name at
least. The first Presbytery was organized in Sialkot
in December 1856. It was supposed to function democratic-
ally with missionaries, pastors and elders all equal in
voting power and authority. This democratic structure,
however, was foreign to Indian society and especially
to the Chuhras who had always played a subservient role.
To adapt to the situation at hand, the missionaries
modified Presbyterian polity by practicing more autocratic methods. Stewart describes the situation as it
evolved:

> The missionary, supposed to be free and
> responsible in his special sphere of labor,
> employs such native helpers, and makes such
> expenditures, as in his judgment are necessary
> to carry on his work with efficiency. If he
> is the ... superintendent of evangelistic
> work, they (his assistants) are all subject
> to his control and can be retained or dismissed
> at his pleasure ... Even elders, theological
> students, licentiates and ordained ministers
> (all but settled pastors) came finally to
> hold the same relation to their work as
> other employees and could be discharged by
> the superintendent if he saw fit--although,
> in the case of ministers, sanction by the
> Mission itself was required to make the
> discharge final. (1896:138)

Such adaptations have been made in every country. A
careful study of the so-called "daughter" Churches will
reveal that often they resemble their "mother" Church
only in superficial ways.

Missionaries are also accused of an undue love of
power that fosters a paternal relationship with the young
emerging Church. Before passing judgment, one should
study this in its historical and cultural context. Had
the U.P. missionaries in the 1880's insisted upon democratic procedures and failed to take decisive action for
the advancement of the Chuhra movement, the Church would
have floundered, remaining weak, ineffective and stagnant.
The national leaders had little experience in making
responsible decisions or solving mutual problems demo-
cratically. Paternalism was reassuring to them at that
stage. They needed all the support and training they
could get, to help them conquer their deeply ingrained
sense of inferiority and dependence. Therefore the outer
structure of the Church remained Presbyterian, but the
practical outworking of it was far more Episcopal, with
the evangelistic missionary acting "Bishop" for his
district.

Stewart considered this modification of Presbyterian
polity a temporary measure to aid church growth in the
early stages, but felt the traditional democratic form of
discipline should be reinstated as soon as possible to
aid in the development of responsible leadership. This
autocratic pattern was dropped as trained pastors and
elders increased, thus preparing the way for the Church
to become self-governing. This will be described in
detail later.

Some Missions advocate a policy of missionaries keeping absolute "hands off" of church organization when a
new Church is emerging. The theory is that this Church
will then be able to work out its own indigenous pattern
of government and discipline. In practice this does not
work satisfactorily. The new national leaders have no
background of experience from which to create their church
structure. Many years of floundering and frustration can
be avoided if missionaries will aid in setting up the

structure they feel is most suited to the situation, but keep it flexible. The weaknesses and flaws of the system will become apparent with usage, and can be corrected as the Church matures. Nevertheless, it provides a framework within which the Church can grow rapidly in the early years.

Punjabi Language Used

As long as evangelistic efforts were concentrated in urban areas on literate people, the literary language, Urdu, was used. When the emphasis shifted to rural illiterate Chuhras, their mother tongue, Punjabi, was essential. An important factor in rapid growth among the Chuhras was that all missionaries were required to learn Punjabi as well as Urdu and use it in their village work.

Dr. Thomas Cummings, a U.P. missionary, developed severe eye trouble while studying Punjabi. Forced to give up all reading and writing for a time, he learned Punjabi solely through listening and engaging in conversation. He discovered to his amazement that he learned far more rapidly and accurately this way. On the basis of his experience he developed a phonetic method for learning Punjabi, known as the "Cummings Direct Method," that has proved helpful to generations of missionaries in the Punjab and is still in use today.

Bible passages for memorization, simplified catechism questions for instructing new Christians, and elders' courses were also prepared in Punjabi. The first Gospel was published in 1885; followed by all four Gospels in 1886; and finally by the whole New Testament in Punjabi.

Many Missions preferred to use Urdu because of its prestige, but using the mother tongue of a people is one of the most effective means of reaching their hearts.

Undelayed Baptism

It is important to note that high standards of knowledge and moral attainments were <u>not</u> required by the U.P. Mission as a pre-requisite for baptism. This was

in sharp contrast to the policies of some neighboring
Missions and therefore a cause of much debate. Converts
were required to publicly acknowledge Jesus Christ as the
Son of God and the Savior who died for them. They were
assured that He welcomes all who turn from idols and
false beliefs to put full faith in Him. Note Gordon's
keen understanding of the situation--an insight that
aided rapid growth.

> Some think a sinner ought to acquire a great
> amount of knowledge, rise to a high standard
> of good character, and almost attain to fit-
> ness for heavenly glory, before our consent
> to his admission into the school of Christ
> here below; but we have aimed rather at the
> simplicity and promptness of Philip who said:
> "If thou believest with all thine heart,
> thou mayest," and of Paul by whom the jailor
> "was baptized, he and all his, straightway."
> (1886:462)

A common belief among missionaries is that inquirers
will learn more eagerly and show a greater desire for
improvement before baptism. It is feared that once they
are baptized they will feel they have "arrived" and will
not be motivated to learn more. Experience has usually
proved the reverse. Until the definite public stand of
baptism has been made, an inquirer tends to vacillate,
always haunted by doubts as to whether he is taking the
right course or not. Once he has made a complete break
with the past and committed himself fully by baptism to
be a follower of Christ, he is free from such doubts and
eager to learn more of what his committment involves.
Baptism must never be allowed to become an end in itself,
but just the first step. Baptized believers must be
given follow-up teaching immediately and prepared for
the next goal of full communicant membership.

Jesus in His Great Commission in Matthew 28:19-20
stressed this chronology in evangelism. He said, "Go ...
and preach the Gospel ... baptizing ... and teaching all
things ..." Note that baptizing comes first; teaching
follows.

The personal records of missionaries of that period
reveal that although large numbers were added to the
Church each year, they were taken in a few at a time,
each one personally examined. Mr. Lytle's diary
illustrates the fact that small groups were baptized
in each center:

> Nov. 15th. Last night Brother Thakar
> baptized two men, five women and one
> infant.
>
> Dec. 8th. Walked over to Dhiliand, held
> public service during the daytime, baptizing
> four men, four women and seven children, all
> belonging to one household.
>
> Feb. 27th. Held divine service in the
> evening and baptized eight men.
> (Gordon 1886:457-460)

Not everyone asking for baptism was accepted auto-
matically as is revealed by the following entrances in
Mr. Lytle's diary:

> Eighteen persons sought admission to the
> Church but were put off for a time, for
> good reasons.
>
> [Of others he wrote:] Think their faith
> too weak to face the trials in store for
> them, and defer the rite for the present.
> (Gordon 1886:460)

It must also be borne in mind that the area in which
the movement was taking place had been the scene of
thorough gospel preaching for a period of some thirty
years. True, the messages had been largely directed
toward the more educated classes; nevertheless, in those
meetings the Chuhras were generally seen standing at a
respectful distance behind the others. Many of them
had heard the message in earlier days but had felt it did
not apply to such outcastes of society as they. Seed
sown in those unproductive years was now producing a
rich harvest.

Obstructions to Growth

Although this period is noted for amazing progress and
a startling increase in church membership, all was not
smooth sailing. There were factors obstructing growth.
As usual, these hindrances came both from outside and inside the Christian community.

Persecution

The diary of Mr. Lytle refers to persecutions sustained
by inquirers and converts alike. The intensity seems to
have varied from village to village. Some suffered from
their own kindred. Stewart describes the baptism of one
convert, Piran Ditta:

> ... his mother began to beat him with a
> stick. He jumped and ran to one side.
> She ran after her son and beat him
> thoroughly, first with a stick and
> afterward with her shoe [a sign of
> disgrace], at the same time weeping
> and giving him the worst kind of
> abusive talk. He just stood and took
> it all. (1896:234)

For the most part opposition did not come from
relatives but from those outside the Chuhra community.
The Hindus feared that the upward aspirations of the
Chuhras would undermine the whole caste system. Both
Hindus and Muslims were apprehensive that as the Chuhras
became Christians they would be lost as servants and
laborers in the fields. They often threatened them with
loss of employment should they become Christians. The
presence of the British government and the respect given
to foreigners acted as a deterrent to extreme acts of
hostility, for all knew these would not go unpunished.
The Chuhras, being the lowest class of society, were of
less concern to the higher castes and therefore came in
for less severe persecution than others. Opposition
never reached the proportions found in the Meg movements.

54041

Neighboring Missions criticized the U.P. Mission for
its work among the depressed classes. This caused doubts
and contention to arise. Many felt these "depraved poor"
could not truly be changed but that work among the higher
classes would bear greater dividends in the long run.
Others feared that the winning of large numbers of "outcastes" would give the Church the mark of being a low-
caste organization and hinder higher castes from joining.
Stewart, writing in 1896, twenty years after the start
of the Chuhra movement, says concerning this:

> Indeed, contrary to the fears of some, our
> work among the depressed classes has been
> a help, rather than a hindrance, to work
> among the higher classes. Chuhras have
> themselves been known to be the agents in
> securing Hindu conversions. And what is
> still more important perhaps, the con-
> versions, education, moral improvement
> and elevation of people, who have for
> generations been almost beneath contempt,
> furnish an object lesson of the most
> striking character ... and this influence
> has had something to do in winning the
> higher classes. (1896:244,245)

Christ's Way to India's Heart by Pickett strongly
reinforces these insights of Stewart. Where Missions
refused to encourage low caste accessions for fear of
replelling the high castes, the Church has not grown. It
remained a small, static conglomerate community. Where
a group movement among the depressed classes was welcomed
and fostered, the Church became a dynamic, growing fellowship, far more likely to attract others. In actuality,
neither approach has been successful in winning large
numbers of high caste people. To this day we have failed
to find the key to effective evangelism among them.

In spite of criticism, the U.P. Mission persevered in
its policy to concentrate on the responsive Chuhras,
and God blessed their efforts with abundant fruit.

6
Retarded Growth (1891-1899)

The statistics for the United Presbyterian Church from
1891 to 1899 reveal a surprising lack of church growth
just when one would expect an acceleration in growth.
(See Figure 9.) Not only did the Church fail to gain
numerically, but by 1898 membership had decreased by nearly
1200 persons. What occurred to retard growth just as
the Chuhra movement was gaining momentum? Were the
Chuhras less responsive? Did mission policy change? Or
is there some other explanation for this seeming regress-
ion? The following are the main reasons for this plateau:

Competition

In 1889 the U.P. Mission Annual Minutes refer to the
arrival of the Roman Catholics and their methods of work:

> ... their object was not the conversion of
> non-Christians, but to lead away by strong
> worldly inducements the Christians in the
> villages. By means of a large expenditure
> of money, they succeeded to some extent and
> secured nominal control in certain villages.
> (A Century for Christ 1955:14).

Their work resulted in considerable numerical loss to the
U.P. Church. No exact figures are available.

The Mission Report to the General Assembly in 1896
notes the efforts of the Reformed Presbyterian Church to
attract to themselves some U.P. native workers. In the
same year the Salvation Army is reproached for encroachin

on U.P. mission area and trying to induce Indian workers
and church members into their group. The Plymouth
Brethren were also active at this time and did not
observe comity lines. It is difficult to determine how
many members left the U.P. Church to join these groups.

This was the beginning of a long history of struggle
as various Missions vied for the allegiance of the
Chuhras. This competition had a healthy effect to the
extent that it stimulated each to provide follow-up
teaching for baptized believers to prevent their being
easily swayed by another group. Nevertheless harm was
done, for attention was diverted from the evangelism of
non-Christians and concentrated upon minor doctrinal
differences among the Christians. Valuable energy was
spent on petty quarrels rather than in seeking the lost.

Transfer

In 1889 a settlement was made with the Church
Missionary Society of the Church of England concerning
the boundary of the Narowal area of the district of
Sialkot. At first U.P. workers had been encouraged by
the C.M.S. to work among the Chuhras in that area. However, Stewart records:

> ... When this work grew to large proportions,
> strong opposition to it arose from our
> brethren in Narowal, and at last we accepted
> the proposition to establish a boundary
> between the two Missions, over which neither
> party should pass. This arrangement left
> the Narowal Mission in undisturbed possession
> of a considerable field in and around that
> city, and entailed a loss on us of eight
> or nine hundred baptized converts. (1896:
> 101-102)

According to the C.M.S. records, 1150 baptized
believers were transferred to them at this time from
the U.P. Church.

Migration

The construction of the Chenab Canal, the greatest
irrigation canal in the Punjab, began in 1892 and gave
employment to thousands of workers indlucing Christians.
Dr. W.B. Anderson writes:

> ... the chief explanation for the shrink-
> age in the church membership was the Chenab
> canal ... I find a great reduction all
> over the field. The canal which is being
> constructed by the government is drawing
> great numbers. Very many take their
> families and move there because they earn
> more there than in their own villages. In
> several places I have found all the Christ-
> ians gone with their families, and this
> has been going on for two years, and has
> reduced the roll very much, all at once!
> (1909:239)

In 1897 when the canal was completed, hundreds more
left to live in the new colonies now opened up for
settlement in the area west of Lahore known as "The Bar."
(See Figure 11.) No Chuhra was given land by the government because they were not classed as agriculturalists,
but non-Christian colonists came to the Bar bringing with
them their Christian and non-Christian Chuhra serfs.
Since the U.P.'s did not have sufficient missionary force
at that time to open stations in the Bar, the Church
sustained serious losses in membership.

Consolidation

Another major cause for lack of numerical growth during
this period was an increasing emphasis upon consolidating
the Church. The task of teaching baptized believers and
organizing worshipping fellowships grew to overwhelming
proportions for the limited personnel available, with the
result that evangelism of non-Christians was neglected.

Many missionaries became convinced that more converts should not be baptized until those already won could be adequately taught. Stewart effectively points out the fallacy of such a policy when he writes:

> ... in other words, keep Christ's lambs out of the fold until that fold is enlarged and put in order, so that every member of the flock can be systematically fed and nicely housed--as if these lambs would not do better in the Church than in the world, however imperfect the former might be; or as if the Lord would make a mistake in regenerating the people too fast and would not, in His providence and by His grace, make abundant provision for the spiritual nourishment and the highest welfare of all His newborn children. (1896:221)

Missionaries enforced strict requirements for baptism and admitted new members with great caution. Anderson illustrates this by quoting from the report of one missionary.

> In one village I took the names of twelve families, some fifty persons, old and young, who are being taught. Several of the men now readily recite fifty pages of short Bible questions. When they have completed the part of the question book relating to the New Testament and have a few more pages of the part relating to the Old Testament, I have promised to receive them into full membership, if there be no other hindrance. It will be noted that these people have already declared their faith in Christ and asked to be baptized. This is the general custom in the whole Mission, to hold back candidates for baptism for further instruction. (1909:420-421)

This evidences a major shift in policy from the day when Stewart described the requirement for baptism as being a simple sincere confession of faith in Jesus Christ. Fortunately, this policy was later revised, or the

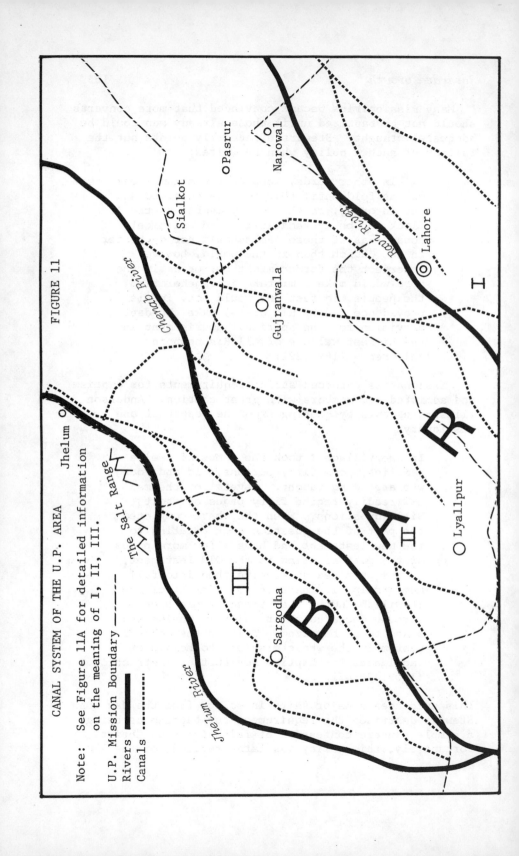

CANAL SYSTEM OF THE U.P. AREA

FIGURE 11

Note: See Figure 11A for detailed information on the meaning of I, II, III.

U.P. Mission Boundary ———
Rivers
Canals ....

FIGURE   11 A

THE CANAL SYSTEM OF THE
U.P. AREA

		Started	First Irrigation	Completed
I.	BARI DOAB* Ravi River			
a.	Upper (Clarkabad)	1849	1860	1878
b.	Lower (Sahiwal)	1906	1914	1917
II.	RECHNA DOAB Chenab River			
a.	Upper (Gujranwala)	1905	1913	1917
b.	Lower (Lyallpur)	1890	1892	1899
III.	CHAJ DOAB Jhelum River			
a.	Upper (Gujrat)	1905	1915	1917
b.	Lower (Sargodha)	1897	1901	1917

The total length of the main lines of these canals --
    9,181 miles

* NOTE: DOAB means the area between two rivers. (BARI
    is an abbreviation of BEAS and RAVI

great growth seen in the next period would not have
occurred.

Rolls were drastically purged. All who failed to
measure up to the standard of Christian conduct set up
by the missionaries were removed from membership after
warning and instruction had been given. Rev. D.S. Lytle
writes in 1899: "I have been reducing and sifting my
roll ... not working for members, but for a better
Church, believing that one solid Christian is better
than ten nominal ones." (Anderson 1945:12)

Removals during this period, for all the above reasons
combined, were as follows:

$$
\begin{array}{ll}
1894 -- & 1,021 \\
1895 -- & 810 \\
1896 -- & 934 \\
1897 -- & 1,201 \\
1898 -- & \underline{902} \\
& 4,869 \text{ Total removed from} \\
& \text{the roll}
\end{array}
$$

At this time the membership hovered between 6000 and 7000,
yet nearly 1000 were removed each year. Had such a large
number been purged merely to purify the Church of nominal
Christians, one would suspect the purgative to be so
strong as to be almost lethal. Many potential group
movements have been arrested by over zealous missionaries
who want to separate the sheep from the goats or the
tares from the wheat and are not content to leave this
to the One who has been given the authority to do so.

During this same period 2,183 persons were added by
confession of faith, and 2,436 more by certificate of
transfer, making a net loss of only 250 people. Had the
U.P.'s immediately established centers in the newly
formed canal colonies; maintained their original
requirements for baptism; and continued efforts to win
non-Christian Chuhras, the graph of growth would have
shown a healthy rise. The reduction in numbers was due
to mission policy, not to any waning in the responsiveness
of the Chuhra people.

7
Accelerated Growth (1900-1930)

From 1900 to 1930 the Church grew 550 per cent, adding
to its ranks a total of 38,000 communicant members on
a base of 7,000--a dramatic ingathering. (See Figure 12.)

Peak Growth (1900-1914)

By 1900 the previous peak of nearly 7,000 was regained
and the movement of the Chuhras to Christ went into its
most accelerated phase. The century began with the
accession of over 1,000 members the first year--a fore-
taste of greater years ahead.

In 1904 the Board of Foreign Missions reported to the
General Assembly of the U.P. Church of North America:

> Our missionary workers in India have been
> fairly embarrassed with the increasing
> number of converts seeking baptism and
> church fellowship. One thousand two
> hundred and fifty-one (1,251) have been
> admitted to the Church this year on pro-
> fession of their faith. (Minutes of the
> General Assembly 1904:49).

We claim that world evangelism is our goal, yet are
"embarrassed" by an influx of only 1,250 a year! Obviously
we aren't expecting results in proportion to our goal or
we would learn to handle far greater numbers.

In 1905 the U.P. Mission, anticipating the possibility
of gathering in the whole Chuhra community of 200,000,
sent out a plea to the American Church for more workers.

Few were sent. By 1914 the communicant membership had
increased to 32,000, a growth rate of 450 per cent over
the first fourteen years of the century. (See Figure 12.)

Following World War I (1920-1922)

After periods of war or stress there often develops
an unusual response to the Gospel. One missionary wrote
that as a result of the keen ministry of army chaplains
and YMCA workers, the "... returned non-Christian soldier
is today the most inviting field in all India for
evangelistic effort." (*Triennial Report* 1916-18:189)
He was probably referring to low-caste labor corps men
who had tasted freedom from the oppression of their
depressed status while serving in the army. They returned
to civilian life determined not to be enslaved again,
searching for better answers to life, and therefore
unusually responsive to the Christian message.

The baptism of 2,135 adults in 1920 was the largest
recorded for several years previous and the largest
witnessed in any succeeding year. Thirty-seven per cent
of these baptisms took place in scattered villages
belonging to unorganized congregations. Seventy-three
per cent were from old established areas where people
listened to the Christian message with increased interest
and response.

1920 was also the year in which the largest number of
new U.P. missionaries ever sent to the India field
arrived--twenty-one in all. They came filled with
evangelistic zeal, inspired by the Student Volunteer
Movement with its famous rallying cry of "Win the world
in this generation."

Distribution of Growth

A comparative study of the districts presently
covered by seven U.P. Presbyteries reveals a striking
contrast in the amount and rate of growth that took place
even in contiguous areas. The total communicant membership of Pasrur Presbytery by 1930 was 12,900--over

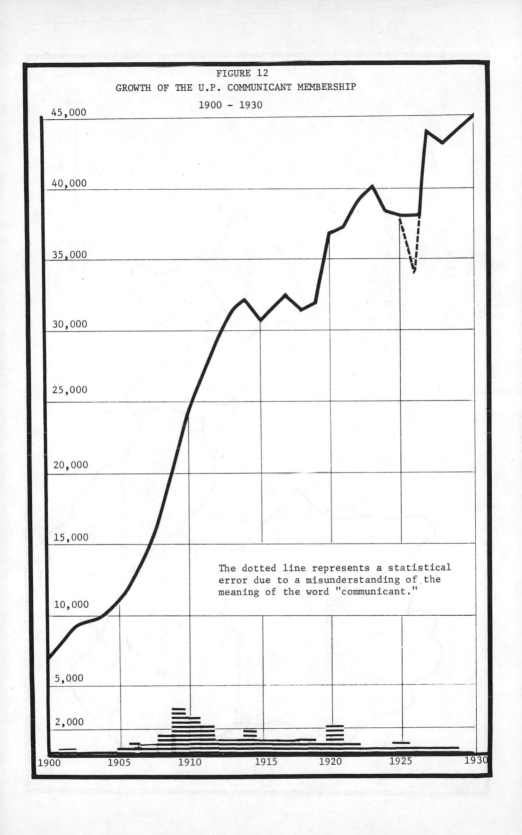

FIGURE 12
GROWTH OF THE U.P. COMMUNICANT MEMBERSHIP
1900 – 1930

The dotted line represents a statistical error due to a misunderstanding of the meaning of the word "communicant."

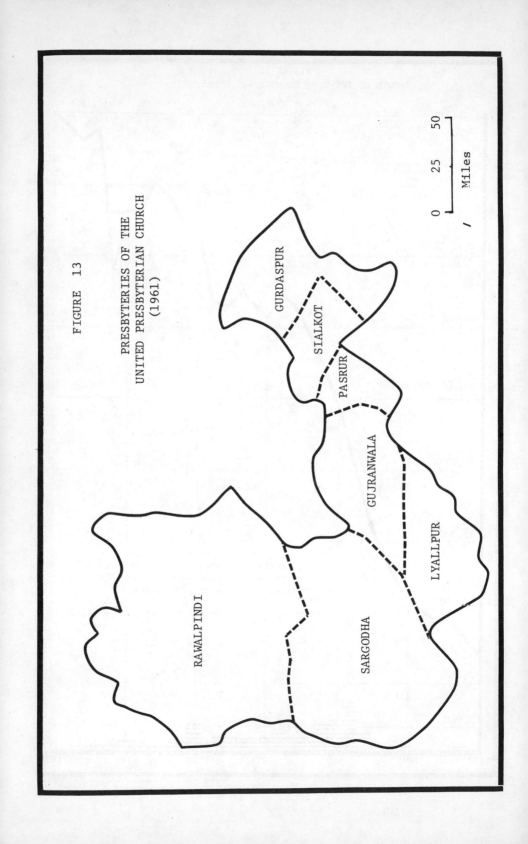

FIGURE 13

PRESBYTERIES OF THE
UNITED PRESBYTERIAN CHURCH
(1961)

GURDASPUR

SIALKOT

PASRUR

GUJRANWALA

LYALLPUR

RAWALPINDI

SARGODHA

0   25   50

Miles

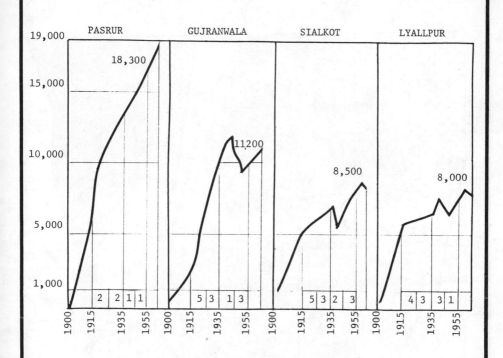

FIGURE 14

COMMUNICANT MEMBERSHIP GROWTH BY PRESBYTERY

1900–1960

Note: The numbers at bottom inside each
graph are the average number of ordained
missionaries for the decades from 1915 –
1955.

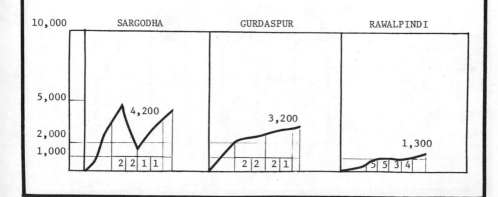

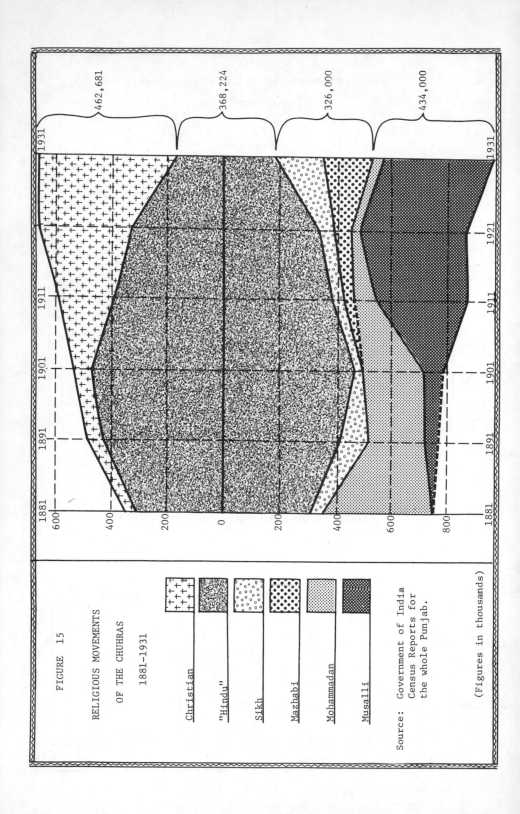

FIGURE 15

RELIGIOUS MOVEMENTS

OF THE CHUHRAS

1881-1931

Christian

"Hindu"

Sikh

Mazhabi

Mohammadan

Musalli

Source: Government of India
Census Reports for
the whole Punjab.

(Figures in thousands)

462,681

368,224

326,000

434,000

fourteen times greater than the 900 members of Rawalpindi
Presbytery, in spite of the fact that Rawalpindi Presbytery
covers an area twelve times larger than Pasrur. (See
Figures 13 and 14.) Gujranwala and Sialkot Presbyteries,
bordering on Pasrur and larger in area and population,
had less church growth than Pasrur. Even Gurdaspur that
adjoined Sialkot Presbytery and was double the size of
Pasrur had only 3,000 communicant members by 1930.

These differences in growth were due primarily to the
fact that converts were not coming from a cross section
of society, but from one group--the Chuhras. Growth,
therefore, was related directly to the population of
Chuhras resident in any one place. It had little to do
with the number of missionaries working in the area.
From 1900 to 1930 an average of two ordained missionaries
were in residence in Pasrur Presbytery, while five
ordained missionaries were working in Rawalpindi Presbytery.
(See Figure 14.) Rawalpindi, however, had few Chuhras,
hence little growth.

When budget and personnel are limited as is true in
almost every Mission, it is imperative that they not be
distributed merely on the basis of the size of population
or area to be covered, but be concentrated on strategic
places where church growth is taking place. Had five
missionaries been assigned to Pasrur to seek and to
shepherd the eager Chuhras, leaving one couple to witness
in unresponsive Rawalpindi district, far more people
could have been brought into the fold.

Reasons for Rapid Growth

There are a variety of reasons for such rapid growth
during this period. The major causes are listed below:

Responsiveness

Without doubt the greatest factor in producing rapid
church growth in this period was the dissatisfaction the
Chuhras felt with their status in society. They were
determined to move from their position at the bottom of

the depressed classes. The most inviting path to progress
open to them lay in changing their religious faith. This
they did in large numbers as is revealed in Figure 15.

In the 1881 Census Report the vast majority of the
Chuhras are registered as Hindus, but even then 379,000
called themselves Mohammadans. They had chosen to align
themselves with the majority community of the Punjab
sometime before that date. Inexplicably the Muslim group
did not gain enough after 1881 to keep up with the rate
of biological increase, for in 1931 they numbered only
434,000, an increase of only 55,000 in fifty years! The
only change was that those called "Mohammadans" who were
loosely affiliated with the Muslim faith steadily changed
into "Musallis" who were recognized as permanent members
of the Muslim community.

By 1881 only 40,500 Chuhras had aligned themselves with
the Sikhs. This number began to increase by 1911 but
the greatest growth took place after 1921. By 1931 there
were 326,600 who considered themselves members of the
Sikh community. Half of them were unofficially aligned
with them, the other half had been ceremonially cleansed
to become "Mazhabi Sikhs."

The most dramatic change took place in the Hindu group.
In 1901 there were 934,553 registered as Hindus; by 1931
this had dwindled to 368,224, about one third of the
original total. Obviously the Hindu Chuhras were rapidly
joining other communities.

The Christians only numbered about 35,000 in 1881, but
steadily increased until by 1931 they totaled 462,681,
the largest single group from among the Chuhras, representing nearly 30 per cent of the entire Chuhra
caste.

Figure 15 clearly illustrates the rapid disintegration
of the Chuhra caste and their eagerness to join other
faiths. This move was not primarily religious in nature,
yet God used these human aspirations to turn them
toward Himself in large numbers. It is significant that
nearly thirty per cent of them turned to the Christian
faith. Conservatives among them must have advocated

remaining Hindu. To align themselves with their Muslim
or Sikh landlords would have been the most logical
change they could have made. Yet the largest group
chose to become Christians, suffering discrimination as
a minority group, and enduring persecution in order to
do so. The gospel message and the work of the Holy
Spirit in their hearts functioned as a powerful magnet
drawing them away from the more natural course of
joining one of the majority faiths. The following
statement made in 1919 is an indication of their overwhelming responsiveness:

> ... 50,000 people in our field in India are
> now asking to be baptized and cannot be
> taken into the church because we have not
> enough workers to teach them ... Another
> mission has 140,000 on its waiting list ...
> Still a third mission has 153,000 on a
> similar list! (*A Century for Christ*
> 1955:31)

The tragedy is that thousands on the waiting lists were
never won. Many lost patience or felt unwanted so
turned elsewhere for the help they so desperately needed.

Follow-up of Migrations

In the late 19th century, new canal colonies were
opened up west of Lahore in the area known as "The Bar."
(See Figure 15   New work opportunities in these
colonies attracted many people and caused a migration
that accelerated after the turn of the century. Encouraged by a new-found self-respect gained at their conversion, and by economic pressures due to persecution,
thousands of Christians of Chuhra background made their
way to the Bar, or were taken there by their landlords.

The Mission followed this migration by opening
stations at Lyallpur in 1895, Hafizabad in 1897, Khangah
Dogran in 1900, Sangla Hill in 1901, and Sargodha in
1905. Lyallpur and Sargodha Presbyteries were formed.
From 1910 to 1930 these two presbyteries received 29,000

Christians on transfer from previous church homes.
During the same period of time about 43,000 people were
removed from the rolls of Pasrur, Sialkot, Gujranwala
and Gurdaspur Presbyteries, presumably because they
emigrated.   The total number of transfers received in
the canal colonies represents about 66 per cent of those
removed from the old presbyteries, indicating that at
least two thirds of the immigrants went to these new
colonies to find employment.   Others settled in areas
served by the Church Missionary Society (Anglican) or
the Associate Reformed Presbyterian Mission.

The Mission discovered that non-Christian migrant
Chuhras were even more responsive than those living in
the old established areas.   History has proved repeatedly
that people uprooted from their traditional environment
and accustomed social structure tend (for a short time
at least) to be open to change and ready to embrace
a new faith.   William Read in his book, *New Patterns of
Church Growth in Brazil*, tells how the Assemblies of
God Church is growing in that country.

> They have discovered the new receptivity of
> the migrating masses.   Continuous uprooting
> and transplanting of a restless people ...
> has created a great sociological void ...
> The assemblies receive these migrating
> multitudes and can attribute much of their
> growth to the unique preparation these
> migrations afford.   (1965:130)

From 1910 to 1930 about 4,000 adults were baptized
in Lyallpur and Sargodha Presbyteries on confession of
faith.   This represents nearly 34 per cent of all the
adult baptisms made in the U.P. Church during that
period.

In spite of the fact that the migrations included
thousands of Scheduled Caste people, in the 1961 Census
Report only 14 are registered in Sargodha District and
308 in Lyallpur.   Evidently during the intervening years
they either became Christians, *Mazhabi* Sikhs or *Musalli*
Muslims.   On the other hand, in the older districts of

Sialkot and Pasrur the numbers of Scheduled Castes are listed as 9,000 and in Gujranwala 1,500. This illustrates the fact that migrant people usually are responsive to change and therefore open to the Gospel.

To follow-up migrations is an important principle of church growth. Today 22 per cent of the members of the U.P. Church reside in the canal colonies. These would have been lost had not the Mission taken the wise and swift action to move with the people as large numbers migrated.

Undelayed Baptism

During this period the U.P. Mission returned to its earlier policy of baptizing quickly. Non-Christians were received and baptized with a minimum of delay upon their confession of faith in Jesus Christ. The main work of teaching was left until after the primary step of baptism. Whenever baptism was delayed until considerable instruction could be given, the majority of the inquirers were lost to the Christian Church. Ernest Campbell in the book, *The Church as Christian Community*, cites the case of the church in Jullundur. He explains that although 5000 people were baptized in the decade from 1915 to 1925, many more might have been, but

> ... the missionaries in Jullundur felt more
> strongly than many that converts should have
> adequate instruction and give evidence of
> individual commitment. Because of this
> many converts were denied baptism until
> better prepared and as a result were lost
> to the Church. (1966:201)

The Psalter in Punjabi

Another aid to rapid growth in the Church, both in numbers and in spiritual depth, was the development of the Psalter in Punjabi. In those days the United Presbyterian Church was adamant in her belief that only the words of Scripture are appropriate for worship. The

Psalms in metrical version plus a few New Testament
verses put to music were the only songs allowed in a
church service. The Rev. I.D. Shahbaz, a pastor in
Sialkot (later honored with a Doctor of Divinity degree),
was a gifted Indian poet. He agreed to translate the
Psalms into Urdu verse retaining the common western tune
from the U.P. Psalter. By 1891 he had completed all 150
Psalms in this form. To the disappointment of all, these
proved unpopular. The Western tunes sounded strange
and unfamiliar to Punjabis, and Urdu, the language of
literate urban people was only partially understood by
village Christians. A few Psalms and hymns that were
written in Punjabi and set to indigenous tunes were far
more appealing to most congregations. In 1895 the
Mission decided to prepare a Punjabi Psalter set to
local tunes. Several missionaries gifted in music spent
long hours in market places and cafes listening to
current Indian tunes and writing them down. Rev. Shahbaz
paraphrased all the Psalms in Punjabi verse to fit the
meter of these indigenous tunes. He made a conscious
effort not to miss a single verse of the Psalms in his
paraphrase.

At first there was considerable opposition to this
method of obtaining tunes, for the words currently known
to those tunes were often obscene. It was feared that
even the tunes set to Scripture would call to mind the
former filthy words and thus prove detrimental both to
worship and to witness. These fears proved unfounded,
for it was not long before the former words faded from
memory and today the Church has a rich heritage of
indigenous tunes set to the mighty themes of the Psalms.
Being in Punjabi, the mother tongue of the Punjab, their
message speaks to even the simplest villager. The tunes
are easy for him to learn because they are of local
origin having familiar tone and rhythm patterns.

By 1905 three thousand copies of a Psalter containing
selected songs in Punjabi were first published in Persian
script in time for use at the Sialkot Convention. This was
a meeting for spiritual quickening for all of the Churches
in the Punjab. It was the center for a revival movement
that had a deep effect on the Church. This will be
discussed more fully in the next chapter. It is

difficult to estimate the spiritual impact of such a
treasure of Scripture set to music and words readily
understood and appreciated by the masses. Not only did
it provide a vehicle for more meaningful worship,
expressing praise, adoration, thanksgiving, confession
and consecration; but it was easily memorized Scripture
with power to guard the heart from temptation and sin.
The work was completed in 1916.

Increased Ordained Ministers

Preceding 1900 there had been a great increase in
evangelistic workers of Chuhra background having a
minimum of secular or theological education. These did
the spade work of teaching new converts by rote memory
the basics of the faith, rooting out idolatrous beliefs
and practices, and training them in Christian worship.
Such workers had to be supervised by missionaries or
national ordained pastors who performed baptisms and
weddings and accepted candidates into communicant membership.

The Theological Seminary that had started in Sialkot
in 1877 moved to Pasrur from 1887 to 1900; then located
in Jhelum with Dr. Robert Stewart as principal. In 1912
a new permanent location was established in Gujranwala
where it has remained to the present. Prior to 1900
there were only 11 ordained Indian pastors for a Christian community of 10,000 in the U.P. Church. Because of
its high standards for admission, the Seminary was unable
to produce ordained pastors at a sufficient rate to meet
the urgent demand. It was impossible for the few
ordained men to adequately care for the people. Many
candidates for baptism had to wait a long time before a
qualified man had time to travel to their village and
perform the baptismal service. This discouraged many who
were on the verge of a decision for Christ, and so
hindered church growth.

In 1894 the Seminary lowered the educational requirements to 5th class pass, enabling more Christians of
Chuhra background to prepare for the ministry. A steady
increase of ordained national pastors began in 1900.
(See Figure 16.) By 1915 there were 45 ordained pastors

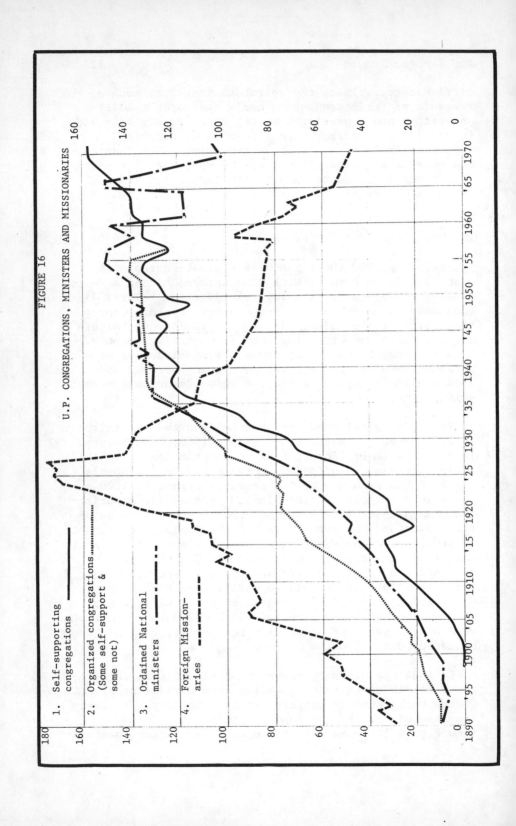

FIGURE 16

U.P. CONGREGATIONS, MINISTERS AND MISSIONARIES

1. Self-supporting
   congregations

2. Organized congregations
   (Some self-support &
   some not)

3. Ordained National
   ministers

4. Foreign Mission-
   aries

engaged in evangelism and the teaching of converts. By
1925 the number had risen to 69; and by 1930 there were
100, many of whom were working in self-supporting
congregations. As early as 1910 these men were performing almost all the baptisms. This is revealed by
the following statement in the *1911 Handbook on Foreign
Missions:*

> Of the more than 1200 persons baptized,
> the missionaries have baptized probably
> not more than one hundred. (61)

Nationals, reaching their own people in increasing
numbers made possible more effective church planting and
encouraged church growth as long as they witnessed to
their own caste or society. Their witness remained
ineffective when directed toward upper class Hindus or
Muslims.

Increased Lay Leadership

Equal in importance with the increase of ordained
pastors was the great progress made in developing lay
leadership in the Church. The Presbyterian system calls
for "elders" to be chosen from each local congregation
and ordained to assist the pastor in all the affairs of
the local church. Elders were chosen, not by missionaries
or pastors, but by the people of the local congregation.
They were usually older men, greatly respected for their
natural leadership ability and spiritual maturity.

Elders were required to complete a four-year course
prepared by the Synod, consisting of Bible study, principles of church government, and their duties as lay
officers. This course had to be designed so that
illiterate men could learn it by rote, for in those days
most of the elders were illiterate. Certificates were
given to those who completed the work satisfactorily.
Only then did their ordination and installation as full
elders take place.

Their duties consisted of calling on the sick, round-
ing up people for worship, collecting offerings to
support the pastor, leading worship in the absence of

the pastor, and settling quarrels within the congregation.
They also took an active part in Presbytery affairs.

The number of elders trained and ordained as lay
leaders increased greatly during this era of rapid growth
in the Church. However, it received its first impetus
during the period of retarded growth, especially from
1894 to 1896, when stress was laid upon shepherding the
flock rather than on seeking lost sheep. (See Figure 17
In 1894 there were 27 elders; in 1895 the number jumped
to 49; the next year it hit a high of 61 followed by
some losses so that by 1900 there were 58 ordained
elders, or a ratio of one elder to every 120 communicant
members. From then on the number rises steadily
paralleling the rapid growth of the Church. Note the
increase over each five year period in the chart below:

Year	No. of Elders	Increase in 5 years
1895	49	
		increase of 9
1900	58	
		increase of 43
1905	101	
		increase of 39
1910	140	
		increase of 127
1915	267	
		increase of 12
1920	279	
		increase of 45
1925	324	
		increase of 74
1930	398	

The greatest increase in elders (127 from 1910 to 1915)
culminates the decade of most spectacular church growth
when the communicant membership rose from 10,000 in 1904
to 32,000 in 1914, an increase of 22,000 persons. From
1920 to 1930 the number of elders increased by 119 to a
total of nearly 400, maintaining the general ratio of
one elder for 110 to 120 communicant members. This took
place at the time when the number of missionaries was at

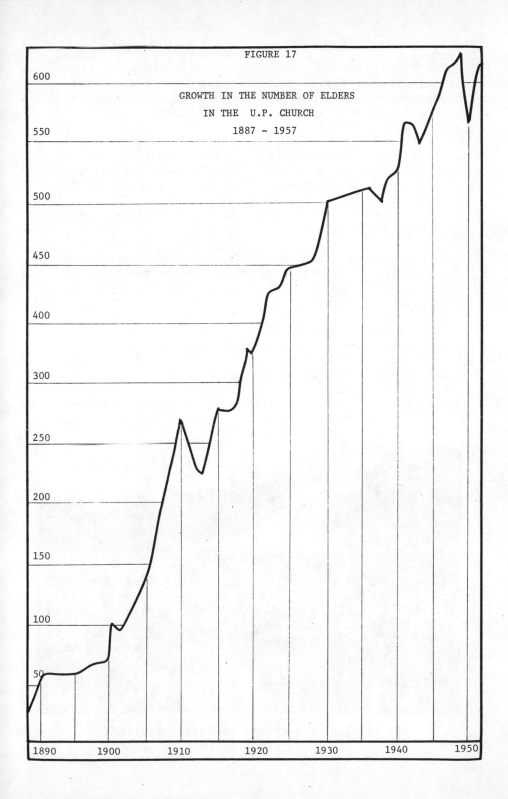

FIGURE 17

GROWTH IN THE NUMBER OF ELDERS
IN THE U.P. CHURCH
1887 – 1957

its height (See Figure 16.)--evidence that the missionaries were not concerned with dominating the Church but
with developing indigenous leadership as fully as
possible.

In 1916 a sudden drop in the number of elders occurs.
Evidently many of these elders, having more initiative
than the average villager, went into the army or obtained
employment at army bases during that period. Their
return is noted by the sharp rise in elders to a total
of 280 in 1920.

Although most elders were illiterate, they were able
to reinforce the teaching given by trained pastors, and
they served to stabilize the Chuhra movement, contributing
to its rapid expansion.

In addition to all of these causes for rapid growth,
was the impetus of a world-wide revival that swept
through many countries during this period and came with
power to the Church in the Punjab during the first decade
of the 20th century. The relationship of this revival
to the growth of the U.P. Church is so significant that
it will be described in detail in the following chapter.

The Sialkot Convention, Center of Revival
-- *from AFTER SIXTY YEARS*

8
Revival

Revival came in full measure to the Church in the Punjab in 1904. For several subsequent years revival swept not only the U.P. Church but all major denominations in North India. Its effect was deep and far-reaching in the life of the Church and its relationship to church growth has great significance not only historically but in terms of the present and the future. What was that relationship?

Keep in mind that significant church growth started through a people movement in the 1880's without the benefit of any special revival in the Church. The Gospel was spread by illiterate villagers persuading their relatives and friends by discussion and example. Stewart writes:

> It is admitted that our people have not been led to profess Christ through the gateway of what is called a "revival"; that is, through the instrumentality of mass meetings in which the Spirit of God has demonstrated His overwhelming power ... We have had no Pentecostal outpourings where individuals exhibited profound conviction of sin, great fear of divine wrath or a strong love for the Savior, or where the mass of the hearers seemed to be swayed hither and thither by the irresistible impulse of a Superior Presence ... Still, that many of the conversions are genuine and that a great work of grace has been going on in our field, can be established, we think, by convincing proofs. (1896:249-251)

By 1904 the U.P. Church alone numbered 10,000
communicant members--evidence of the work of God's
Spirit. Then in the midst of this group movement a
classic revival came. It did not initiate church growth
but it certainly stimulated further growth. Two powerful forces were interacting at this time among the
Chuhras--the group movement and the reviving power of
the Holy Spirit.

The socio-economic factors that caused some Chuhras
to become Muslims or Sikhs propelled others into the
Christian fold. These had made a genuine decision to
leave idolatry and follow Christ, but it had been done
without a deep sense of sin or experience of the power
and presence of God. After baptism, however, they
received follow-up teaching which brought distinctively
Christian factors into operation. A sense of sin arose
as they memorized the Ten Commandments. An awareness
of God's fatherly care deepened as they prayed the Lord's
Prayer in public worship. They began to find freedom
from fear of evil spirits. Their children went to
school and learned to read the Bible. The plateau that
marked the 1890's was ended and rapid growth had begun
again, bringing many new converts into the fellowship.
The thrill of seeing hundreds and thousands of family
and clan members leave idolatry and pledge allegiance
to Jesus Christ filled the hearts of Christians with
praise and adoration and a sense of expectancy that
prepared them for a deeper work of the Spirit.

Without doubt the revival sparked even greater church
growth. The decade following was a period of peak
growth, with 22,000 communicant members added from 1904
to 1914. (See Figure 12.) Church members deepened in
faith and filled with the power of the Holy Spirit were
eager to witness to their non-Christian relatives and
friends, bringing many more to declare their faith in
Christ. In this way the revival acted as a catalyst
working through the rapidly growing group movement and
stimulating further expansion.

What led to this revival and how was it manifested?

A *Spiritual Awakening in 1896*

In February 1896 General Booth, the great founder of
the Salvation Army, held meetings for spiritual quickening in Amritsar. His interpreter was a Muslim convert
whom he had met previously in England--Ihsan Ullah,
pastor of the Anglican congregation in Narowal, forty
miles from Sialkot. One Saturday evening as General
Booth was vigorously denouncing sin, Ihsan Ullah became
so convicted of the formality and pride in his own
ministry that he felt he could not continue to interpret.
Bursting into tears he said, "I cannot go on." The
General replied, "Brother, don't think of self now.
Think only of other poor sinners and afterwards we will
discuss your case." That night after the meeting Ihsan
Ullah surrendered anew to the Lord and pledged himself
to obey the Holy Spirit no matter what the cost.

Sunday morning he openly shared his experience with
his congregation in Narowal. Many confessed their faults
with tears, begged forgiveness of neighbors with whom
they had quarreled, and left with a new-found power and
joy. Revival spread to villages in the area.

A few days later Ihsan Ullah met two United Presbyterian seminary students, Mallu Chand and Labhu Mall,
visiting their home villages for Easter vacation. Having
known them since they were boys, he asked each with deep
concern, "Brother, are you saved?" Irritated, they
began to answer affirmatively when suddenly they felt
such conviction of sin they fell at his feet weeping and
crying for mercy. They arose new men. Returning to the
seminary in Sialkot they shared their experience with the
other ten students, who then spent one whole night getting
right with God. Their wives overhearing their weeping
were greatly puzzled as to what was happening. The next
day, however, they too experienced a time of humble
confession and renewal.

On March 24th, 1896, Sialkot Presbytery met at Pasrur
to study the first and second chapters of Acts. In
closing, the speaker urged the men to accept the gift

of the Holy Spirit. Immediately some fell on their faces
weeping. Several hours of earnest prayer and confession
of sin were followed by a deep sense of joy and praise.

Synod meeting in Jhelum was the scene of more such
meetings as the work deepened in the hearts of many
pastors and elders. The working of God's Spirit was
also evident in Bible schools for pastors and evangelists
held in Zafarwal the end of April, in Gujranwala in May,
and in Sialkot. Several men left the meetings to make
right old enmities at home before returning to share in
the joy of forgiveness.

Simultaneously, a spirit of earnest prayer and longing
for a deeper walk with the Lord was developing in the
Girls' Boarding School in Sialkot. Prayer groups met
each night and Bible study took on new meaning. One
Sabbath in June Ihsan Ullah was invited to speak to the
Sialkot congregation where the school girls attended.
His message on the Holy Spirit struck a responsive chord
with them. At the Wednesday night prayer meeting the wife
of a seminary student felt convicted of disobedience to
the Holy Spirit in not praying aloud in the meeting. She
had hesitated to do so as no woman had ever prayed
audibly before men in a public meeting before. As the
meeting closed, before the school girls had filed out,
she began to pray aloud. Soon all the girls were weeping,
under deep conviction of sin, followed by the assurance
of forgiveness and cleansing. These students shared
their experience by letter with their parents, with the
result that God's power was demonstrated in many
scattered villages of Sialkot district.

One evening Labhu Mall and Mallu Chand, the two
young seminary students won by Ihsan Ullah, felt led to
hold a meeting in the Christian Training Institute, the
boys' boarding school in Sialkot. The management, misunderstanding the revival and feeling they should guard
the boys from emotionalism, refused to allow the meeting
to be held. Labhu that night prayed specifically, "Oh,
Lord, please grant that the place where we were forbidden
to speak tonight may become the center from which great

blessings shall flow to all parts of India." His
prayer was abundantly answered as the C.T.I. compound
later became the site of the famous Sialkot Convention,
designated by some as the "Keswick of India."

The revival of 1896 is especially significant as the
impetus to the development of a self-supporting pastorate.
This will be explained more fully later.

Stewart in 1899 in the Addenda to the second edition
of his book summarized this awakening as follows:

> A striking work of grace (what we generally
> call a revival), among native workers,
> students, and the more highly educated
> classes of the people, began at a meeting
> of the Sialkot Presbytery in Pasrur,
> March 24, 1896, and has been continued
> from time to time in various places from
> that day to this ... The highly spiritual
> character of this movement has been mani-
> fested in deep contrition for sin, in
> the confession of faults one to another,
> in restitution for wrong done, in strong
> crying and tears, in a love of prayer,
> praise and other means of grace, in attach-
> ment to God's Word, in affection for the
> brethren, in greater consecration to Christ's
> service, in tithe-giving, in diminished
> covetousness, in a willingness to serve
> God without promised pay, and in other
> ways. And both sexes have been affected
> alike ...
>
> And yet it may still be said that revival
> influences have only to a very slight
> degree reached the common people. (1899:
> 415-416)

Revival among church leaders peaked in 1896. The next
notable peak is 1904.

The Punjab Praise and Prayer Union

A deep hunger for greater blessing persisted from
1896 until 1904 with occasional demonstrations of the
Spirit's working in small scattered areas. In April 1904
two seminarians and a number of missionaries felt burdened
for a closer walk with God themselves, and for revival
in the Church as a whole. A meeting for prayer and
devotions was held in Sialkot, resulting in confession,
cleansing of sin, and deep spiritual refreshment. Those
present agreed to meet the following year at the same
time and place and invite others to join them. This
was the beginning the the Punjab Praise and Prayer Union
which has greatly influenced the spiritual life of all
denominations in the Punjab. Those who became members
were asked to sign the following pledge in the form of
questions:

  1. Are you praying for quickening in your
      own life, in the life of your fellow
      workers, and in the Church?

  2. Are you longing for greater power of
      the Holy Spirit in your own life and
      work, and are you convinced that you
      cannot go on without this power?

  3. Will you pray that you may not be
      ashamed of Jesus?

  4. Do you believe that prayer is the
      great means for securing this spiritual
      awakening?

  5. Will you set apart one-half hour each
      day as soon after noon as possible
      to pray for this awakening, and are
      you willing to pray till the awakening
      comes? (*A Century for Christ 1955:24*)

The longing for a widespread quickening in the whole
Church resulted in a general invitation to all Christian
workers throughout North India to come together in Sialkot
for a Christian Life Convention in the fall of 1904.

The Sialkot Conventions of 1904 and 1905

The foundation for the first Sialkot Convention in 1904 was laid in prayer. For thirty days and nights prior to the convention John ("Praying") Hyde of the American Presbyterian Church, McCheyne Paterson and George Turner of the Church of Scotland, and Ihsan Ullah of the Anglican Church spent much time in earnest prayer.

> Through these servants, especially, God
> opened the flood-gates of confession,
> restitution, and illumination, almost a
> living over again of the glory on the
> Mount of Transfiguration ... The secret
> of the convention lay in the prayer room
> in which many joined, both missionaries
> and nations, not the least of whom was
> 80 year old Kanaya who spent three of
> the ten nights in prayer and was mightily
> used of God in scattering the Holy fire
> wherever he went. (*A Century for Christ*
> 1955:24)

During the Sialkot Convention of 1905 there was an even deeper work of the Holy Spirit reviving all those present. Approximately three hundred missionaries and national workers were in attendance. Some nominal Christians experienced the new birth; many earnest believers discovered greater dimensions to faith. Miss Emma Dean Anderson in her book, *In the Shadow of the Himalayas,* writes of the occasion:

> ... lives were changed; many missionaries
> who were counted "good missionaries" before,
> became missionaries of power. All night
> long the hall remained full of people
> praying and praising; and I can testify
> to the fact that our Mission and Church
> have been different ever since that night
> when God so graciously poured out His
> Spirit upon His people. (1942:203)

In this way the Church in the Punjab enetered into the
world-wide wave of revival which Dr. J.E. Orr refers to
as the early 20th century Evangelical Awakening. It
was an amazing working of the Spirit of God in such far
removed areas of the world as China, Korea, Wales,
Scandinavia, Los Angeles, Australia and India. Each
followed a similar pattern of deep conviction of sin,
confession, and cleansing, followed by spontaneous joy
and praise. As Dr. Orr says:

> ... its sources were in the springs of little
> prayer meetings which seemed to arise spon-
> taneously all over the world, combining into
> the streams of expectation which became a
> river of blessing. (1973:188)

Revival Spreads

The Sialkot Convention, originally intended for church
leaders, was expanded in 1906 to include all interested
Christians of every denomination. That year over 1300
attended, many coming from great distances. An overwhelming conviction of sin and the need for cleansing
was created in the hearts of those present. Many would
groan and cry in great distress as they became aware of
their sins and failures. They were eager to confess
their faults publicly in order to obtain release and
pardon. When assured of forgiveness, they broke out
into such joyous laughter and singing the meeting tent
fairly rocked. Pengwern Jones of the Welsh Khasi Hills
Mission came as one of the speakers and made this report:

> No doubt the great power of the Convention
> was centered in the Prayer Room and not
> the Preaching Hall ... The voice of
> prayer and praise was constantly heard
> day and night, during the whole days of
> the convention ... All who entered the
> Prayer Room felt that it was a sacred
> spot, that Christ Himself was present
> for the very atmosphere seemed to be full
> of the spirit of praise and prayer ...

> It is very remarkable how the Convention
> ended with praise. During the first days
> there was a great deal of singing going
> on but not much praise; the last days there
> was less noise but more praise, there was
> a ring of joy and praise in every sound.
> One of the speakers ... scores of times
> said: "Surround men with an atmosphere of
> praise and the evil one cannot get at
> them."   (Reports and Letters to the Board
> of Foreign Missions of the Presbyterian
> Church U.S.A. Vol. 164-33, 1906)

Revival spread as the fire was carried back to cold
congregations and mission stations.

By 1908 the attendance at convention had grown to
2000 and people came with a deep sense of expectancy that
God would bless them there. John Hyde was powerfully
used by God until his departure for America in 1911.
Hyde at that time was leading an average of four persons
a day to put faith in Jesus Christ. Who were the
persons being won? They were largely Chuhras. The power
of the revival was enhanced by the people movement then
in full swing. The tinder was dry. Christians of Chuhra
background revived by the Convention witnessed to interested relatives and friends who rapidly caught fire from
their enthusiasm. John Hyde himself said:

> The revival has so stirred and given such
> visions of the blood and revealed such
> mighty workings of Christ in many lives
> that the hope is very definite of Jesus
> being about to open the eyes of the
> Hindus and Mohammedans. (Miller 1955:
> 89)

It is clear from this statement that Hindus and Muslims
were not as yet being reached through the convention
revival. There was just renewed hope that they would
be. Unfortunately this hope was not and has not yet been
realized. There was no people movement among Hindus
or Muslims where the fire could catch. The tinder was
still green. Even the power of this great revival was

not sufficient to break through caste barriers or to
reach into another caste channel to begin a group movement among the high castes. This is another indication
that revival in the Punjab did not initiate a group movement, but worked like a catalyst in the midst of an on-
going movement.

Figure 18 points up some more interesting facts that
shed light on the relationship between the Sialkot Convention revival and the Chuhra group movement. After
the first burst of growth, peaking in 1886, there was
a distinct lull in adult baptisms. This reflects the
period when the Mission felt overwhelmed by the rapid
ingathering and deliberately avoided baptizing inquirers
until they could perfect those already baptized. At the
turn of the century, another growth spurt began that
peaked dramatically from 1908 to 1910, just toward the
close of the Sialkot Convention revival period. This
striking fact could easily lead to the conclusion that
the peak growth was caused primarily by the revival.
It is important to examine this more carefully.

Note in Figure 18 the number of adult baptisms that
took place in Sialkot Presbytery. They remained almost
constantly at 300 to 350 a year from 1884 to 1910. The
only sharp rise came in 1886 when it jumped to about 750.
The revival years of 1904 to 1910 show no sudden increase
in numbers, although the Sialkot Convention would naturally have had its deepest effect upon the people of
that locality who attended in large numbers. They undoubtedly gained much spiritual insight and blessing,
but no appreciable difference is seen in the number of
non-Christian Chuhras being won in Sialkot.

On the other hand, the largest spurt of growth from
1904 to 1910 was taking place in the Lyallpur-Sheikhupura
area, more than 100 miles from Sialkot, a lengthy and
difficult trip in those days. Only a few from this area
could possibly have attended the Convention meetings.
Yet, the Church grew by leaps and bounds. Obviously
other forces were at work turning non-Christians to Jesus
Christ. The revival undoubtedly stimulated growth but
was used primarily to deepen the lives of those already
in the fold.

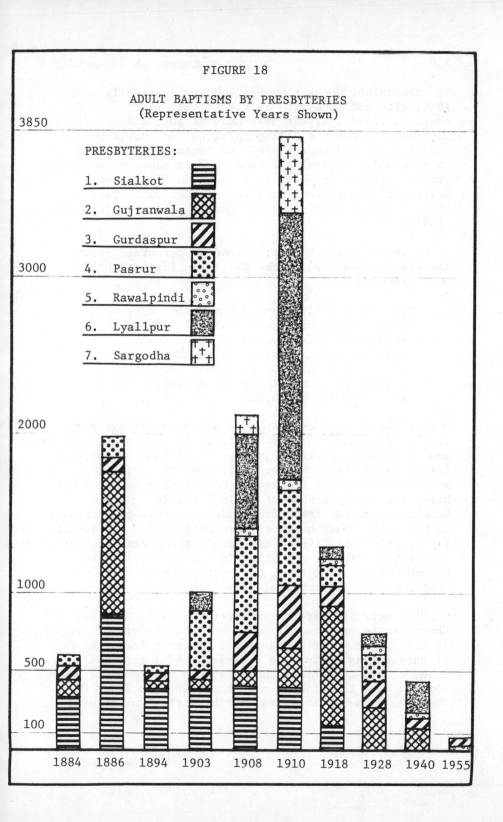

FIGURE 18

ADULT BAPTISMS BY PRESBYTERIES
(Representative Years Shown)

PRESBYTERIES:

1. Sialkot

2. Gujranwala

3. Gurdaspur

4. Pasrur

5. Rawalpindi

6. Lyallpur

7. Sargodha

3850

3000

2000

1000

500

100

1884 1886 1894 1903 1908 1910 1918 1928 1940 1955

The Sialkot Convention has been held annually since
1904, with the exception of five or six years when
cholera, floods, or war have made it impossible. It has
continued to exert a strong spiritual influence on all
the Missions and Churches of the Punjab. However no
such sweeping revival has come from it since those early
years. Its waning power is in part due to increasing
neglect of the prayer room; but another vital reason is
that there has been no active people movement since the
1930's.

In recent years Christian leaders concerned about
the static condition of the Church in Pakistan have
been prone to say:

> "If only a revival would come, then the
> Church would grow once again. If these
> second and third generation Christians
> would be baptized afresh with the power
> of the Holy Spirit, they would reach out
> and win their non-Christian neighbors as
> their forefathers did."

Revival has been looked upon as an essential pre-requisite
for healthy church growth. Efforts have been concentrated
upon providing opportunities for Christians to deepen in
faith. Much prayer has been offered for revival, and a
succession of committed men of God, including Dr. Akbar
Haqq, the "Billy Graham of India," the Rev. Robert
Cummings, and two teams from Indonesia have been brought
to Pakistan. They have held Conventions for the deepening of spiritual life in the hope and expectation that
a spirit of revival may arise in the Church. These
brought blessing to many, but neither revival or
church growth has resulted.

What hope is there for another revival? What can the
Church do to prepare for one? The history of the Church
in the Punjab would suggest that the most likely means
of encouraging revival is to search out a responsive
group of non-Christians and in simple obedience to God's
command seek to bring them to know and love Jesus Christ.
When the present Christian Church reaches out to others

and experiences the joy of seeing non-Christians come
into the fellowship in large numbers; and when Christians of all denominations fall on their knees in earnest
confession and prayer, there is great hope that revival
fire will once again sweep the Church.

9
Self-Support

Winning converts and baptizing them into the fellowship
of the Church is only a first step in discipling a
people. The second essential missionary task is to
establish a self-supporting, self-governing and self-
propagating Church.

In the *Minutes of the General Assembly* of the United
Presbyterian Church in North America as far back as 1868
is this important statement on mission policy:

> ... the idea should be constantly kept in
> view that the present system of conducting
> foreign missions should be regarded as
> introductory to the more permanent and
> efficient system by which the work will
> be mainly carried forward by native teach-
> ers and missionaries and from home (Indian)
> sources of support. (498).

The General Assembly of 1896 reiterated this stand:

> A native self-supporting, self-propagating,
> independent church must be the goal toward
> which all missionary efforts shall tend.
> The sending out of foreign missionaries is
> not to be perpetual. (*Minutes of the General
> Assembly of the U.P. Church of N.A.* 1896:59)

Plan for Self-Support

As early as 1890 the Mission appointed a special committee known as the "Evangelism and Self-Support Committee" whose main goal was to develop self-support in the U.P. Church as soon as possible. By 1894 the Mission reported that this subject had come to be called the "U.P. Mission specialty." Each year this committee prepared Bible study materials and memory programs to be taught in all congregations in an effort to train the Church in essential doctrines and especially in stewardship.

In 1898 in order to implement the development of self-support the following resolutions were taken:

1. To encourage all Christians to be witnesses and work voluntarily for the spread of the Gospel.

2. To teach laymen systematic and liberal giving to support a local worker or pastor.

3. To not increase the number of Christian helpers employed by the Mission for instructing new converts, but to try to get this work on a self-supporting basis within four years.

4. To organize village Christian groups into evangelistic circuits large enough to support a national worker.

5. To choose suitable workers to take charge of these circuits, drawing their living from their people.

6. To encourage each circuit to choose their own lay leaders to serve without pay. After sufficient instruction, these leaders will be ordained as elders.

7. To install a pastor in a congregation when the people can assume his full support; only special cases to receive aid from the Mission.

8.   To urge the national Church to assume all expenses
in connection with building and repairing their own
churches.

9.   To employ a limited number of Mission-paid evangelists
to work among non-Christians under the supervision of a
missionary.

10.   To establish village schools only where 12 or more
children attend and a Christian teacher can be secured.
Students must furnish their own books.

Delay in Self-Support

There was considerable delay in putting the above
resolutions into practice.   Until 1896 the emphasis on
self-support was promulgated almost entirely by
missionaries.   Following the revivals of 1896 and 1904,
national leaders began to show greater enthusiasm for
it.   Nevertheless, only one self-supporting congregation
had been established by 1901, although there were at that
time 8,022 communicant members, 24 organized congregations
and 15 ordained Indian ministers.   The Church in the
Punjab remained definitely dependent for some time after
it had made significant growth.   Why?

During the 1890's controversy developed in the Mission
over self-support.   Some missionaries felt the policy
of paying Indian workers had been a mistake from the
beginning.   Workers should be required to depend for
their support solely upon the contributions of the people
they serve.

Note that this position was not forcefully presented
in the early stages of growth.   At that time it seemed
clear to all that evangelistic helpers would have to be
paid by the Mission if the overwhelming task of seeking
and shepherding was to be done at all.   Had they not
paid workers, no movement would have taken place, for
during that early period there were not enough Christians
in any congregation to support a national pastor.

Adobe Home and Courtyard of a National Pastor in Khangah Dogran
--from *IN THE SHADOW OF THE HIMALAYAS*

Local Christians Tear Down a Shrine to the Smallpox God

The first twenty years of service netted only 153
communicant members. These were usually disinherited
by their families and found it difficult to support
themselves, much less a pastor. At the same time the
need for national workers to help sow the seed over a
widely scattered area was urgent.

As the Chuhra group movement accelerated, there were
greatly increased numbers of converts, but these were
not concentrated in centers. Christians were scattered
in villages, often at great distances from one another,
and could not easily be gathered into a congregation
that one man could pastor.

Another difficulty was the low economic level of the
Chuhras. Due to their illiteracy, lack of training,
and degraded social background, few could obtain
lucrative employment. The monthly income of most
village Christian families was approximately five rupees.
Being share croppers or unskilled farm laborers they
were usually paid in crops, not in cash. They received
a share of each kind of produce at the time it was
harvested, plus frequent handouts of food.

The missionaries in teaching stewardship had to devise
opportunities for the Chuhras to give offerings in kind.
One common method was to have a woman put aside for God
a handful of flour out of every ten she kneaded into
bread for her family, or to set apart a chicken or a
lamb as an offering. At the harvest thank-offering
service a percentage of the harvest income was given to
the evangelistic worker. Such training took time and
patience, but slowly began to bear dividends.

During the 1890's the U.P. Church employed seven
ordained ministers. These had been highly trained in
the Theological Seminary so received from 30 to 120
rupees a month as salary, the average being about 55
rupees. The demand for pastors greatly exceeded the
number of men trained for the ministry. Various Missions,
both Protestant and the newly arrived Roman Catholics,
were short of Indian workers. Frequent attempts were made
by competing Missions to entice away workers with promises
of higher salaries. To counteract these inducements the

U.P. Mission had to pay comparatively high salaries.
This did not encourage self-support, for it would take
more than 100 tithing Chuhra families with an income of
five rupees a month to support the average pastor
receiving 55 rupees a month. It is a mistake to have
pastors on a much higher financial, social and educational
level than the people to whom they minister. The Chuhras
could hardly be expected to contribute sacrificially to
maintain a pastor at a standard so much above their own.

The presence of foreign missionaries with seemingly
endless resources, and connections with influential
government officials, also predisposed the Chuhras
against giving much from their own sparse earnings.
Why should they scrimp to provide an evangelistic worker
with sufficient funds, when the Mission could easily
support him from foreign funds? Self-support could not
become a reality until these prejudices were broken down
and the Chuhras gained a vision of their responsibility
to carry on the Lord's work themselves.

In 1891 the Mission formed a committee to bring the
matter of self-support emphatically and forcefully before
the national pastors in Presbytery. They worked out a
sliding scale by which the churches would become self-
supporting in ten years. The pastors felt increasingly
threatened as the Mission pressured them concerning self-
support. Bitter feeling arising from this issue coupled
with frustration at the autocratic rule of the Mission,
resulted in the Sialkot Presbytery sending a memorandum
directly to the 1892 General Assembly in the United
States complaining that the missionaries were fostering
a "master - slave" relationship in the Church. They
accused the Mission of exercising absolute power in
dispensing foreign funds, with no regard for the wishes
of the Church. They pleaded for a more "just and
equable" use of mission money, especially regarding
salaries for pastors and evangelists. This incident
climaxed the growing rift in the relationship between
the missionaries and the Indian pastors and greatly
hindered the progress of self-support. It may be that
God used this conflict to make both parties acutely

aware of their need for cleansing and revival, preparing the way for the deeper work of His Spirit in 1896 among both pastors and missionaries.

U.P. missionaries differed among themselves as to the advisability and feasibility of the Church becoming self-supporting. Some felt that pastors should be sent out "without purse or script" to become Christian *fakirs* or *sadhus* on the same pattern as many Hindu and Sikh religious leaders. Others believed that the national Church could and should support a regular pastor living in their midst. On the other hand, Stewart voiced the opinion of many that the policy of paying pastors was a practical necessity on a temporary basis until the Church had grown in numbers sufficient to support its own pastors, and had been thoroughly trained in stewardship. The attitude expressed by Stewart was held by all the neighboring Missions who were not much concerned with encouraging self-support at this time. None of them had such a large number of Christians or national workers, so had not yet faced the difficulties and financial strain of such a policy. The conflict of opinion undoubtedly slowed down the development of self-support in the U.P. Church.

Revival Sparks Self-Support

In 1896 a special work of the Holy Spirit began among U.P. Indian pastors and leaders at a meeting of the Sialkot Presbytery in March. This was an indirect result of the previously described revival in the life of the Rev. Ihsan Ullah, the C.M.S. pastor in Narowal, forty miles from Sialkot. Both the Presbytery meeting and the Synod meeting a few weeks later were marked by a spirit of prayer, deep sorrow for sin, confession and a longing for spiritual power. Revival spread to the students in the seminary in Gujranwala and was apparent in the summer Bible Schools that year.

Up until this time the policy of self-support had been urged by the missionaries but resisted with considerable resentment by Indian pastors. Now on the crest of this revival, came a turning point.

In August of 1896 a prayer retreat was held in the
home of the Rev. W.T. Anderson, missionary in charge of
Zafarwal district. A number of those blessed by the
Sialkot revival were present. On short notice an
invitation was sent out to the Rev. Ganda Mall, the
second son of one of the first Meg converts, Kanaya,
asking him to lead some meetings in the prayer retreat.
He had heard rumors of the revival through his sister,
Maryam, a teacher in the Girls' Boarding School in
Sialkot. She had been used of God to bring new life
and consecration to a number of her students and had
recently been specifically praying for a special blessing
upon her pastor brother. Ganda Mall was suspicious of
the "emotionalism" accompanying the revival and was
tempted to refuse the invitation. He consulted his wife.
To his amazement, his wife, who usually stayed home to
care for their six children, said, "We will go." As
Ganda Mall saddled the horse, she called in a neighbor
to watch the four oldest children and prepared the two
youngest to go with them. They arrived that night after
the close of the evening service.

Next morning they attended their first meeting. The
subject of the conference that morning was "Self-Support"
--a touchy issue in the Church in those days. When the
subject was first presented, the people had little to say.
They couldn't think of any practical ways to increase
their giving. As discussion went on and specific
suggestions were made, interest grew. Ganda Mall who
usually enjoyed discussion and argument was strangely
silent throughout. He was passing through a great inner
struggle as God dealt with him.

In the evening a consecration service was held. Ganda
Mall's head drooped lower and lower. At the close he
rose with great effort and cried out, "Brothers, pray
for me! God wants me to do something and I don't know
what it is." Several prayed. After prayer the meeting
broke up, but a few stayed behind for further prayer.
Ganda Mall was in great distress, praying with sobs.
The circle interceded earnestly for him unaware of the
reason for his struggle. Finally he drew his wife to
the back of the church and talked quietly with her for

a few minutes. Then he announced, "I know now what it
is God wants me to do. God wants me to give up the
eight dollars a month salary I have been receiving from
America and to take just what my own poor people can
give me, in order that our people may learn to support
their own work."

Ganda's wife stood with downcast eyes a few minutes,
then said to her husband, "Father of Khalil, don't do
anything hastily. Think of me and of our six children."

All night long Ganda paced through the fields thinking
and praying. Next morning the family went home. Little
was said on the journey. That night after the children
were in bed Ganda's wife came to him and said, "I am
willing now. I knew yesterday that God wanted you to
give up your salary, but I was afraid to consent. I
felt we would suffer, perhaps starve. I am willing now
for you to take this step, for if God wants you to do it,
will He not provide?"

Ganda Mall was so overjoyed he woke the four older
children and told them of their decision. Their oldest
son, Khalil, said, "Thank God for such parents. We
cannot do much to help you, but if the time should come
when there would not be much to eat, we will not cry or
trouble you in any way." Then the family knelt down
and thanked God for the victory won.

The following evening Ganda Mall called together his
congregation to tell them of his decision. Would they
resent his placing such a financial burden upon them,
when they had so little? An elder rose to respond,
"Thank God for such a pastor!" he said, "We have known
for a long time we ought to do more. If God will forgive
us the past, we will do better in the future ... Pastor,
you know we do not have much, but when you are hungry
we will be hungry too. We will divide the last crumb
we have with you."

That year the two seminary students who had been
challenged by Ihsan Ullah to a deeper committment of
their lives, Labhu Mall and Mallu Chand, (see page 129.)
were finishing their seminary course. They too were led
to trust God for their support as they served in village

congregations. In 1905 Rev. Labhu Mall was chosen to
become a professor in the Theological Seminary. He
reminded Synod that he had promised God not to use any
foreign money for his support. Synod accepted this new
challenge, stepped out on faith and agreed to raise his
salary from local sources. This was the start of the
"Home Mission Fund" and a further step toward total self-
support.

In spite of this promising beginning, it is disappoint-
ing to note that by 1900 there was only one congregation
entirely self-supporting. Due to severe famine, the
others continued to receive some foreign aid.

The Sialkot Convention revival from 1904 to 1910
gave great impetus to self-support. Pastors were
strengthened in faith and encouraged to trust God instead
of the Mission for their financial needs. Revival also
stimulated the laity to better stewardship. Villagers
were encouraged to give in kind when they had little
cash. The women set aside the first handful of flour
each meal when measuring it out for bread. They began
to give the pastor a proportion of their grain at harvest
time. Offerings increased, making self-support more
feasible. The Mission Minutes for 1910 reports a 27
per cent increase over the previous year in local church
giving. This new spiritual dimension found in the Church
was due to the influence of the revival.

Probably the most significant contribution to self-
support by the revival was increased converts from among
the Chuhras. Sialkot Convention instilled in the hearts
of many simple Christians a profound concern for the lost.
They witnessed with greater zeal to friends and neighbors,
causing a sharp rise in baptisms. Congregations greatly
increased in size as the Church grew from 7,000 in 1900
to 32,000 in 1914. (See Figure 12 Most important,
enough Christian families were concentrated within a
short radius to facilitate their ability to support a
national pastor. So revival gave the self-support
movement new impetus, not only by increasing zeal and
sacrifical concern but by multiplying supporters.

Church Organization Spurs Self-Support

A foundational step to making self-support feasible was to organize congregations into circles that one man could pastor, and to train lay leaders (elders) to work with the pastor in shepherding those congregations. Many missionaries made this task their major concern during this period. The high priority given to organization and the choosing of lay leaders in the Church is revealed in the Triennial Report for 1919-1921:

> We are cranks on church organization. We
> believe that when people become Christians
> they should be quickly organized into a
> congregation and not get the habit of
> having their preacher paid by the Mission.
> A short time ago we baptized the people
> in the village of Rana. After the baptisms
> we had them elect their elders. (147)

An organized congregation consisted of at least two elders, and a pastor who acted as moderator of the governing body of the local congregation, the session.

It is significant to note the close correlation between the establishment of organized congregations and the number of congregations that became self-supporting. (See Figure 19.) Note how rapidly the percentage of self-supporting congregations rises as shown in five year intervals.

During the first decade of the 20th century, the number of organized congregations more than doubled, increasing from 20 to 43. The percentage of self-supporting congregations rose dramatically from 5 per cent in 1900 to 65 per cent in 1910. During World War I only 13 new congregations were organized and no progress was made toward self-support. After the war the number of organized congregations steadily increased, and from 1925 to 1935 the percentage of self-supporting congregations jumped from 54 per cent to 90 per cent.

To organize believers rapidly into worshipping congregations with their own indigenous leaders is of utmost
importance as a step toward a self-supporting Church.

"Home Rule" and Self-Support

Starting in 1918 there was an increasing emphasis
upon "Home Rule" or independence for India. Gandhi was
one of the outstanding leaders of this movement. It
gained momentum for several years and then temporarily
diminished with Gandhi's imprisonment in 1924. This
emphasis upon independence was a further stimulation to
self-support, for nationalistic spirit ran high, bringing
to the Church the desire to stand on her own feet and
cut loose from the apron strings of the "Mother Church"
in America. Financial independence was one aspect of
this. Note that the number of self-supporting congregations more than double in the 1920's, rising from 32
in 1920 to 71 in 1930. (See Figure 19.)

The Great Depression

As early as 1925 the United States was facing a
financial crisis that led to the stock market crash in
1929, followed by the Great Depression of the 1930's.
Mission budget was cut drastically; by 1926 it had been
reduced by 25 per cent. One result was a dramatic rise in
self-supporting congregations. In 1925 there were 48 self-
supporting congregations (54 per cent of the total); by
1935 the number had risen to 111 or 90 per cent of the
congregations. Every congregation since that time has been
expected to support its own pastors and program. Only a
few "Home Mission" centers received outside aid.

This goal was reached at considerable sacrifice
on the part of national pastors and their families--a
tribute to their great courage and faith. A lady
missionary happened in on a village pastor's wife as she
was cleaning a conglomerate mixture of grains in
preparation for grinding it into flour. Surprised to
see such a mixture, as usually each type of grain is

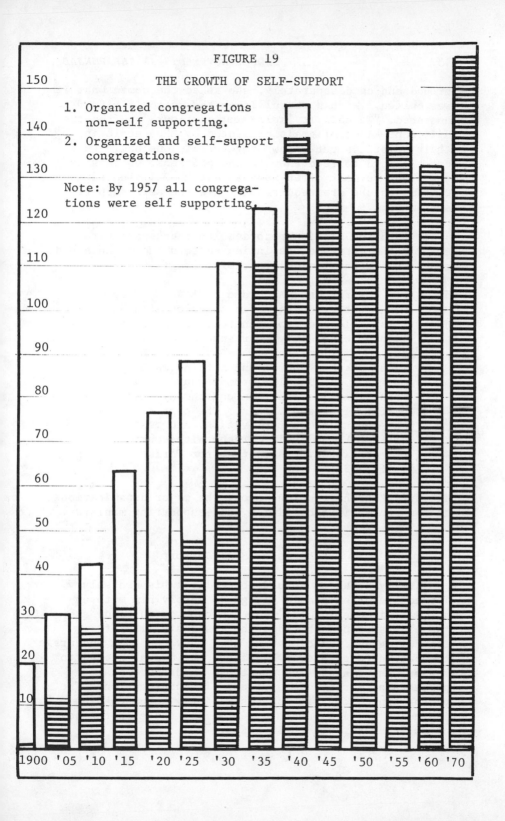

FIGURE 19

THE GROWTH OF SELF-SUPPORT

1. Organized congregations non-self supporting.

2. Organized and self-support congregations.

Note: By 1957 all congregations were self supporting.

ground and used separately, she asked the woman what it
was called. With a rueful laugh the pastor's wife
answered, "We call it 'self-support flour.' Often the
different kinds of grain presented by the people in
their offerings get thrown together in one bag. We
can't afford to feed them to the chickens, so this is
the flour we most often have to eat." Daily sacrifices
of this nature are required to make the self-support
system work.

In 1933 the Mission recorded its thanksgiving to
God for the attitude the Indian pastors and workers had
shown during the financial crisis:

> ... the response accorded by Indian fellow
> workers to reductions in salaries afford
> infallible proof of consecrated spiritual
> life which greatly heartens us; confirming
> our convictions that our God is in the
> midst of this Church and nothing shall
> move her ... The indigenous Church has
> maintained its position under many
> difficulties and trials. The pastors
> have endured great privation, and most
> of them borne their burdens with courage
> and fortitude. (*A Century for Christ*
> 1955:38-39)

The U.P. Church is unique among the major denominations
in the Punjab in achieving a self-supporting ministry.

Problems of Self-Support

Ideally a pastor should not collect his own salary.
The congregation should pledge to supply him with an
adequate income for the year (in cash or in kind) and
the elders should shoulder the responsibility of
collecting and administering it. They can then encourage
the people to give over and above the amount needed to
support the pastor, and use these funds for local
projects or for needs outside their congregation. The
pastor can concentrate on his ministry unburdened by
financial worries, and his people can share in the joy
of outreach through their gifts.

Unfortunately in the U.P. Church in Pakistan such an ideal has been practiced only by larger city churches. Rural congregations have seldom been able to follow this pattern. Although self-support is recognized as an important goal for every Church to achieve in order to be truly indigenous, it does involve a number of difficulties and dangers as seen below. These apply primarily to the past, but mark the present as well.

1. Presbytery often gives a minister too large an area to pastor in an effort to include enough people to support him. This is self-defeating, for as the people are neglected, they give less and less to their pastor.

2. Elders have often proved dishonest in handling pastoral funds, using some of them for their own family needs. The poverty of the average Christian family, the unbelievable pressure relatives can exert on a man entrusted with funds, and lack of experience in handling money for an organization make it difficult for these men to administer funds with complete integrity. For this reason most rural pastors collect their own support. Some congregations have solved this difficulty by keeping church funds in a strong-box with two locks. A key to one lock is given to each of two unrelated elders so the box cannot be opened unless both are present. This makes it easier for a man to withstand the pressures of his relatives.

3. Perhaps the greatest temptation for pastors is to focus their attention primarily upon raising their own salary. Such pastors preach frequent sermons on stewardship and make extended pastoral calls when harvest offerings are due, showing considerably less diligence at other seasons of the year. Following an experience of spiritual renewal, one pastor commented to the writer: "When I was running after funds, they always ran faster and I could never catch up with them; but now that I am serving my people without thought of money, the funds run after me and I find I always have enough."

4. Self-supporting congregations often become self-centered, engrossed in their own needs. Since the pastor gathers the funds himself, the people suspect that their offerings are used exclusively to support his family and are not likely to be sent on to some other project. They then lose interest in the larger mission of the Church. It is vital to the spiritual health of a local congregation to retain a vision of needs beyond its boundaries.

5. In order to raise his own support, a pastor is put into the awkward position of a beggar. He is tempted to judge the worth of his church members by their generosity to himself, and to treat them accordingly.

6. Since the pastor collects his own income, and much of it is in kind, his congregation have no accurate knowledge of how much he gets. They tend to overestimate what he is receiving, and any complaints on his part are interpreted as greediness or lack of management. If the local session handled the funds, they would be aware of lacks and responsible to make them up.

7. Church members in a self-supporting congregation can exert undue influence upon their pastor to accede to their wishes in matters contrary to his own moral principles. They can pressure him into swearing falsely in their favor in a civil court, into performing marriages on illegal grounds, or countless other questionable practices. He knows that to stand by his convictions means alienating supporters and may result in considerable financial sacrifice. Few have the courage to abide by their principles consistently in the face of these pressures.

8. Pastors having difficulty in raising their own support are easy prey to divisive denominations that entice them to join their ranks by offering them a generous salary. This has proved a major problem in the U.P. Church since 1968 when Carl McIntire of the Bible Presbyterian Church in the U.S.A. began to pour into Pakistan large amounts of foreign funds, promising salaries to all pastors who would join his movement. Nearly half of the U.P. pastors left the Church to join

him, in contrast to relatively small numbers that left
other major denominations in which salaries had always
been supplemented from foreign funds. Undeniably the
security of having a guaranteed income from abroad was
an important factor in encouraging U.P. pastors to join
McIntire. However, there were other more potent factors
in the situation that will be discussed in detail later.
Nevertheless, the self-support system is vulnerable to
this kind of attack.

9. When a pastor is supported by his congregation rather
than from a central fund, the Presbytery or superior
church court has little control over his activities or
location no matter what their opinion may be of his
ministry. If he can maintain the good will of his
people, he is practically beyond effective discipline
by the church courts. In recent years Presbyteries
have declared certain pastors unfrocked from the ministry.
Nevertheless, as long as their congregation will support
them, they carry on in defiance of this decision.

These problems are not unknown in North America, but
especially plague the Church in Pakistan because of the
low economic level of the people. In spite of them,
however, the U.P. Church has maintained an average of
more than 90 per cent self-supporting congregations
since 1935. Should foreign funds be cut off suddenly
from all denominations in Pakistan, the U.P. ministry
would be among those best prepared to survive.

Home Mission Work

An important milestone in the development of self-
support in the U.P. Church was the formation of the Board
of Home Missions of the Synod of the Punjab in 1907. For
two years prior to this the Synod had been supporting an
Indian professor, the Rev. Labhu Mall, in the Theological
Seminary. Now they took a new step in evangelistic
outreach by appointing one of their strongest pastors,
the Rev. Yusaf, to be a pioneer in the town of Mianwali,
85 miles north of Sargodha. It was so remote in terms of
the available transportation of that day, that it took
a day and a night to reach it by train from Sargodha.

Shortly after the Rev. Yusaf established residence as
nearly the only Christian in this strongly Muslim town,
his small daughter died. He was forbidden to use the
Muslim cemetery, but a Christian friend who had arrived
unexpectedly on the morning train helped him dig a little
grave outside of town in which to lay the precious
remains. When Muslim fanatics threatened his life,
Rev. Yusaf replied, "You may kill me, but the ones who
sent me will send two in my place. If you kill them, they
will send four." His courage won their respect and in
time he came to be so revered that when he lost two sons
just a day apart during the influenza epidemic following
World War I, his Muslim neighbors flocked to show their
sympathy and help with the burial arrangements. Later
the government granted him 112 acres of land in recognition of his services.

Although the Muslims became increasingly friendly
with the Rev. Yusaf, they continued unresponsive to the
Gospel. However, by 1918 a small congregation of 66
members had been established among the Chuhra and
Balmiki sweepers who were open to evangelism.

In 1916 the Synod voted to make Hafizabad a Home
Mission area. It lies about 30 miles west of Gujranwala.
They sent the Rev. Ganda Mall, the first pastor to
relinquish foreign support, to be in charge of the work
there. He had friendly relations with the high caste
Hindus among whom he lived and worked, but it was the
Chuhras who were willing to be baptized and openly declare
themselves Christians. Ganda Mall wisely turned his
attention from the resistant high castes and concentrated
upon the responsive Chuhras, building up a good sized
Christian community in Hafizabad and the surrounding
district.

The *Triennial Report on the Foreign Missions of the
U.P. Church of North America, 1919, 1920, 1921* reports
another step taken by the Synod of the Punjab in an
effort to make their outreach more effective:

> The New World Movement was set in motion
> by the Synod of the Punjab in March, 1920 ...
> The objectives are very practical: ninety-

> nine new church buildings; 85 new parsonages;
> 75 of an increase in ordained ministers;
> 330 elders taught, trained and ordained;
> one hundred more congregations organized;
> a Sabbath School in every congregation;
> 50 per cent of the Christian community in
> the Sabbath School; 50 per cent of the
> Church members pledged intercessors;
> family altars in 50 per cent of the homes;
> all parents and guardians pledged to put
> away the heathen marriage customs; 10,000
> pledged to give the tithe; ... a scholar-
> ship fund of at least 15,000 rupees to help
> forward education; a church building fund
> of 50,000 rupees; and a Home Mission fund
> of 35,000 rupees ... in five years. (172, 173)

This ambitious program was inaugurated on the crest
of the wave of enthusiasm to "Win the world for Christ
in this generation." The idea came from the West as
part of the post World War I forward movement in missions.
It was undoubtedly put through Synod by missionary
enthusiasts who still influenced the decisions of Synod
to a large degree. The goals were beyond the thinking
and expectations of the Indian Church and never became
a motivating force in the Church. The increases attained
by the end of 1925 were far short of the objectives as
can be seen in the table below:

	Objectives	No. Attained
New church buildings	99	13
New parsonages	85	18
Newly ordained pastors	75	20
Newly ordained elders	330	44
Newly organized congre- gations	100	14

Nevertheless some progress was made. It is better to
have an unattainable goal than no goal at all. "If you
aim at nothing, you are sure to hit it every time."

The Khangan Dogran district, northwest of
Sheikhupura, was turned over to the Synod by the Mission
in 1926, with the understanding that Synod would supervise the work there for a trial period of five years.
To take on responsibility for such a large area required
dedication and sacrificial giving on the part of the
national Church which at the same time was becoming
more and more self-supporting. The *Annual Report for
1931* gives a summary of all the Home Mission Board was
supporting--a tribute to the vitality of the Synod of
the Punjab at that time.

> One reason for growth is the missionary
> activity of the Church. Synod's Home
> Mission Field covers four districts in
> which there are nine organized congre-
> gations and a membership of 3,417. In
> this field entirely supported by the
> Synod there are nine ordained ministers
> and fourteen evangelists employed.
> Synod's budget this year, which corre-
> sponds to our missionary budget in the
> home Church, amounts to Rs. 17,262.
> The largest share of this goes to the
> Home Mission work, Rs. 10,462. The next
> largest share is for the support of the
> two Indian professors in the Seminary,
> Rs. 2,750; then comes Rs. 2,500 for
> church buildings and parsonages; Rs. 1,000
> for ministerial relief; and Rs. 550 for
> the work of the Synod. (115)

The Home Mission program developed in the Church a
sense of responsibility and self-respect as well as
concern for others that had great psychological and
spiritual value--resulting in a vital, outreaching Church.

10
The "407" Movement

In October 1902 the U.P. Mission submitted to the Board
of Foreign Missions an analysis of their field in India,
pointing out that their mission area covered 24,223
square miles containing over five million people. In
the light of these facts, they proposed a plan for
evangelizing the field. Anna Milligan in her book,
Facts and Folks in Our Fields Abroad, states the goal they
had in mind:

> ... we believe it to be the duty of our
> Church to secure the evangelization of
> this field within the period of a single
> generation--that is, so to bring the
> essential principles of the Gospel to
> the attention of all classes in that time
> that no one of mature understanding could
> say that he was not acquainted with the
> way of everlasting life. (1921:40)

To accomplish this goal, the Mission felt it needed
a minimum of one male missionary and one lady evangelistic missionary for every 50,000 people in the U.P.
mission area, plus a much enlarged force of Indian
evangelistic workers. To obtain this proportion of
missionaries to the population, they appealed for 180
more evangelistic missionaries--90 men and 90 unmarried
ladies--to be distributed as shown on Figure 20. The
distribution of workers was solely on the basis of
population not taking account of responsiveness. This
appeal was combined with similar requests from other
mission fields under the U.P. Board of Foreign Missions,

making a total of 407 new evangelistic missionaries
needed. For this reason the effort to send this many
new workers to the four U.P. mission fields came to be
called the "407 Movement."

The General Assembly of the U.P. Church in 1903,
recognizing that these unusual requests were stimulated
by the Holy Spirit, encouraged the Church to rally to
this challenge. Many conventions on mission were held;
mission-minded leaders gave stirring messages; yet no
unusual response came from the Church for fifteen years.

In 1919 the "407 Movement" received new impetus.
World War I demonstrated to the United States that
isolation from the problems and responsibilities of the
world was no longer possible. This helped stimulate
new interest in work overseas. A "407 Prayer League"
was formed of more than 1500 people who pledged to pray
for the accomplishment of this task. Prayer Councils
were held in many places throughout the Church. Inspired
by the strong Student Volunteer Movement in the colleges
and universities, many young people offered themselves
for mission work. By 1926 a total of 170 new recruits
had been sent to the four U.P. mission fields. The
largest number of new missionaries (21) came to India in
1920. For the next six years the numbers of new recruits
remained high, reaching a total of 66 by 1926--21 men
and 45 unmarried women. This was just a little over
one-third of the number asked for. Since several deaths
and retirements had taken place in the meantime, the net
gain was not adequate to accomplish the high goal of
evangelizing the whole field. Nevertheless, it was an
encouraging step forward, and many of the outstanding
missionary leaders of recent years came through that
effort.

Unfortunately the "407 Movement" had to be abandoned
near the end of the 1920's due to the Great Depression
that necessitated a serious retrenchment in all Missions
in the 1930's.

FIGURE 20

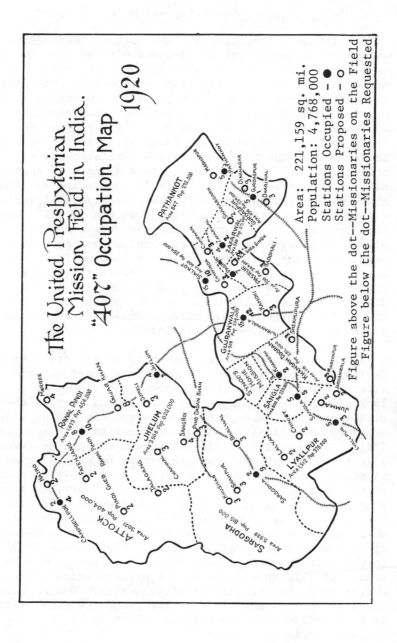

The United Presbyterian
Mission Field in India.
"40°" Occupation Map
1920

Area: 221,159 sq. mi.
Population: 4,768,000
Stations Occupied – ●
Stations Proposed – ○

Figure above the dot—Missionaries on the Field
Figure below the dot—Missionaries Requested

Equalitarianism

The vision of reaching all men with the message of
salvation and providing an adequate witness for each
segment of population was a worthy one. If the total
number of new recruits had been forthcoming, this plan
to scatter the missionaries equally in proportion to the
population might have been a wise one. However, it took
24 years to gain even one third of the hoped-for rein-
forcements. The Mission was faced with limited personnel
to accomplish the task. When such limitations are
present as they usually are, it is a mistake to apportion
missionaries solely on the basis of population or land
area, not taking into account the receptivity of various
segments of society to the message of the Gospel. There
is a legitimate place in mission work for continual
effort to evangelize even unresponsive people, with the
persistent hope that they will turn to find life in
Christ. On the other hand, it is unwise not to observe
priorities in the use of <u>limited</u> resources. As Dr.
McGavran states in his book, *How Churches Grow;* "If the
Church is to grow we must direct maximum resources to
areas of maximum growth." (1955:174)

There were thousands of low-caste people pressing for
Christian teaching. These should have received priority
attention until all were discipled. Instead, due to
lack of teaching, some of the Chuhras and many of the
other potentially responsive depressed class groups never
embraced Christianity, but later chose to join some other
faith. The Mission in its well-meant concern to evangelize the whole area in one generation by providing equal
witness to each segment of society, left the responsive
areas short handed. Pasrur Presbytery, where the greatest
church growth was taking place, received only an average
of two evangelistic missionaries throughout this period,
while unresponsive Rawalpindi Presbytery had an average
of five evangelistic missionaries. (See Figure 12.)
Undoubtedly Rawalpindi covers a much larger geographical
area, but this should not be the primary criterion for
determining the location of missionaries. Had an adequate
force of workers been sent to the group movement centers,
it is possible that the U.P. Church today would be twice
the size it is at present.

11

Periods of Decline

The Graph of Growth of the U.P. Church from 1900 to 1930
(See Figure 12.) reveals within this era of rapid
expansion, two periods when church membership declined.
The first coincides with World War I (1914-1919); the
second occurs from 1924-1926. What were the reasons for
those two brief periods of decline?

World War I (1914-1919)

   No net growth in the U.P. Church took place from
1914 to 1919 the period coinciding with World War I,
yet adult baptisms numbered nearly 1000 a year. Various
depressed classes continued to be responsive as is seen
in the following report:

> Another caste, the Batwal, is showing
> unusual interest in the Gospel and
> constitutes still another great challenge.
> ... (The Triennial Report 1916-1918:147)

   There are several reasons for the fluctuation in the
number of communicant members during these years in
spite of continued baptisms.

Migration

   A new tract of land was opened for settlement in
Montgomery District (now known as Sahiwal) in 1915,
attracting new migrations of Chuhras. Many of the most

ambitious and capable Christians emigrated from
Gurdaspur, Sialkot and Gujranwala districts, weakening
those congregations. The Associate Reformed Presbyterian
Mission working in Montgomery faithfully sought out and
pastored these new immigrants, so they were not lost from
the fold.

Many Christians found their way to the limits of the
Frontier Provinces. Alexander McLeish writing of the
Muslim frontier in his book, *The Frontier People of
India*, said:

> ... the sweeper Christians ... are by far
> the largest section in the Christian
> communities of the Frontier ... These
> mass-movement Christians have immigrated
> from the Punjab in large numbers in
> search of work. (1931:33)

In this way many who were converted as United
Presbyterians moved to other parts of the country and
have become the backbone of the local churches of every
denomination. These migrations proved to be by far the
greatest reason for the sudden leveling off of the
accelerated growth up to 1914.

During the years of World War I thousands of Chuhra
Christians joined the army. At first they hesitated
to enter this open door, but once a start was made,
enlisting became popular, and almost 6,000 were under
arms, besides the many who enlisted as transport drivers,
hospital assistants, laborers and clerks. The war was
another opportunity to take a step forward into new-
found freedom and social advancement. Previous to
World War I Chuhras had been barred from the army. Now
Christians of Chuhra background rose to second and third
place in proportional enlistment in districts like
Gujranwala, Sialkot, and Gurdaspur. A generation before
this would have been incredible and impossible.

Many whole families moved to military centers to obtain
employment. A number of these never returned to their
homes but became permanent residents in their new location.
Thus colonies of Christians were scattered across the land.

After the war many men returned from military service
with a new sense of self-respect, became leaders in the
life of the Church, and sparked church growth. They had
seen the world, returned as heroes, and their word
carried weight.

Competition

The Seventh Day Adventists started missionary work in
the district of Khangah Dogran in 1916, drawing away
U.P. church members. *The Triennial Report for 1916,
1917, 1918* reports encroachments from other groups as
well. Sangla Hill serves as an example:

> In the absence of a regular staff of
> missionaries for the district since
> 1916, proselyting sects such as the
> Salvation Army, the Roman Catholics,
> Peter's Men, the Seven Brothers,
> Jesus' Army, the Brethren, and the
> Seventh Day Adventists have done real
> harm to the work. (166)

Had each of these Missions chosen an unreached responsive
caste such as the Doms or Chamars, concentrating evangelistic efforts upon them instead of competing for the
Chuhras, a movement could have been fostered in many of
the depressed classes. What a pity that energy was spent
in squabbling over the few "found" sheep instead of
seeking the many more that were still lost!

Not only were Christian groups competing for the
Chuhras, revived non-Christian religions too began to
vie for their allegiance. The British sought to give a
measure of self-government to the Indian people by
creating a Legislative Assembly on a communal basis.
Each religious community was assigned a number of seats
in the Assembly in proportion to the number of their
adherents. Numbers became an important factor in
political power. This led to the unexpected result of a
revival of Hinduism and Islam. A strong sense of
competition developed between the various faiths for the
allegiance of the depressed classes. As early as 1912

these religions renewed their efforts to win the Chuhras
and incorporate them into their respective communities.
In some districts the Arya Samaj claimed to have won
several thousand Chuhras back from Christianity. The
Chuhras were faced with more options than ever before,
giving them a greater sense of importance and lessening
their responsiveness to Christ.

Consolidation

   During this period emphasis was placed on nurturing
and establishing the Church rather than on winning the
lost. This was not an intentional change of policy in
the Mission, but the result of having limited personnel
to do a limitless job. *The Triennial Reports for 1919,
1920, 1921 and for 1916, 1917, 1918* have this recurring
theme:

> (Gujranwala) Most of our work has been
> done among the Christians and inquirers ...
> there has been little time for direct
> effort among the non-Christians. (1921:133)

> (Sialkot) Owing to the pressure of work
> among the more than 4000 village Christ-
> ians, we are able to give but scant
> attention to the non-Christians. (1918:176)

> (Zafarwal) Our time ... as in previous
> years has been given chiefly to the
> Christian community. (1918:182)

   Building up the Christian Church, an essential aspect
of mission work, took most of the time and energy of
the evangelistic missionaries. Inevitably non-Christian
work was neglected--an unfortunate trend, for there were
still many responsive Chuhras ready to align themselves
with one of the major religions of India. The same
Triennial Reports cited above mention this:

> (Khangah Dogran) ...[The caste] in which
> our work has met with most response is
> the sweeper caste. There are 15,000

> of these in the Khangah Dogran Tehsil
> who are still sweepers, while 5,000
> have become Sikhs, 2,000 Mohammadans
> and 4,000 Christians. (1918:139)

> (Lyallpur) There are 55,000 low caste
> people, of whom 34,000 have not embraced
> any of the great religions; 14,000 have
> become Christians, 6,000 have become
> Mohammadans and 1000 Sikhs. Thus about
> 25 per cent of these have been won for
> Christ. (1921:157)

These figures prove that the work of witnessing and
ingathering was far from complete.

Influenza

The influenza epidemic of 1918 took a heavy toll on
the Church of the Punjab. *The 1919 Handbook on Foreign
Missions* reports:

> The influenza made sad inroads on the
> membership of the Church this past year.
> As many as ten per cent of the members
> in some districts were taken. More than
> 500 died in the Gujranwala district,
> leaving many orphans. (62)

A total of 3,452 were removed by death from the rolls in
1918 alone.

Although the Church was depleted in numbers, it was
deepened in faith by these experiences, as is evident
in the *Triennial Report:*

> The influenza epidemic paralyzed everything.
> God substituted some special lessons in
> mortality, eternal life, and the comforting
> Jesus ... Among both Christians and non-
> Christians the hearts of many who seemed
> to have been indifferent to everything but
> mere earthly pleasures and duties, have

been softened and many have been led to
think more seriously of life and death.
Church services and special meetings were
well attended. (1918:152, 149)

Nationalism

   In 1919 wide-spread riots broke out over India fanned
by anti-British feeling. The Punjab had provided nearly
half a million recruits for World War I, had suffered
heavily from influenza, and was now torn with discontent
that centered on British rule. On April 10th at
Amritsar an unruly mob protesting the arrest of two
local leaders began to loot, burn, and disrupt communi-
cations. Order was restored with difficulty by
Brigadier-General Dyer and his troops. April 13th,
the day of the *Baisakhi* festival, Dyer determined to
teach the rebels a lesson. His troops marched into an
unarmed holiday gathering in the walled compound of the
Jallianwala Bagh and fired 1,650 rounds in ten minutes
into the trapped crowd. Nearly 400 persons were killed
and 1200 injured. For months after this the British
heaped indignities and harsh penalties on Indians,
particularly the educated, politically conscious classes.
This triggered more mob violence until Martial Law was
declared to put down the revolt.

   These tensions put a damper on the work in 1919, but
nevertheless the stage was being set for an encouraging
beginning to the next period. The war with its unsettled
conditions caused people to seek for stability. Riots
and unrest shattered their complacency and made them open
to the Gospel. From 1920 to 1922 over 6,000 communicant
members were added to the U.P. Church.

The Decline of 1924-1926

   From 1924 to 1926 U.P. church membership declined
sharply. Few adult baptisms were performed. (See
Figure 12). Over 9,000 people were removed from the rolls
in 1923 alone, either by transfer or by suspension. This
purging of the rolls took place because Synod raised the
standards for membership. Many rural Christians no

longer met the stricter requirements, so were dropped
from the roll. Pruning "dead wood" from church rolls
is a necessary procedure from time to time, but raising
the requirements for baptism is of questionable value
if it excludes any true believer. Miss E.D. Anderson
tells of an old woman who asked to be baptized. The
missionary answered:

> No, Mother, you do not know enough yet;
> you must wait until I come next year
> before you are baptized. She went back
> to her seat on the floor ... lifted up
> her voice and wept, saying, "I am too
> old to learn, but I know Jesus Christ
> died for me and I love Him." The mission-
> ary called her back and baptized her with
> the rest of the inquirers. (1942:278)

There was an unusually large number of deaths from
bubonic plague in 1924. From Baddomali one missionary
wrote:

> Plague has been an affliction more than
> once, but the summer of 1924 will long
> be remembered as the most terrible of
> its visitations here, thus far. The
> total Christian community numbers about
> 7,000. About one-tenth died last summer
> within three months. *(The Triennial
> Report for 1922, 1923, 1924:134)*

In all U.P. mission districts a total of approximately
5,000 people were removed from the rolls by death from
1924 to 1926.

Pentecostal Controversy

In 1924 just when the Mission had the strongest force
of missionaries in its history, and a bright prospect
for evangelistic work, a controversy arose over the
baptism of the Holy Spirit and speaking in other tongues.
A group of about twenty of the U.P. missionaries were
blessed with a Pentecostal experience and convinced

that speaking in tongues was the sign of the baptism of
the Holy Spirit. They began promulgating this doctrine.
The Mission took action to curtail their influence, as
is reported in the *Annual Meeting Minutes* for 1925:

> Your committee appointed by the Executive
> Committee respectfully report that it has
> held a number of conferences with those in
> the "Pentecostal" group, and after much
> prayer and consideration recommends that
> the Mission express its disapproval of
> the peculiar tenets and practices of
> "Pentecostalism" as held and practiced
> by the "Pentecostal" group in our Mission,
> and that all members of the Mission be
> asked to refrain from teaching and propa-
> gating these tenets and practices. (336)

This created a furor in the Mission. Some of the
"Pentecostal" group felt their conscience would not allow
them to refrain from teaching what they believed to be
biblical truth. A few were tactless and outspoken,
antagonizing mission members unnecessarily. On the
other hand, many missionaries who had not had the
Pentecostal experience felt sympathetic to those under
censure and objected to restrictions being place upon
them. The Mission was torn by dissension, with inevitable
repercussions felt throughout the national Church.

In 1926 severe action was taken requesting the Board
of Foreign Missions to recall one couple who were leaders
in the movement. This led to the resignation of four
couples and three single ladies who felt they could no
longer work whole-heartedly with the U.P. Mission. This
unfortunate split, with its undercurrent of bitter
feelings, took a tragic toll on the morale and spiritual
power of the Mission.

Summary of 1900-1930

The period from 1900 to 1930 was a time of unprece-
dented growth in every basic phase of church life. The
chart that follows shows the figures for the beginning

and end of this era with the percentage of increase in
each category. It speaks for a vigorous and dramatic
growth of the Church.

Number of:	1900	1930	Per Cent of Increase
1. Missionaries	59	137	132%
2. Ordained Indian Pastors	12	100	733%
3. Evangelistic Workers	139	279	100%
4. Ordained Elders	58	398	586%
5. Organized Congregations	20	111	455%
6. Self-Supporting Congregations	1	72	
7. Communicant Members	6,987	45,002	543%
8. Christian Community	10,361	96,203	828%
9. Evangelistic Fund of Indian Church	Rs. 3,681	Rs.17,770	382%

It is thrilling to see the growth of those first
thirty years of the 20th century. The U.P. Christian
community grew by more than 85,000, while communicant
members increased by 38,000. A total of 78 more missionaries and 228 additional Indian pastors and evangelists
worked to shepherd the flock. Ordained elders, the
mainstay of local congregations, increased by 340. There
were 91 newly organized congregations; 72 that were self-
supporting. The Church was bearing more and more of the
financial load in evangelism. One cannot help but praise
God for a record such as that--the outcome of the
dedicated labors of many faithful servants of God, both
Indian and foreign.

12
Internal Growth (1930-1973)

From 1930 to 1973 the U.P. Church made no significant
progress numerically. The period is made up of two
plateaus in growth with small temporary fluctuations.
The first plateau is from 1930 to 1947 when the communicant membership of the Church only grew from approximately
45,000 to 46,500 in 17 years! Then for three years a
spurt in growth occurred, with over 6,000 added to the
role. Since 1949 the Church has made numerical progress
merely by biological growth, gradually increasing from
53,000 to a peak of 55,835 in 1965. Due to a schism in
the Church in 1968, the membership decreased, reaching
a total of 53,240 in 1971. (See Figure 21.)

Although the Church did not grow in numbers much during
this period, she took two steps toward maturity by
becoming self-supporting and self-governing, independent
from the U.P. Church in the U.S.A. It is important to
study the effect these two steps have had on church life
and growth. Also it is imperative to analyze the reasons
why the U.P. Church is not self-propagating at present,
and look for a solution that in the providence of God
may change the present static Church into a vital growing one.

The First Plateau (1930-1947)

In 1930 the Church began with 45,002 communicant
members and by 1947 it had 46,491--an increase of only
1,489 or 3.3 per cent over a period of seventeen years.
Twice there were drastic decreases of over 2,000 members,
followed by the recovery of them soon afterward.   The

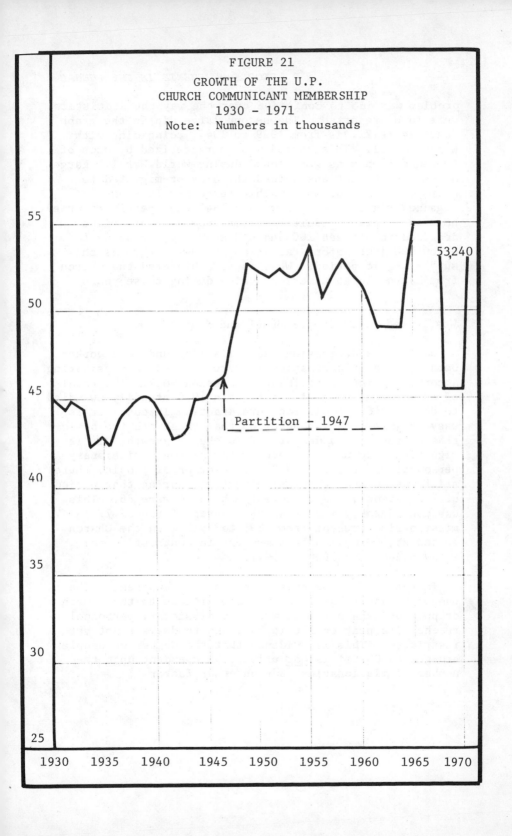

FIGURE 21

GROWTH OF THE U.P.
CHURCH COMMUNICANT MEMBERSHIP
1930 - 1971
Note: Numbers in thousands

Partition - 1947

53,240

problem was due to confusion over the way the statistics
were to be reported. The second large dip in the graph
(See Figure 21.)is from 1939 to 1944, coinciding with
World War II. This period was characterized by much of
the same trends as were found during World War I. Large
numbers of Christians joined the army or migrated to
camps in search of work. This temporary loss was
regained right after the war in 1945 when people returned
home once again. Adult baptisms from non-Christians
declined to between 200 and 400 annually, dropping to
below 100 just before Partition in 1947. Why was this
such a static period? What factors hindered the Church
from making large numerical gains during these years?

Was it reduction in personnel and funds?

During the depression years mission funds and workers,
both missionary and national, were reduced, necessitating
a corresponding curtailment of mission work. The total
of 137 U.P. missionaries active in 1930 steadily dwindled
to 86 by 1946. Funds too were drastically cut. It is
easy to jump to the conclusion that these are the basic
reasons for the sudden arrest in church growth. It is
significant to note, however, that although missionary
personnel was reduced by 37 per cent or 51 people, there
still was an average missionary force during that period
of 112 persons, and at lowest ebb there were 86. This
was considerably more than the average force of 77
missionaries present from 1895 to 1915 when the Church
gained 25,000 communicant members in contrast to the
1,489 added from 1930 to 1947.

In the 1920's the same phenomenon is apparent. The
number of adult baptisms and acquisitions to the Church
dropped off sharply just when the missionary personnel
reached its peak of 176 in 1925 and funds were not yet
restricted. This is evidence that the number of people
brought to Christ is not primarily dependent upon the
number of missionaries, but on other factors.

Was it lack of concern for evangelism?

In 1931 Bishop J.W. Pickett with a team of workers
sponsored by the National Christian Council of India
came to Pasrur to study the movement among the Chuhras.
The study was published in 1933 in a book called *Christian
Mass Movements in India*, a most significant analysis of
people movements in the subcontinent. Bishop Pickett's
report created in the U.P. Mission a sense of expectancy
of a large harvest from the depressed classes not yet won,
just as there had been from the Chuhras. In 1936 the
Mission urged all workers to give priority to evangelistic work among these castes. In 1937 each district
missionary was asked to make a detailed survey of the
Scheduled Castes in his own district, noting the number,
location, and responsiveness of the various castes other
than the Chuhras. Synod set aside one of its most able
pastors to concentrate on evangelizing these depressed
people.

In 1941 the Mission's Future Policy Committee
recommended that intensive work be done among the Chamars.
A committee was formed to study the situation and plan
a strategy for winning them. Funds were appropriated
for this work. In spite of these efforts, conversions
from other castes were not encouraging. Instead of the
thousands who had been coming to Christ in the previous
era, an average of less than 100 a year were added in
these 17 years. Lack of growth was not due to lack of
concern. What then was the primary reason for these
meager results?

Were the Chuhras less responsive?

The *Census Report* for 1931 gives the numbers of
Chuhras that were left in various districts along with the
religious community they claimed as theirs. It is
interesting to note that the number of people who
claimed to be Chuhra Christians were far fewer than the
actual number of Christians. This reveals that the

the baptized Christians no longer considered themselves
Chuhras, but felt they had risen above that category.
Those calling themselves Chuhra Christians were probably
not as yet even loosely affiliated with any Church.

Some registered as *"Ad Dharmi"* in order to claim
their old Chuhra faith as distinct from being Hindu.
Their purpose was not religious but political, as this
was an attempt by the Scheduled Castes to obtain an
electorate of their own apart from the Hindus. For this
reason the *Ad Dharmi* are included with the Hindu figures
below in the understanding that they were not actually
Hindus but retained their old status as a depressed
class. All figures in the table below have been rounded
off to give a general picture of the situation.

THE CENSUS REPORT ON CHUHRAS, 1931: 286,287
(U.P. MISSION AREA)

District	Hindu	Sikh	Muslim	Christian
Sialkot	300	---	30	1,100
Gujranwala	1,300	8	30	345
Jhelum	450	20	---	200
Rawalpindi	2,700	70	280	---
Gurdaspur	8,000	1,100	100	1,100
Sheikhupura	10,000	500	600	70
Lyallpur	21,000	6,000	500	5,000

(OTHER MISSION AREAS)

Lahore	43,000	12,300	11,800	10,000
Amritsar	25,300	5,000	10	1,400
Montgomery	12,500	550	14	1,000
Multan	2,800	250	550	1,200

The center of the Chuhra group movement, Sialkot
(including Pasrur and Zafarwal) and Gujranwala, had
scarcely any Chuhras left. Jhelum never did have
significant numbers. Rawalpindi was gaining a few by
migration, but less than 3000 scattered over the large
Rawalpindi district did not actually constitute much
of an evangelistic challenge. Therefore, little growth
could be expected in these centers from the Chuhra caste
channel other than biological growth.

Three U.P. areas still had a large number of unaligned
Chuhras--Lyallpur with 21,000; Sheikhupura with 10,000;
and Gurdaspur with 8,000. By far the largest group
claiming to be *Ad Dharmi*,10,000 in all, were in Lyallpur.
Montgomery had 4,5000 and Sheikhupura had 3,000. This
indicates that the Chuhras in those centers were politically minded and had placed their hopes for social
advancement upon getting more representation in the
National Assembly. This made them far less responsive
to the Gospel than they had been previously.

In other Mission areas, however, there were still
many Chuhras to be won. Lahore, Amritsar and Montgomery
had specially large Chuhra communities. It may be that
these too were placing more confidence in politics than
in religion to help them escape from their depressed
condition.

Were other Scheduled Castes responsive?

Through the years small groups from among the Megs,
Doms, Chamars, Sansis and other Scheduled Castes had
been baptized, an indication that they were potentially
winnable. Yet, although they were restless and searching,
they seemed less ready to come to Christ as a community.
Even when special efforts were directed toward them,
they failed to respond in significant numbers. Why?
There are two basic reasons for this:

1) Each caste, even among the depressed classes, is
strongly cohesive, with a clear understanding of its
position in the caste structure. To eat or associate
closely with members of another and especially of a

"lower" caste is anathema. The Christian Church was made
up almost entirely of Chuhras, one of the lowest groups
on the caste scale. Other groups were expected auto-
matically to integrate into this Church. Most were
unwilling to hurdle this barrier.

Had the Mission realized all the implications of this,
they could have overcome the difficulty by taking the
following steps: a) Set aside workers to evangelize
one caste exclusively having as little contact as possible
with any other caste; and b) Organize believers from
that caste into separate worshipping groups, not trying
to integrate them into the existing (Chuhra) Church.
This appears to be a denial of the brotherhood stressed
by Christ, yet it is necessary at least as a temporary
phase in mission work for the purpose of more effective
evangelism. As God's Spirit works and the Word of God
takes root in a young Church, these caste barriers
gradually break down. This cannot be forced.

2) The second reason for lack of response among these
other castes was the effect of "Home Rule" upon them.
The "Home Rule" nationalistic movement under Gandhi was
pressing for political independence during this period
(1930-1947). The Hindus became concerned about losing
the depressed classes, thus diminishing Hindu numerical
majority in the National Assembly. For this reason they
sought to "save the depressed classes for Hinduism" by
developing programs to uplift the poor, and by making
concessions and promises to them. As a result the
Scheduled Castes were hesitant to align themselves with
any non-Hindu religion, especially with Christians who
would have no political power after independence. They
were tempted to wait and see which religion could offer
them the most in the realm of social status, political
advantages and economic gain, or to form their own
separate electorate to fight for their rights.

A highly educated member of the depressed classes,
Dr. Ambedkar, became the outstanding spokesman for them.
He denounced Hinduism and vowed to lead his people into
some other faith. This caused great political and communal
concern. Gandhi started a fast to the death to prevent
the depressed classes from forming a separate electorate

from the Hindus. After Gandhi had fasted for three weeks
and thousands of telegrams were pouring in, Ambedkar
finally yielded and accepted promises from Gandhi on
behalf of the low caste peoples.

These factors undoubtedly played a significant part
in keeping other low castes from responding during the
1930's and 1940's as they anticipated the great day of
independence that seemed to be just on the horizon. Their
consuming desire was for freedom from oppression and a
rise in social status. At first they looked for it in
religion; now they believed it would come through political
"seats" in the Assembly. They were sure this would solve
all their problems.

Responsive people do not remain responsive indefinitely.
Fruit unpicked when it is ripe falls off and is lost. The
great opportunity to win many more thousands to Christ had
slipped through the fingers of the Christian Church. "The
harvest is past and we are not saved." (Jer. 8:20)

Partition (1947-1949)

In August 1947 Great Britain granted independence
to her territories in India, terminating the colonial
era. This was the culmination of years of agitation for
"Home Rule" championed by Gandhi. Prior to independence,
the Muslim minority in India, led by Mr. Mohammad Ali
Jinnah, demanded a separate state for Muslims. Districts
having a Muslim majority population were designated as
Pakistan with the exception of the eastern portion of
Kashmir which remained part of India in spite of its
strong Muslim majority. This has been a source of
contention between the two countries ever since.

The areas given to Pakistan consisted of two widely
separated portions--West Pakistan, between Afghanistan
and Iran on the west and India on the east; and East
Pakistan, located on the eastern side of India just north
of the Bay of Bengal. (See Figure 1.) The two portions
of Pakistan were separated geographically by 1100 miles
of Indian territory; and culturally by differences in
ethnic background, language, and life style. Adherence

to the Muslim faith was their chief bond of unity. The
Province of the Punjab, where U.P. Mission work is
centered, was also partitioned into two parts--the
eastern portion located in India, the western in Pakistan.

Communal Riots

   Prior to Independence Day, Muslims living in India,
and Hindus or Sikhs living in the areas to become Pakistan
had vague fears as to their status under the changed
conditions. Loathe to leave their ancestral homes or
thriving businesses, many suppressed these fears, convinced that the differing religious communities would
continue to live side by side in relative harmony as
they had for centuries. When Partition became a fact,
however, on August 14, 1947, they soon discovered how
tragically wrong this assumption had been.

   In areas such as east Punjab, where the population
was nearly evenly divided between Muslims on the one
hand, and Hindus and Sikhs on the other, one group would
plan to kill or frighten out as many of the other as
possible to insure their own majority and to secure that
district for their country. Murder and pillage began
on a massive scale. As word spread of killings on both
sides of the border, panic stricken families left everything to flee to their respective countries. An
estimated twelve million people migrated within a few
weeks. Nearly one million were massacred on the way.

   Christians, being neutral in the struggle and not
the target of persecution, did not migrate in great
numbers, but were used of God to minister to the
wounded, sick and needy of all religious communities
often at risk to their lives. They marked their homes
with crosses and identified themselves by sewing a
cross on their clothing, testifying later as to how
the cross had saved them from physical death--an
illustration of the power of Christ's cross to save
from eternal death as well.

Changes Caused by Partition

After peace was restored, the Church in West Pakistan
found itself in quite a new atmosphere. The Christians
were now the largest minority group but represented only
1.4 per cent of the population, surrounded by a resistant
Muslim majority of 97.2 per cent. This brought several
significant changes in the life of the Church.

The newly formed government of Pakistan was faced
with the monumental task of resettling thousands of
Muslim refugees who had left land and homes in India to
flee to Pakistan. They helped solve the difficulty by
dividing up large tracts of land abandoned by Hindu and
Sikh landlords and parcelling them out in small lots to
these Muslim refugees. Many rural Christians who had
worked for Hindu and Sikh landlords lost their means of
support, for their services were no longer required on
the smaller plots of land. This created a serious
economic hardship for rural Christians and weakened
village congregations.

The more ambitious Christians began to move to the
cities in search of employment. This trend continues to
the present day. Being unskilled farm laborers, they
are ill-equipped to make a living in the city. They tend
to cluster together with friends and relatives in crowded
unsanitary ghettos where the sweeper Christians live.
Some find jobs in mills and factories, but their lack of
specific technical skills, coupled with the natural
discrimination faced by all minority groups, makes it
difficult for most to make a satisfactory living. Some
become sweepers; others work as day laborers whenever
they can get employment. The ghetto atmosphere in
which they live encourages drinking, gambling, drug
addiction and loose morality.

The area of the Punjab that became part of Pakistan
always had a Muslim majority. Prior to Partition,
however, British influence and the presence of large
Hindu and Sikh minorities encouraged an atmosphere of
religious tolerance. Although few high caste Hindus
accepted the Gospel, they usually listened to it with
respect and interest and the minority groups bolstered

one another's morale. After 1947 the Christians were
virtually the only minority left in the Punjab. Nearly
an equal number of Scheduled Caste Hindus were left, but
mostly in Sindh.

Pakistan is officially a Muslim state, yet its
constitution guarantees freedom to the minorities, not
only to worship and practice their own faith, but to
propagate it as well. No official restrictions have been
placed upon methods of evangelism. Muslims, however,
have always been resistant to Christianity. Christians
in order to win them must not only overcome theological
objections but hurdle formidable social and cultural
barriers, handicapped by the natural feeling of inferiority
experienced by all minorities. This inability to have an
effective outreach to the majority community has deeply
affected the life of the Church.

A Surge of Growth

From 1947 to 1949 the U.P. Church made a net gain of
6,200 members. Most of these were by certificate of
transfer, for during communal riots at Partition, all
who could prove their status as Christians were safe.
Relief supplies were also distributed according to the
number of members in a congregation. Nominal and loosely
affiliated Christians made sure their names were on the
roll and began taking a more active part in church
activities. Adult baptisms, however, numbered 1,491, the
largest recorded since 1921. More than half of these
took place in Lyallpur district. A number of low caste
people, probably Balmikis or Mazhabi Sikhs, who had been
undecided about their allegiance, felt it best to align
themselves with the Christians and take no chance of
being classified as Hindus. The crisis situation was
used by God to encourage hesitant inquirers to take
their first step of faith. These required much follow-
up teaching.

Immediately preceding and shortly following Partition
at least a dozen new Missions began work in Pakistan
increasing the missionary force by about 100 persons.
Many of these new groups were allotted areas of the
country that lay within the comity boundaries of older

denominations but had been neglected due to limited
personnel. The northern sections of the U.P. Mission
area, including Abbottabad and Campbellpur were turned
over to The Evangelical Alliance Mission in 1949. With
this new influx of missionary personnel and a deeper
spirit of inquiry evident among the people, the stage
was set for a period of great church growth. Sad to
say, it has been followed by the longest plateau in
growth since the beginning of U.P. mission work in 1855.

The Second Plateau (1950-1973)

From 1950 to 1973 the U.P. Church made a net gain of
240 communicant members! (See Figure 21.) This actually
respresents a serious decline in growth, because it is
far less increase than even mere biological growth should
yield. The decline is due primarily to factional strife
leading to a major schism in 1968. The strife is rooted
in two significant developments in the life of the Church--
self-government and indigenous management of Christian
institutions. These should have led to great maturity
and stability in the Church, but instead have proved
detrimental in many ways. The following chapter will
attempt to analyze the reasons why they have produced
such negative results.

Village Congregation with Newly Built Place of Worship

13
Pakistani Leadership

In the early days of the Church although all national
ordained pastors and an elder from each congregation were
voting members of the Synod of the Punjab; practically
speaking, the ordained missionary men governed the Church.
Even as late as the 1920's the pastors, evangelistic
workers and elders from each mission district tended to
vote like the missionary in charge of that area. Dr.
R.A. Foster described a Synod meeting of that era as
follows:

> The debate was heated. Dr. McConnelee from
> Gujranwala vigorously supported the issue.
> The workers from his district nodded their
> heads in agreement. The Rev. Crowe of
> Sialkot just as vehemently opposed it. His
> workers shook their heads too. I was sitting
> at the back of the hall counting the nods
> versus the shakes as each man spoke. I
> slipped in beside Dr. Connelee and whispered,
> "You're going to lose by three votes."
> Sure enough, when the votes were counted,
> he was three short. (Interview)

This situation gradually changed as more capable
leaders were developed. The Theological Seminary in
Gujranwala had a national principal, the Rev. Wazir Chand,
in the 1940's. The second Pakistani principal was the
Rev. K.L. Nasir who held this position from 1958 until
he led his party to join with Carl McIntire in 1968.
In 1954 the Theological Seminary became interdenominational, with the Methodists, Anglicans, Lahore
Church, and the Associate Reformed Presbyterians

cooperating in sending students and providing staff as
well as taking part in the managing Board. The standards
for admittance into Seminary were raised in the 1950's
requiring candidates for the ministry to be 10th class
graduates with a Matriculation certificate. An increasing number of college graduates have been taking
advantage of the advanced level program offered by the
Seminary that leads to the Bachelor of Divinity degree.
These leaders are capable of managing church affairs
and seldom look to missionaries for guidance any more.

Christian schools and hospitals had also been administered by missionaries until this period. One by one
as Pakistani leaders were trained they took over the
administration of these institutions, so that today no
missionary is the chief administrator of any institution
in the U.P. Church area. This was an important step
forward but had unfortunate results as well, as we shall
see.

Self-Government in the Church

The era of missionary domination of Synod passed as
the Church became self-supporting, the pastorate more
highly educated, and elders better trained in their
rights and responsibilities. Before 1930 the Church
had made great strides organizationally. Local congregations had their official sessions with trained elders.
There were six Presbyteries making up the Synod of the
Punjab that was responsible to the General Assembly of
the U.P. Church of North America. National leaders
demonstrated increasing ability to manage ecclesiastical
affairs, though occasionally a knotty problem was
referred to the General Assembly in the U.S.A. for a
solution.

As the spirit of nationalism grew in Pakistan, this
structural tie with a foreign organization became
increasingly embarrassing to the Church. In 1960 the
Synod requested total independence from the U.S.A. Church.
The General Assembly granted their request. It took
effect at an impressive ceremony on April 11th, 1961 in
Gujranwala.

Since achieving independence from the U.S.A. Church,
the U.P. Church of Pakistan has been plagued with
increasing internal strife. Christians are such a small
minority in the country that they have practically no
opportunity for leadership in politics or inter-community
affairs. Therefore, positions of leadership and
authority in the Church are greatly coveted. This is
seen on all levels of church life. The election of
elders in a city congregation sparks a political campaign
throughout the Christian community with each candidate
emphasizing his superior qualifications for the position.
These do not always coincide with Paul's description
of a good elder as found in I Timothy 3! The annual
struggle for the position of Moderator of Presbytery or
of Synod causes deep rifts in relationships that destroy
the loving fellowship so essential in a Church. Bribery
has been used to gain votes; Synod often has to decide
which of many contenders are the legal delegates from a
local congregation; and most unfortunate of all, a number
of decisions made in church courts have been contested
in the civil courts—an ugly demonstration of Christian
enmity and strife before non-Christians.

Factionalism, an integral part of the caste system,
permeates society on the Indian subcontinent. That
it is found in the Church does not so much reveal sub-
Christian behavior as it represents a true picture of
the way their culture operates. There seems to be a
deep psychological need among the people of Pakistan to
join a "party" to provide moral support to individuals.
As long as the Mission was in control of the Church,
they were able to maintain a superficial unity. When
self-government was achieved, indigenous cultural factors
exerted their influence, and party factions became
dominant in the life of the Church.

Not only is this tendency to factionalism found in
church life, it is apparent in the country as a whole.
The Western concept of individualism is unpopular.
Decisions are made by family and clan groups, or by
"parties." Individuals are expected to follow along
regardless of personal convictions. To object results
in ostracism and social pressure difficult for the

Western mind to comprehend. A person who refuses to belong to any "party" is suspect by them all, not welcome anywhere.

The Presbyterian system of democratic church government allows full scope for the development of party spirit, for there is no autocratic control over it. Therefore, in recent years the U.P. Church of Pakistan has been sadly torn by dissension. Several presbyteries have divided into two separate church courts along party lines, each one claiming to be the legal body. Each party then proceeds to declare the members of the other party "disgowned" or "unfrocked," i.e. divested of their ordination. These pronouncements are ignored and all the "unfrocked" pastors and elders continue their ministries as before, with the result, however, that people have lost much of their respect for the ordained ministry.

Many have attempted to bring reconciliation and unity to the Church, with only partial success. Perhaps God will bring a wide-spread revival or use a time of severe persecution to accomplish this much needed task. Or perhaps the Church should accept factionalism as an ingrained characteristic of the local culture, and learn to use it constructively to bring about greater church growth.

Administration of Institutions

Since the 1930's, the U.P. Mission in Pakistan has trained national leaders with the goal of turning over to them the administration of Christian institutions as quickly as possible. After Partition the Mission centered her attention on the development of a satisfactory organizational scheme whereby the educational and medical institutions could be administered by nationals. This has involved a great deal of time, effort and patience.

In 1946 the Mission invited the Synod to appoint an Administrative Board to assume all responsibility, authority, and ownership of properties for mission institutions. The Board was to consist of nationals and missionaries appointed by and responsible to the Synod.

At first Synod accepted this offer and began to draft a constitution for the establishment of the Administrative Board. Due to the confusion of Partition, and the weakened psychological and financial position of the Church in the newly established nation of Pakistan, Synod voted in 1950 to postpone the inauguration of the Administrative Board indefinitely.

In 1961 the Administrative Council Scheme was substituted for the previous one and proved to be a mutually agreeable plan. Its purpose was to enable nationals to carry on all of the major work formerly administered by the Mission. It provided that educational and medical institutions be administered by boards composed of a certain proportion of representatives from the Mission and the Synod, as well as capable Pakistani laymen. The basic difference between the Administrative Board and the Administrative Council schemes was that the latter provided for educational and medical boards directly responsible to the Board of Foreign Missions in New York rather than responsible to Synod. In this way the large sums of money needed for institutional budgets were kept out of the hands of church officials. Inaugurated in 1961, the Administrative Council marked an important milestone toward complete Pakistani control.

In order to put the Administrative Council into operation, the Mission ceased to function as an administrative body except in matters affecting only missionaries--a tragic decision, showing a lack of understanding of the need for a separate mission body to carry on evangelistic work among non-Christians. This has hampered missionaries in developing creative plans to accomplish work not being done by Synod, especially in the field of outreach.

The policy of placing institutions under the direction of the Church, even indirectly, has borne bitter fruit. The most educated and able pastors became involved in an increasing number of committee meetings dealing with institutional, financial and property matters little related to their work in the Church. They had to be absent frequently from their congregations so that pastoral work suffered. Not only were they absent physically, but their thoughts and concerns became

centered on the administration of institutions and the
dispensing of large amounts of money. It was a great
source of irritation to men on self-support, getting
relatively low salaries, to see how much money went into
institutions and the salaries of their administrators.
They wanted to channel these funds into areas of more
direct benefit to the Church. The pastors asked to have
the Educational and Medical Boards under the direct
control of Synod. They argued that the primary purpose
of Christian institutions is to build up Christians and
be an arm of the Church for witness to the non-Christian
community around. They felt Synod control was essential
to guarantee the fulfillment of this spiritual purpose,
and to prevent the institutions from becoming secular
in emphasis.

Several church leaders requested the Board in New York
to institute a new General Council scheme enabling Synod,
directly or indirectly, to choose most of the members of
the Educational and Medical Boards, and make these Boards
answerable to Synod as well as to New York. In this way
the Church could exercise considerable influence upon
the budget and administration of these institutions.

The proposed General Council scheme created deep
apprehension in the national staff and administrators of
the institutions. They were well aware of the power
Synod could wield over their policies and activities
should such a plan come into effect. The security of
their position and employment was threatened. They would
be under constant pressure to comply to the desires of
Synod leaders regardless of whether the policies suggested
were educationally or medically sound. If they didn't,
they risked being replaced by those willing to toe the
party line no matter what their qualifications might be.

When the General Council scheme was presented to the
Board in New York (then called The Commission on Ecumenical
Mission and Relations) they ruled it contrary to their
policy. Unhappy experiences of similar schemes in other
countries, placing institutions directly under the control
of the Church, had stimulated them to formulate a policy
statement favoring autonomous boards for mission
institutions. However, they were anxious not be autocratic or overbearing in their attitude toward any

scheme originated by nationals. Rather than giving a
decisive negative answer, they couched their rejection
of the G.C. plan in such tactful language that their
reply was misinterpreted to mean that the G.C. scheme
would be acceptable with a few minor changes. Synod
leaders renewed their efforts to gain the upper hand over
the institutionalists.

To meet this threat to their security, the administrators and employees of the educational and medical institutions formed a party to combat Synod control. Those
pastors and elders who were disgruntled with the leadership in Synod that had dominated the affairs of the
Church for some years, joined the opposition party until
the adherents of both groups were nearly equal in number.
Each party threatened to oust the leaders of the other
group from their positions in the Church, the Seminary
or the institutions. Leaders of both factions knew their
financial security and social status depended heavily
upon the outcome of this struggle. On this foundation
of fear and insecurity the competition became intense
and bitter. Relationships grew so strained that finally
a rift developed and two separate Synods were formed,
each claiming to be the legal one. Constructive church
work was forgotten, and the stage was set for Carl
McIntire.

The McIntire Schism

In the spring of 1968, at the height of the party
strife within the U.P. Church of Pakistan, the leaders
of Synod realized that the Board in New York had no
intention of granting them administrative control of the
educational and medical institutions. Fearing reprisals
from the institutional party should they gain control,
the Synod Party began searching for a face-saving escape
from their predicament. Carl McIntire of the Bible
Presbyterian Church in the U.S.A., notorious for creating
schism throughout the world, provided them with just
such an escape. He offered them ample funds for pastors'
salaries and administrative expenses on condition they
join him in decrying liberalism in the U.P. Church, in

repudiating the Revised Standard Version of the Bible,
and in denouncing the World Council of Churches. The
Synod party of approximately 60 pastors began to receive regular stipends from McIntire, accused the
theologically evangelical U.P. missionaries of liberalism, and declared themselves the only true U.P. Church,
rightful heir to all the property. Nearly half of the
pastors of the U.P. Church took this step, not because
they believed in it, but because their "party" had done
so, and a guaranteed salary was tempting. They expected
a reconcilation on favorable terms within a few months
and looked upon the salary provided, not as a permanent
way of life, but as a little extra "gravy" for the moment.
These pastors were not able to carry all members of their
congregations with them. Many laymen, disgusted by the
seeming greed of the pastors for money, and their slander
of friends, refused to join them. About a third of the
laymen of the U.P. Church went into the McIntire movement.
Over the years a few dissident pastors of other denominations have joined the McIntire schism, but not in large
numbers.

Since such a large group of U.P. pastors left the
self-support system to join McIntire, it might seem that
the self-support system is primarily to blame for such
instability. A careful study of the "party" system,
however, indicates that factionalism is the chief culprit.
There is no discernible difference in the number of good
or poor pastors, lazy or diligent pastors, greedy or
self-sacrificing pastors in the U.P. Church and the
McIntire schism. Those characteristics are found equally
in both groups. The split had nothing to do with doctrine,
and little to do with guaranteed salaries. It was a
party struggle over leadership in the Church, particularly
over the control of funds for Christian institutions.
Other issues were raised simply as a smoke screen. Both
parties anticipated an early reconciliation, but the years
that followed have witnessed a widening of the breach,
until only a slight possibility remains that they will
ever reunite.

14

Self-Propagation

Self-support and self-government have become realities in
the U.P. Church, with both beneficial and harmful results.
In the realm of self-propagation, however, the Church
has made no progress in recent years. A variety of
reasons account for this. Non-Christian Chuhras proved
much less responsive after 1930, probably because they
began to pin their hopes on politics rather than religion
to solve their socio-economic problems. Also a new
strategy in mission began to evolve.

   At the start missionaries geared all their efforts
toward winning non-Christians. When a rapidly growing
Church emerged, follow-up teaching was urgently needed.
Gradually the time-consuming job of nurturing the Church
displaced all but token efforts at evangelizing non-
Christians. This gave rise to a new philosophy in
Missions--that the primary function of the missionary is
to strengthen and train national Christians so that they
can win the rest of their countrymen to Jesus Christ.
It was thought that their proficiency in the language,
greater understanding of local culture, and deeper insights into the religious beliefs around them would
enable them to be far more effective evangelists than
foreign missionaries could be. This has proved to be
a false assumption, not taking into consideration the
formidable barriers of social status and class prejudice
that Christians must hurdle in order to witness effectively to the majority community. Nevertheless, this
philosophy has deeply affected mission work in recent
years. Evangelistic personnel has steadily declined

and institutional work has received top priority as a
means of developing national leaders. Dr. Harris J.
Stewart wrote of this in 1954:

> As far as the foreign mission is concerned,
> we may say that there is no longer any
> plan or effort on the part of the church
> in America or of the mission on the field
> to occupy our unevangelized territory.
> Mission personnel have been absorbed
> more and more into institutional work, to
> the neglect of district and other evange-
> listic work. (Annual Meeting Minutes
> 1954:47)

The few evangelistic missionaries not involved in
institutions have been preoccupied with building up the
Church. Bible teaching, training of elders, adult
literacy, stewardship instruction, and youth work have
been major concerns allowing little time for evangelizing
non-Christians. This situation is not unique to the
U.P.'s but is sadly typical of most Missions in the
entire Indian sub-continent. Eugene Hillman in his book,
The Church as Mission, refers to this common problem as
follows:

> The successful evangelization of large numbers
> of people in one or another region, especially
> when this achievement is coupled with a
> chronic shortage of personnel, is apt to
> result in the total stagnation of mission-
> ary expansion among the remaining non-
> evangelized people. So many missionaries
> are taken up with the pastoral care of the
> converted that further expansion is "choked."
> ... Among missionaries in India, this has
> come to be known as the "Choke Law." (1965:29)

"Evangelism" now refers primarily to bringing nominal
Christians into a vital relationship with Christ.

Evangelism Among Nominal Christians

In recent years both missionaries and national church
leaders have placed major emphasis upon building up and
reviving the Church. This has been done in a variety
of ways:

Urban Evangelism

Since Partition many rural Christians, unable to earn
a living in the villages, have migrated to the cities.
Colonies of Punjabi Christians are now found in every
major city in Pakistan, with large groups living in
Karachi and Lahore. The U.P. Mission was alert to the
urgent need for following up these migrating people. In
1961 the Evangelistic Committee of the Mission drew up
the following recommendation:

> Keeping in mind the movement of Christ-
> ians from rural areas to the cities, and
> the necessary restrictions imposed upon
> us by limitations of personnel and budget,
> we hereafter concentrate evangelistic
> efforts upon the following centers:
> Taxila-Wah, Rawalpindi; Jhelum, Gujranwala,
> Sialkot, Sargodha, and Lyallpur. (Annual
> Meeting Minutes 1961a:52)

The above quotation reveals that "evangelistic efforts"
implied reaching nominal Christians. It is a pity that
it had become so limited in connotation, for in addition
to the hundreds of Christians migrating to the cities
from rural areas, there were thousands of non-Christians
doing the same. Surveys around the world have shown
that a non-Christian uprooted from his traditional society
is unusually responsive to the Gospel for a limited
period, differing according to the situation. When he
has established himself into a new urban pattern, he is
not nearly so open to change. Had the U.P. Mission, in
carrying out the above resolve to "evangelize" the
cities, concentrated on these new comers from rural
areas; provided services to aid them in finding employment; helped them with literacy; and given them

Christian teaching, this evangelistic effort might have borne much fruit among non-Christians. No such programs were worked out, for evangelistic vision was limited just to providing worship for Christians.

In the late 1960's a program of "industrial evangelism" was started in Karachi on an interdenominational basis by a U.P. missionary. This program helps Christians find employment, learn technical skills needed in factories, and receive legal advice in labor-management struggles. It is a much needed effort in social work but not truly evangelistic in purpose.

Women's Work

Bible women have been used in evangelistic work since early days. Single lady missionaries chose and trained promising widows for this work. Even though they had little education or training they proved helpful in teaching the women and children.

In 1939 Miss Marian Peterson with her national assistant, Mrs. Samuel, started a U.P. training school for Bible women in Rawalpindi. The first class had five students, two of whom were converts. In 1947 the school moved to permanent quarters in Gujranwala and became a union institution known as the United Bible Training Centre. Ten denominations cooperate on its board but about 50 per cent of the students have continued to be from the U.P. Church. Approximately one hundred women have completed the two year course and gone out to serve in rural and city congregations as well as hospitals, usually under the supervision of a lady missionary. They have been invaluable in teaching the women and children and have made a significant contribution to upbuilding the Church. Those working in hospitals have reached many non-Christians as well with the gospel message.

As soon as the United Bible Training Centre was established in Gujranwala a course was offered to seminary wives to prepare them to help their husbands in the ministry. This continues to the present. About 1968

the regular two-year course for Bible women was discontinued because few congregations could afford to support
both a pastor and a Bible woman, and few evangelistic
lady missionaries were left.

In recent years the United Bible Training Centre has
developed a new creative program of varied short courses
for teachers, nurses, new literates and college students.
Their staff members travel to centers throughout Pakistan
to hold leadership training courses in schools, churches
and hospitals. These have stimulated the Church to
develop more effective programs for Christian education.

Spiritual Life Conventions

The Sialkot Convention has continued to be held
annually with a few exceptions due to war or floods. The
Billy Graham system of counselling and follow-up has
been used as a pattern. Counselors are trained during
the pre-convention period and many decisions are made
each year. The prayer room continues to be a powerhouse
of blessing to those who use it regularly.

Since most of the Christian community cannot take
advantage of the Sialkot Convention because of distance,
many congregations located in larger cities have started
their own conventions. These should be of greater
benefit to the local community. However, most of these
conventions lack solid prayer backing, counselor training
and follow-up procedures. Often the topics chosen are
geared for Muslims, while 99 per cent of those who
attend are Christians. Such conventions don't speak to
the needs of those attending, so fail to revitalize the
Church.

In 1960 Dr. Akbar Haqq, the "Billy Graham of India,"
toured Pakistan holding conventions in most of the
larger cities. Counselor training and follow-up
materials were used. Many dedicated their lives to
the Lord, and various denominational groups experienced
a close working fellowship in their local situation for
the first time.

The next year the Rev. Robert Cummings held conferences
for pastors at the invitation of the U.P. Church. He
was one of the U.P. missionaries who resigned in 1926
over the Pentecostal controversy, but was greatly used
by God in the Assemblies of God Church. The meetings he
led resulted in renewed dedication among many of the
pastors. Dr. Paul Lindholm, formerly a Presbyterian
missionary in the Philippines held training sessions in
stewardship both in 1963 and 1966 that challenged many
laymen to more sacrificial giving and pastors to more
faithful pastoral work.

In 1968 and 1970 teams were sent from Indonesia to
minister in many conventions throughout Pakistan. As
Asians they had insights into the needs of the Church in
Pakistan beyond that of most Westerners. Their ministry
produced fruit in the deepened lives of many. Yet none
of these efforts have succeeded in overcoming the
factional strife that is destroying the spiritual life and
witness of the Church.

Adult Literacy

Much of the spiritual lethargy found in the U.P. Church
of Pakistan can be traced to the fact that 85 per cent
of her members are still illiterate, unable to read their
Bibles. In 1938 Dr. Frank Laubach of the Philippines
visited Pakistan and helped to prepare materials to enable
adults to learn to read their own language in a short
time. These materials have been revised and expanded
many times and have proved beneficial. Many who learn
to read as adults find that the Bible takes on new meaning
for them, and their faith is strengthened.

For many years most of the adult literacy teaching was
done by a few paid workers. This proved unsatisfactory
because there were too few teachers, and many of them did
it as a means of earning a living, not out of concern for
their pupils. Readers learned slowly and shortly afterwards lapsed back into illiteracy. During the last few
years an extensive drive to train volunteer literacy
teachers in large numbers throughout the Church has
found good response. Some of the best volunteer teachers
are those with little education but a real love for the

Lord and concern for the illiterate around them. Today
there are many small literacy classes scattered throughout
the U.P. Church area taught by volunteers but supervised
by trained paid staff from the Adult Basic Education
Centre in Gujranwala. One of the greatest obstructions
to rapid learning is that Punjabi, the mother tongue
of the Punjab, cannot be used. Literacy materials, as
well as almost all literature in the country, are in the
national language, Urdu, not well understood by many
illiterates.

Although not spectacular in leading to sudden conversion, literacy has done a great deal toward revitalizing
small groups of Christians and making them open to
further teaching. It has also been used as a means of
evangelism to a few non-Christians who join the reading
classes.

The Team Approach

In order to take full advantage of the responsiveness
of the newly literate, a team ministry to Christians was
begun in 1960. Two teams made up of missionary and
national workers in evangelism, medicine, and village
uplift concentrated for six weeks to three months in
centers where adult literacy campaigns had preceded them.
A good series of Bible study workbooks and verses for
memorization, translated from Navigator materials, were
adapted for the newly literate, and formed the backbone
of their teaching program. Certificates were given for
the completion of each stage of the course. Special
attention was given to training layleaders in Bible
study, memory work, Sunday School work, Christian Home,
sanitation, and economic uplift, with the intention that
these leaders would carry on the effort after the team
left. Follow-up visits were made at intervals to check
on the progress made, to give out certificates, and to
encourage the people to keep on learning. Subsequent
visits have revealed that many rural lay leaders leave
their villages shortly after the team has trained them
and move to urban centers. Here they don't have the same
position of leadership they had in their local communities,
so are not the pillars of strength to the Church the
team had hoped they would be.

Adult Literacy Class by Alice Hill

Adult Literacy Class in Marwari by Anita Vance

Village Primary School

Flannelgraph Lesson Taught by Laura Reynolds

The Team approach has deepened the spiritual understanding and commitment of the congregations where it has
ministered. It has been discontinued, however, due
primarily to the extreme factionalism in the Church.

Each of the methods mentioned above have brought
blessing to many congregations and new life in Christ to
individuals who were nominal Christians, but they have
not brought lasting revival to the Church. As long as
church leaders are engaged in factional disputes rather
than in shepherding the flock, not only will the Church
fail to grow, but there is serious danger of a severe
decline in membership in the near future.

Evangelism Among Muslims

Although a majority of the U.P. missionaries in recent
years have worked in Christian institutions or directly
with the Church, a few have felt a special call to evangelize Muslims. The Church each year participates in various
efforts designed to win Muslims, and a few individuals
have proved gifted in this ministry.

Methods

A variety of methods for winning Muslims have been
used, some of which are mentioned below, but none has
succeeded in discipling any sizable group of them.

An apologetic approach is most often used with Muslims.
Many tracts and booklets have been prepared and distributed
dealing with Muslim objections to Christianity and com-
paring or contrasting the two faiths. Conventions for
Christians held annually in many cities often choose a
topic geared for Muslims and send arguments out over the
community from loud speakers. In 1961 a famous Muslim
convert, Abdul Haqq, an expert apologist, and the father
of the Indian evangelist Akbar Haqq, was invited from
India to hold meetings throughout the Punjab. Muslims
flocked to hear him and he dealt ably with many difficult
questions they threw at him. This approach is stimulating
to the intellect, reinforces the faith of Christians, and

may have convinced some Muslim minds of the superiority
of the Christian faith, but it has been unfruitful in
reaching the heart and bringing men to accept Jesus as
Savior and Lord.

A closely allied but more psychologically sound approach
has been to present the Gospel positively to Muslims,
attempting to avoid controversy. Cattle fairs or religious
gatherings in honor of Muslim saints are visited by teams
of Christians who distribute literature and give messages
on the Christian faith with no attempt at dispute.
Usually they find attentive audiences and sell a fair
number of tracts and Gospels.

For many years the West Pakistan Christian Council
sponsored an annual "Commando Campaign," lasting from two
to six weeks, with the purpose of making a concentrated
witness to Muslims in one specified area each time.
Nationals and missionaries from many Churches cooperated
in this effort. These have had a healthy effect on the
Churches, diverting attention from their own difficulties
and needs, creating concern for the lost, and giving
them the joy of close meaningful fellowship with Christians of other denominations. No visible fruit in terms of
open converts have resulted, but the seed has been sown
which we trust will eventually produce a harvest.

In 1967 the Christian Study Centre was established in
Rawalpindi to interpret the Muslim faith to Christians and
train them in more effective ways of witnessing to Muslims;
and to explore the possibilities for dialogue with Muslim
scholars, not aiming at conversion, but toward mutual
understanding. They publish a bi-monthly journal, *Al
Mushir,* for both Protestants and Roman Catholics, dealing
with subjects related to Muslim and Christian theology
and missiology. They believe a low-key approach to
evangelism among Muslims will bear more fruit in the
long run.

Perhaps the most effective tool in Muslim evangelism
in recent years has been Bible Correspondence Schools.
Special courses geared for Muslims have been prepared and
Muslim subscriptions have soared from a few hundred to
to several thousand on the current rolls of the various
centers. A Muslim can study the Bible at home without

creating undue suspicion among his relatives. He is at
greater liberty to seriously consider the gospel message
and the claims of Jesus Christ without pressure from
any human source. Responses received to questions in the
courses reveal the deep impact the Scriptures are having
on many lives, resulting in a number of secret believers.
Several attempts have been made to get such believers
together where they could be encouraged by one another's
faith. As yet this has proved unsuccessful. They fear
the consequences of an open declaration of faith too
greatly to risk meeting together. If this productive
method of seed sowing could be combined with some means
of reaching whole family units, it could result in
considerable church growth.

False Assumptions

The Christian approach to the evangelization of Muslims
in Pakistan is based on several false assumptions, leading
to unproductive strategy. Some of them are as follows:

First, we have failed to realize that Muslim society
is not monolithic. It is divided into many segments--
various sects of Muslims, a variety of tribal groups,
class strata, different cultural and linguistic backgrounds. We approach them all alike, scattering the seed
willy-nilly. We make no attempt to "test the soil," to
distinguish which segments of society are more responsive,
better able to hear and accept the Gospel. It may well be
that sweeper Muslims, or certain hill tribes, or the
student class are more open to the Gospel than others.
Once we discover where the fertile soil is, we should
concentrate on planting the seed there.

So far most Muslim evangelism has been directed at
individuals apart from their family environment. They are
urged to make a personal decision for Christ that inevitably
leads to ostracism and social dislocation, with all the
psychological upheaval this involves. The extensive use
of literature rather than oral evangelism has resulted in
winning more young, educated, urban men, who as yet have
little status in the power structure of their society.
They are unable to effectively influence the elders of
their families, but rather are looked upon as upstarts,
disgraceful rebels. If evangelism could be geared to

win the natural leaders of potentially responsive segments
of Muslim society so that they could influence their whole
clan to accept Christ as a group, conversion could be
without severe dislocation. These natural leaders are
usually the older men, many of whom are illiterate or
scarcely literate, but who wield great power in the family
structure. Different methods of evangelism will be needed
to attract them.

Too often we assume that theological difference are
the primary barriers to winning Muslims. This has been
repeatedly disproved. Many are theologically convinced
of Christianity, but cannot hurdle the social and
cultural obstacles to faith. Probably the greatest
single barrier converts face is the necessity of inte-
grating into the established Church with its depressed
class background. This is not just because of prejudice
ingrained from childhood, but because it requires a convert to adjust to a completely different culture, way of
thinking, pattern of worship, religious vocabulary, and
status in society. Because we have won individuals
apart from their families, it has been impractical to set
up a Christian fellowship for Muslim converts apart from
the established Church. The community would be too
unbalanced. When, by the providence of God, whole
families are won, it is crucial to organize them into a
separate communion structured according to their cultural
orientation. This will make it far easier for them to
win their friends and neighbors and become a growing
Christian community.

The following quotation reflects some of the possible
adjustments that could be made to make them feel at home
without compromising the essentials of the Gospel.

> Consider for example the merits of the
> formation of a homogeneous church com-
> posed totally of Muslim converts. The
> ritual of this worshipping community
> would follow as closely as possible the
> form prescribed for worship in the mosque.
> This would minimize spiritual disorientation
> on the part of the young converts. For
> instance, is there a definite regulation
> in Scripture that God must be worshipped

> in corporate fashion only on Sundays--or
> could not Friday be retained by the
> convert as a meaningful day to come apart
> and meet God? It has been said that
> cleanliness is next to godliness, so
> perhaps it would be appropriate for the
> Muslim convert to continue his ritual of
> washing prior to his prayer time. Would
> it not be permissible to remove one's
> shoes before worshipping the Lord--even
> as Moses was commanded to do? Is there
> anything unscriptural about praying five
> times a day? Direction of prayer is
> important to the Muslim. Could not
> Jerusalem replace Mecca--not as an object
> of veneration but rather as an expression
> of respect for a part of the world that is
> pregnant with sacred memories for the
> Christian. The Bible expressly declares
> fasting is a spiritual exercise acceptable
> to God. Muslims could retain the month
> of abstinence as an integral part of their
> worship form. (Parshall   1974:349)

It is imperative not to encourage syncretism regarding
basic truths of Scripture, but we must be careful not to
confuse our cultural trappings with the central eternal
message of Jesus Christ.

We also assume that the Urdu Bible so meaningful to the
Church will have the same effect on Muslims. We are unaware
that the translation uses religious terminology geared
primarily to people of Hindu and Christian background, not
to Muslims in spite of the fact that two of the translators
were Muslim converts. Muslims have different names for
God, Jesus, John the Baptist and others of the prophets.
They never refer to a prophet without adding the phrase,
"may peace be upon him." A special translation using such
terminology is urgently needed. Tracts, books, and
Bible correspondence courses should all be prepared in
vocabulary meaningful to them.

It may be that the traditional resistance shown by
Muslims to the Gospel is more due to our faulty methods
of evangelism than to their hardness of heart. May the

Lord make us flexible and teachable as we obey His command
to make Jesus Christ known to the majority community in
Pakistan.

Evangelism Among Scheduled Castes

Although the present Christian Church in Pakistan has
come almost entirely from the depressed classes, nearly
a century of Christian teaching and influence has lifted
the Christian community to a status considerably above
the Scheduled Castes remaining in Pakistan. Through
mission institutions a good sized Christian middle class
has developed, so that Christians are found in almost
every profession and branch of government service in the
country. For this reason the Christian Church feels
superior to the Scheduled Castes, not inclined to evangelize them, and not eager to welcome them into their fellowship. One pastor when urged to seek out a Scheduled
Caste group that had shown a responsive spirit, replied,
"Are there no other lost sheep to be sought?"

In spite of indifference, neglect, and rejection on
the part of the Church, small groups of several Scheduled
Castes have become Christians in recent years in the U.P.
Church area. A few cases are recorded below:

The Mazhabi Sikhs

In 1953 Mr. and Mrs. Ross spent twelve days teaching
groups of Mazhabi Sikh sweepers in Lyallpur. These were
originally Chuhras, but had loosely aligned themselves
with the Sikhs. Unsatisfied with the inferior position
they continued to occupy, bereft of the Sikh community
that migrated to India in 1947, and lacking a meaningful
religious experience, they proved unusually responsive.
Seventy-eight professed to believe in Christ as their
Savior; fifty-eight were baptized. Small numbers of
Mazhabi Sikhs have become Christians in other districts
as well.

The Balmikis

The Balmikis are a Scheduled Caste of sweepers,
closely related to the Chuhras, perhaps originally a
sub-caste of the Chuhras. They are found in most major
cities and many small towns, often living in the midst
of or adjacent to communities of sweeper Christians. They
continue to worship their special deity, Bala Shah.
They construct a mud platform and place small oil lamps in
niches at the front end of it. Regular offerings of food
are presented to Bala Shah in order to assure his help
in everyday needs. Many Balmikis are not earnest in
their faith. Small groups of them have been won to Christ
in many different centers. Wherever a congregation has
a large group of Christian sweepers, Balmiki converts have
integrated into it happily. In places where the congregation consisted of middle class Christians, Balmikis did
not feel at home and were not made welcome. Efforts to
win any Scheduled Caste community can be furthered by
establishing separate worshipping groups for them at the
beginning, rather than attempting to integrate them into
middle class congregations.

The Gagare

The Gagare are a group of the depressed classes
scattered throughout the Punjab. According to the 1911
Census Report there were 3,155 Gagare largely in Lahore
Division. They are among the most despised of the
Scheduled Castes because of their occupation as scavengers.
They collect rags and papers, and dispose of the carcasses
of dead animals, selling the hides to tanneries and the
bones, horns and hooves to fertilizer factories. They
also catch, keep, and apply leeches for medicinal purposes.
Many still eat carrion since it is readily available to
them in their occupation, and are also known for eating
rats. This habit degrades them most in the eyes of all
other communities. Some Gagare are nomadic, living in
small quilted tents stretched over bowed branches. Their
furnishings consist only of mats for sleeping. Others
live in shacks or simple adobe brick homes in ghetto
areas.

In 1955 a group of the Gagare living in Wazirabad area
contacted a U.P. missionary at the Sialkot Convention
and asked for teaching. As Wazirabad was in the Church
of Scotland Mission area, the U.P. missionary referred
those inquirers to the Sialkot Church Council. Nevertheless he obtained from them the names of other Gagare
families living in the outskirts of Gujranwala city.
These welcomed teaching and one of the first converts was
a Gagara leader, Sain Chamba. His leadership greatly
influenced others and a group of about 20 adults and
at least an equal number of children were baptized.
There were about one third of the group living in that
section of Gujranwala.

In the light of this challenging opportunity, the U.P.
Mission set aside Miss F.E. Brown to concentrate on
evangelizing this tribe. She worked among them from
April 1959 until she was transferred to Lyallpur in May
1961. None were baptized during this period, but rather
seemed to become more and more hardened, steeped in
idolatry and *pir* worship. Students from the Theological
Seminary and Bible teachers from the United Bible Training
Centre worked with her during that time and continued
contact after she was transferred, but the local Christian
congregation, pastor or session took little interest in
the effort. The Gagare worshipped separately and were
not welcomed into the fellowship of the other Christians
in town.

After Miss Brown was transferred to Lyallpur she
contacted a group of at least 200 Gagare who lived next
to the sweeper Christian colony. The Headmistress of the
Christian primary school tried to introduce some of the
Gagare children into school, but the other children
wrinkled up their noses and said, "They smell!" The
Gagare requested a school of their own, but it was never
started. Due to the press of other assignments in
Lyallpur, Miss Brown was unable to give the Gagare work
much attention. Had the local congregation taken an active
interest in reaching them, they would probably have reaped
a rich harvest, for the Gagare were eager for teaching and
ready to respond. Their leader in Gujranwala told Miss
Brown that there were about 500 Gagare in the Lyallpur area,
an even larger group in Sahiwal, and a total of several
thousand in all of Pakistan.

In 1969 a daily prayer meeting began in Sargodha growing out of blessing obtained through the Indonesian team
ministry. The responsiveness of the Gagare in other
districts was brought up as a matter for prayer coupled
with a concern that the Gagare in the Sargodha area be
reached as well. An illiterate night watchman, Aziz, felt
convicted and spoke up, "I feel that God would have me
make the first contact with the Gagare here," he said.
"I can't teach them much, but at least I could get the
work started. Pray with me for ten days about this, that
we may have God's guidance as to how this can best be
done."

Five days later Aziz' water buffalo fell ill. The
buffalo provided milk for the family and represented a
major financial investment for them, but in spite of
careful doctoring, she died. Aziz, dazed by this loss,
started off to call some Christian friends to help him get
rid of the carcass, when suddenly he remembered that
disposing of dead animals is the traditional occupation
of the Gagare. As he was returning with two of their
men he asked, "What is your faith?"

They replied, "We have no faith any more. Our trust
in idols is gone. We are interested in becoming Christians
because some relatives in another district are receiving
Christian teaching, but we have nobody to tell us what it
is all about."

Aziz returned radiant and said, "I have lost a buffalo
but have gained a ministry."

The Gagare in Sargodha listened with great interest.
Some even traveled distances to persuade relatives to
come to hear the Good News. Several Christian laymen have
continued to teach them regularly and Aziz faithfully
rounds them up for worship, but the local pastor and
session have not yet been persuaded to baptize them or
accept them into the Church. It is urgent that those who
have been taught and are ready to confess their faith be
baptized quickly. Constant postponement results in
hardening of heart.

If the U.P. Church in Pakistan would only recognize the opportunity on their doorstep in the form of the Scheduled Castes, and take advantage of it, significant church growth from among them is abundantly possible.

15

God's Answer for Today

In summary, what is the situation in the U.P. Church in
Pakistan today? What diagnosis can be made of her
problems? What are the possible solutions for her
factionalism and lack of growth? These are questions
that have been on the hearts of many deeply concerned
nationals and missionaries. We believe the history of
this Church has provided insights that can lead to constructive answers to the present dilemma, if the Church
has the faith and courage to act upon them without delay.

The Rural Church

In spite of constant migrations to the city, at least
75 per cent of the U.P. Church still live in thousands of
scattered villages, working mostly as tenant farmers,
share croppers, or day laborers. In the old centers of
the Chuhra movement (Sialkot, Zafarwal and Pasrur) the
people have suffered repeated disasters from war and flood,
resulting in great poverty. Migrations from these areas
have been heavy. Christians in the canal colonies of
the Bar are better off financially and more stable.

When evangelistic missionaries were in charge of each
district--itinerated, held annual Bible schools in each
congregation, gave regular monthly instruction to national
evangelistic workers and pastors, and played a supervisory
role throughout each presbytery--the rural Church was quite
well taught and staunch in faith. Such "district" missionaries have gradually been phased out and since the 1960's
the major burden of rural church work has fallen on self-
supporting pastors and their elders. An increasing number
of village elders are now literate, and they continue to

be the backbone of the rural Church. Most of them are
truly concerned for their people and do what they can to
build up the Church to the limit of their ability, training and resources. The majority of rural pastors have
tried to be faithful, but have too many villages in their
congregation to do an adequate job of teaching and
pastoral calling. When "party" spirit grew to major
proportions, both preceding and following the McIntire
schism, rural pastors were drawn increasingly into church
politics; courted, and even bribed for their votes; and
kept in such a psychological turmoil that they have had
little time or heart for shepherding their flock. Village
congregations have become demoralized by the factionalism
and lack of solid teaching. Those earnest in their
faith are attracted to the Pentecostals, Brethren, or
Roman Catholics; others turn to the worship of Muslim
pirs, ("holy men"), the wearing of fetishes, and faith
in black magic.

In spite of neglect, meager knowledge of the Scriptures,
and frequent discrimination from the majority community,
Christians have remained amazingly steadfast in times of
crisis. During both the 1965 and 1971 wars, some Christians were accused of loyalty to India, imprisoned and
tortured; many were pressured to become Muslims; but few
turned their backs on their faith.

The Urban Church

Most urban congregations consist of two distinct
groups--the middle class professional people, and the
sweepers. Sometimes they worship together; more often
the sweeper community worships in their own section of
town.

Most city congregations have a Sunday School program,
women's group, youth group, choir, and elders who are
educated and gifted in leadership. Some pastors feel
threatened by the increasing capability of the laypeople
in the congregation, but many are glad for their help
and make good use of them. In recent years, unfortunately,
city elders have become embroiled along with their
pastors in "party" struggles. Politically ambitious

laymen strive for eldership in order to take a more
active part in the fray. Most congregations, both rural
and urban, have been split by the McIntire schism. Often
an evangelist or pastor is provided for the same congregation by each faction, resulting in confusion, divided
loyalties, and endless court cases over the ownership
and control of church properties.

The intense factional strife within the U.P. Church
absorbs so much of the time and energy of church leaders
that evangelistic outreach has come to a standstill.
Local congregations, disenchanted with Synod, no longer
contribute to Synod Budget. Home Mission work, formerly
supported from the budget of Synod, has been discontinued.
No worker has been employed by them since 1965.

As rural Christians are easily led to put faith in
magic and fetishes due to lack of a vital teaching
ministry in the Church, urban congregations are plagued
with growing secularism. Middle class Christians, if
not grounded in the Scriptures, tend to ape Muslim ways
to avoid being classed with the sweepers. They gradually
drift away from the Church and sometimes their children
become Muslims. There has been an alarming increase in
recent years in the number of educated Christian girls
who are married to Muslims and lost to the Church.
Christian schools for girls have outnumbered those for
boys because girls' education was neglected by the
government in the early days. This has resulted in a
higher number of educated girls than boys in the Christian community. Many parents arrange for a less educated
bride for their sons so that she will prove a more
docile daughter-in-law. This leaves a large number of
Christian nurses and teachers with the choice of marrying a less educated Christian or a Muslim of equal
educational status. Too often they choose the latter.
A demoralized community is in great danger of increasing
disintegration of this kind. This is the critical
situation faced by the U.P. Church today.

A Diagnosis

Many modern missionaries looking at the present U.P.
Church--rent by factions, declining in numbers, and
filled with poorly taught nominal Christians--lay the
blame for this upon the group movement strategy of
Missions. Their argument is as follows: "If the early
missionaries had not baptized and taken into the Church
such hordes of untaught illiterate people, but insisted
upon each believer making an individual personal decision
for Christ and being 'born again,' the Church would not
be in such a state today." Is this valid?

The analysis made in this study clearly demonstrates
the fallacy of such a conclusion. The Church made up of
thoroughly taught but isolated converts who had made an
individual personal decision in accordance with Western
ideas of propriety, turned out to be weak, static,
dependent, and prone to immorality and apostasy. When
missionaries were forced (by their continual knocking
at the door) to let in whole families of Chuhras, it was
not done carelessly. Records of the evangelistic tours
of the district missionaries from early days up through
the 1950's reveal the care they took to interview all
candidates for baptism, to provide follow-up teaching,
to prepare elders for their local responsibilities, to
train and supervise evangelistic workers, and to organize
worshipping fellowships to strengthen believers. Illiteracy and the overwhelming numbers involved made the
task monumental, beyond the capacities of the limited
personnel available.

Still, the resulting Church had all the characteristics
of a vital growing fellowship. Up until the 1930's they
were rapidly becoming self-supporting and both laymen
and pastors were winning many each year to the Lord.
The group movement method enabled converts to remain a
part of their social structure. This gave stability
and strength to the Church, so that even today only a
small percentage apostatize in spite of many inducements
to do so.

Why does the Church not show the same growth and
vitality today?

It is easy to jump to the conclusion that the Church
is now ineffective in witness because it is filled with
unsaved, nominal, 4th and 5th generation Christians who
have no concern for the evangelization of the non-Christians around them. The U.P. Mission Minutes in 1955,
referring to the lack of growth in the Church, makes the
following unfavorable comparison between the Church of
today and the poor unlearned villagers, Ditt and Kanaya,
who:

> ... witnessed to their families, fellow-
> villagers ... and brought thousands of
> non-Christians to Christ. Since that time
> the tendency has been more and more to
> leave the work of evangelization to the
> professionals. (15)

Is this a fair criticism?

Such a conclusion is not only an over-simplication
of the problem, but contains a false judgment of the
Pakistani Church. In spite of all her weaknesses, the
U.P. Church is filled with thousands of Christians who
know and love the Lord, read or memorize the Bible, give
sacrificially, serve the Church with loyalty and devotion,
and witness to their non-Christian neighbors. Even many
of the leaders most involved in party strife deplore the
system and long to escape from the meshes of factionalism.
What then is wrong?

The criticism quoted above does not recognize one
factor basic to the situation. Ditt and Kanaya who
witnessed so effectively and "brought thousands of non-
Christians to Christ," were working among their own caste
and clan, all of whom were restless, on the march, looking
for a new faith. Megs brought Megs, and Chuhras brought
Chuhras to the Lord. They were not witnessing in a
cross-cultural situation.

There are few non-Christian Chuhras left in Pakistan
today, so Christians are cut off from the opportunity of
winning non-Christians from among their own caste channel.
Now they are forced to witness across many barriers.
Their background, culture, thought patterns, religious
vocabulary, and social standing are all different from

that of the majority community. Often their witness is
ridiculed and rejected; seldom does it bear visible fruit.
To continue witnessing when response is poor or negative
takes great courage, persistence, and love; yet many do
it. It is true that some fear too active a witness may
threaten their security in a Muslim land. Others,
having suffered discrimination and the many disadvantages
of a minority group, are tempted to keep to themselves
their one advantage, their "spiritual heritage." They
are loathe to share it with those who have so many
visible benefits. But the major reason Pakistani Christians have been unable to win large numbers of converts
is because they now have to witness across social, cultural
and religious barriers that have proved formidable
obstacles to missionaries as well. The Church cannot
be justly criticized in this, for the facts indicate
that as many Muslim converts are being won today as were
won in previous years. Until a group movement begins
in some segment of the majority community in Pakistan,
it is unlikely that large numbers will be brought to
Christ.

The development of factionalism is closely related
to the above problem. Because the Church has been unable
to reach out effectively, she has become hemmed in,
absorbed in her own affairs. Just as a pond without an
outlet becomes stagnant and germs multiply, so a Church
without outreach becomes static and ripe for all kinds
of evil influences. In place of the thrill of bringing
others to Christ, leaders seek satisfaction in striving
for position in the Church. Self-government gives
scope to the factional spirit indigenous to the culture,
so that many are unwittingly embroiled in party strife
and don't know how to extricate themselves from it.
This has brought the U.P. Church to its present state.

A Remedy

What can be done to change the current situation that
is leading to demoralization and disintegration in the
U.P. Church? Is there a solution?

Many look to revival as the only means of saving the Church from her present dilemma. For this reason concerned church leaders in every denomination have spent much time, money and prayer on spiritual life conventions, bringing revival teams from India and Indonesia. Many individuals responded in repentance and consecration at these meetings, but the Church situation as a whole has not improved. Why?

Revival, although desperately needed, is only a partial remedy and unlikely to have its full effect until another condition is fulfilled. The Church must look beyond herself and her problems and become deeply involved in winning others. Then cleansing and revival can come. Can pure rain from heaven make a stagnant pond clean and healthy? Of course not. It only stirs up the mud and dirt. Just receiving fresh water is not enough. The pond will be cleansed when it <u>both receives and gives out</u> water, when it becomes a flowing stream.

The problem in the Church today has been traced to lack of effective outreach. The solution is obvious. Just as a pond must receive and give out water to become a life-giving stream, so the Church must receive and give out spiritual blessing in order to be cleansed and revitalized. The Church must find an effective outreach for the Gospel. And just as revival came to the U.P. Church in the midst of growth, not as its initiating cause but as a crucial deepening influence that led to greater growth, so revival can come today <u>when the Church begins to grow</u>. We have seen it happen in the lives of individuals who have become immersed in the work of outreach. As they give out to spiritually receptive people, their own faith is deepened and their sense of expectancy of what God will do is heightened until they truly are revived by the Holy Spirit. We firmly believe it can and will happen to the Church if she will turn her full attention upon making disciples in obedience to Christ's commission. She will become a stream of living water to the land of Pakistan, receiving life from the Lord and passing it on to others.

How can the Church grow? Where can effective outreach
be made? We have seen that the Church is stymied in its
efforts to win the majority community. There are too many
theological, cultural, and social barriers to overcome.
New approaches need to be explored in Muslim evangelism
that may produce increased fruit. Nevertheless, let us
not fail to learn the lesson it took so many years for
God to teach to the early missionaries. Let us not keep
looking to the "high and mighty," but open our hearts
and the doors of our churches to the "weak and lowly,"
the Scheduled Castes, who have shown ample evidence of
spiritual hunger and potential responsiveness. If God
has prepared their hearts, who are we to call them
unworthy and unclean? Let us humble ourselves and
reach out to them, having the mind of Christ who humbled
Himself all the way from His throne in heaven to death
on a cross in order to win us.

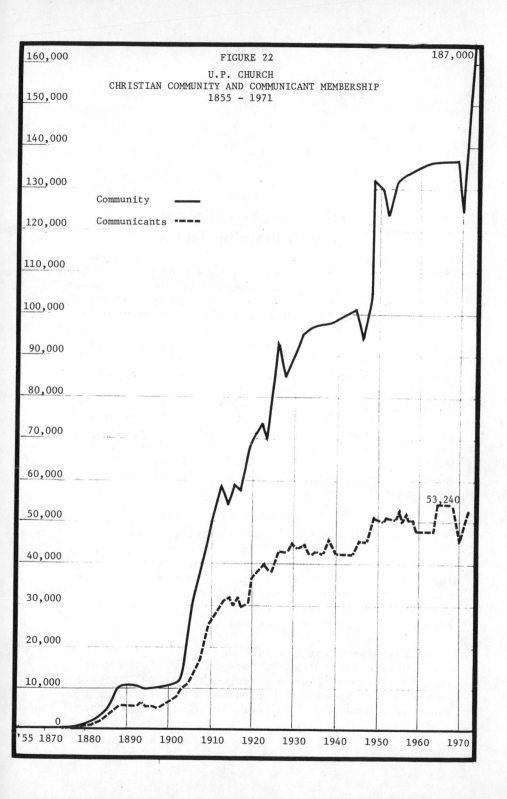

FIGURE 22
U.P. CHURCH
CHRISTIAN COMMUNITY AND COMMUNICANT MEMBERSHIP
1855 - 1971

16
Principles Essential for
Church Planting Today

The study and analysis found in this book have not been
made merely for historical interest in the development
of the Church in Pakistan, but primarily to provide
guidelines for present evangelism and church planting.
"He who fails to learn from history is doomed to repeat
its errors." A look at present evangelistic efforts in
Pakistan makes the truth of this statement painfully
evident. The methods that have failed for 120 years
still dominate our approach to non-Christians, with
predictable lack of fruit. May God grant all Missions
and Churches the courage to examine their work in the
light of history; to test it for tangible results in
terms of people won; and to seek the guidance of the
Holy Spirit in how to apply the principles of church
growth to the present situation. Essential principles
are outlined below:

Recognize Numerical Church Growth as God's Will

In these days many are offended at the idea of gathering large numbers into the Church, convinced that it
can only be done by accepting hordes of nominal Christians
who have no true spiritual life. Do large numbers
necessarily mean poor spiritual quality?

In the history of the U.P. Church in Pakistan it is
abundantly evident that periods of slow growth when
individual converts were given much personal attention,
were times of spiritual barrenness as well. When thousands were baptized each year, the Church experienced

revival, developed a deep life of prayer, progressed
toward self-support, and had an active Home Mission
program of discipling non-Christians of their own caste
in new areas. Quantity, rather than reducing quality,
was used by God's Spirit to create a vital growing
fellowship so essential to spiritual depth. Present
nominality and lack of quality in personal experience
cannot be blamed upon the period of rapid growth, but
upon the last forty years when the Church has become
stagnant, not winning others.

God is definitely interested in numerical church growth.
We are called not just to be faithful, but to win people.
Quantity as well as quality should be our goal in mission
work. Jesus commanded, "Go ... and make disciples,"
implying that it is both possible and expected. We cannot deny the validity of God's call to certain individuals to work in spiritually barren fields of the world
where only the occasional convert is possible. However,
the majority of Missions are located in areas of great
growth potential and cannot claim "faithfulness" as an
excuse for winning only a few souls. God yearns as a
father for all of His children. He is not content with
a few highly polished "quality" Christians, but opens
His arms to gather in all who will come.

In Jesus' parable in Luke 15, the shepherd left 99
sheep in the fold to search for one lost one. In most
of Asia today Missions hover tenderly over the one or
two per cent who are in the fold, paying only nominal
attention to the ninety-eight or ninety-nine per cent
still wandering outside. If all heaven rejoices when
one sinner repents, how much deeper the joy will be
when many are won! God is interested in numerical church
growth, because to Him they are not "merely numbers,"
but His children, infinitely precious in His eyes.

Make the Discipling of Non-Christians a _Primary_ Goal

When missionaries first go to a foreign country,
their one absorbing goal is to win non-Christians. They
are following the clear command of the Great Commission

to "go...preach...baptize...and disciple." As people
are converted and the Church is established, the need
to nurture the new Christians is crucial, and absorbs
more and more of the missionaries' time and thought.
Gradually evangelism of non-Christians takes a minor
place in their priorities, because there is so much to
do among the Christians. The Church grows and matures
and her leaders become increasingly able to manage their
own affairs. Missionaries talk about "working themselves
out of a job," i.e. training a national to do the church
job the missionary has been doing. The original goal
of evangelizing non-Christians has by this time dropped
out of the picture entirely. The tiny per cent of the
population who have become Christians have blotted out
the vision of reaching the majority who do not yet profess to believe in Jesus Christ.

Let us get back to the original goal given by Christ,
to disciple all the nations. With over 2 billion left
in the world who do not profess Christ even nominally,
the chances of "working ourselves out of a job" are slim
indeed!

Search for Responsive People

Never assume that non-Christian society is monolithic.
It is made up of many different social segments and class
strata. Each has distinct characteristics that determine
the reaction of its members to the message of the Gospel.
The first step toward an effective evangelistic program
among non-Christians is to discern which segments of
society are receptive to the Good News. God loves all
and longs that all come to know Him, but for reasons
beyond our comprehension, He has prepared some groups to
accept Him now, while others will be ready at another time."
Wise strategy in evangelism as in farming is to place
few workers in unripe fields, and concentrate on those
fields that are "white to harvest," reaping them before
the grain spoils from being over ripe.

How can such responsive segments of society be
recognized? Certain sociological situations greatly
increase a group's readiness to accept the Gospel.

These should be noted as clues in searching for the people whose hearts have been prepared by the Holy Spirit. Some of the clues are as follows:

1) Animistic people are usually more open to change of faith than members of one of the major religions of the world.

2) Groups who have only recently joined a major religion and still are kept on the fringes of their society are often winnable.

3) Socially depressed groups dominated by an oppressive force--economic, political, religious, or racial--are looking for better answers to life and often ready to accept the Christian solution. Those living in peace and security are satisfied with the answers they have, not seeking for new ones.

4) People who have recently moved are open to change and therefore to accepting a new faith. Refugees from war, flood, famine or oppression; migrating populations to newly irrigated land; rural people moving to the city in search of employment; college students away from home; and service men have all proved fertile fields for the Gospel. Such people must be reached soon after dislocation before they have had time to create a new structure of society satisfying to them, for then they no longer are as ready to change.

5) Cities that are new and growing present better prospects for evangelism than old established ones. Those parts of the city that have transient or newly arrived residents have great church growth potential.

6) Certain isolated tribes, especially in mountainous or remote areas, have proved responsive. Scarcity of land often causes economic pressures that drive them to look for new answers to life. They begin to realize their isolation and need to "catch up with the world." These natural desires are used by God to open their hearts to His Word.

7) The poor usually turn to God more readily than the
rich, so Christian evangelists should pay special
attention to the poor. Jesus pointed out this unique
feature of the Gospel in describing His own ministry to
the disciples of John the Baptist, when he said, "Tell
him ... that Good News is preached to the poor."

8) Those who take their non-Christian faith seriously
are more approachable than secularly minded people to
whom religion is unimportant. Rural, illiterate people
often fall into this category more than their sophisti-
cated cynical urban brothers.

Even though these factors are basically sociological
rather than religious in nature, God uses them to stir
up men's hearts and turn them to Himself. His Spirit
causes them to seek Him in the perplexities and problems
of life. We need to be aware of these forces and take
advantage of their power to propel men into the Kingdom
of God.

Is it not unscriptural to make distinctions between
people, to neglect some and concentrate unduly on others?
No. God has always been selective in His dealings with
men. Jesus in sending out His disciples two by two
gave them these instructions: "Don't go to the Gentiles,
or the Samaritans, but only to the people of Israel ...
Any city or home that doesn't welcome you--shake off the
dust of that place from your feet as you leave."
(Matt. 10:5,14)

Jesus urged the disciples to go to the most potentially
responsive--the Jews, who had the spiritual background
to understand their message. Even among them, family
units and whole villages would prove unfertile ground
for the Gospel. These were to be left so that time and
effort could be spent where it would count the most and
produce the most fruit.

The Apostle Paul repeatedly applied this principle.
In a new city he looked up the Jews, having the most in
common with them and considering them the most likely
to accept his witness. When they resisted and refused
to listen, he left them and concentrated on the Gentiles.

Such strategy is thoroughly biblical, for God is interested in people coming to Christ in as great numbers
as possible.

Give Priority to Responsive People

When a receptive group has been located, the discipling
of that group should become a priority goal of the whole
Mission. Too often it is treated as an interesting side-
line, not the mainstream of mission concern and effort.
In the U.P. Church when the Gagare movement started,
one missionary was assigned to that work for two years,
then it was dropped. After 500 Bajanias were baptized
in Sindh from 1939 to 1941, the one Anglican missionary
involved in this movement was transferred and the movement starved to death for lack of follow-up teaching.
(See Appendix, page 246.) Today no Christian from that
group has been located. Such unnecessary tragedies have
been repeated many times over in the history of Pakistan
and India, but should never be permitted to do so again,
by God's help.

In order to give priority to new responsive groups,
it is necessary to take a clear hard look at existing
work and close down those that are not bearing fruit and
show little promise of doing so. Peter Wagner in his
book, *Frontiers in Missionary Strategy,* applies the
Parable of the Barren Fig Tree to missionary work in a
revealing way. The owner of the fig tree is interested
in one thing--obtaining fruit. Finding none on the tree,
he is ready to cut it down immediately. However, the
gardener has spent many hours planting, watering and
tenderly caring for that tree. He has an emotional
attachment to it because of the years of labor it represents. Besides it has lovely leaves and looks so
decorative in the garden--an attractive sight to show
visitors. He pleads to have the tree preserved in the
faint hope that in the future it may produce fruit,
though an honest appraisal would have forced him to
admit the slim chance of fruit from that tree.

What a picture of so much mission work today! The
buildings, the organization, the plan and structure of
various institutions and projects look beautiful to us,
but when examined closely are found to be leaves, not
fruit. Yet we cling to these programs and methods with
an emotional fervor generated by the hours of loving
labor spent on them, and are loathe to obey the Master's
command to cut down unfruitful trees.

The Lord wants to see fruit. The prepared hearts of
receptive people are adequate evidence of the priority
He places upon them. How urgent it is that Missions
too make it a priority concern, not just through prayer,
but by transferring a significant amount of personnel
and budget into discipling such people.

Aim at Winning Family Units

Most missionaries, ingrained from childhood with the
Western concept of individualism, convinced of the
necessity of each inquirer making a personal decision,
find it difficult to accept the validity of a group
decision for Christ. Yet the history of the Church in
Pakistan from the early days until the present has provided ample proof that individual extraction conversions
do not result in a stable, growing Church, able to win
others. On the other hand, when a whole family or clan
decide to become Christians, the social structures that
gave stability to their society before are transferred
to the Church. In this way caste becomes a means of
rapid spread of the Gospel. The extended family
connection provides a natural channel for witness among
those most likely to be influenced by a convert's
testimony. When a large enough group is won together,
the power of ostracism and pressure to recant are greatly
reduced. Fellowship and moral support are available to
strengthen each member of the group, and marriage
arrangements can be made. All these help to create a
stable Church, attractive to others of the same caste.

Baptize Without Delay

Church growth is deeply affected by the amount of time that elapses between an inquirer's confession of faith and his public baptism. This is especially true when whole groups are involved. The Missions that severely restricted those eligible for baptism, placing them on interminable waiting lists, and requiring the memorization of many truths and Bible passages, found them increasingly indifferent to the claims of Christ. Many were lost to other faiths. Constant delay was interpreted by inquirers as reluctance to accept them, and not having made a public confession of their new faith, they were prone to waver and to wonder if they were making the right decision. Missions that accepted the Chuhras readily, baptized them without long periods of probation, and then provided immediate follow-up teaching, found their Church growing rapidly both in numbers and in eagerness to learn. Although newly baptized converts were weak in scriptural knowledge, their old prejudices against Christianity were gone, and they were anxious to learn as much as possible about their newly avowed faith. Missions today too often revert to the unproductive method of long periods of probationary teaching. It is essential to learn this lesson from history so that potentially large movements to Christ will not be dwarfed and stunted by unwarranted zeal on this point. In the Great Commission we are commanded to baptize and then teach. This scriptural order produces a far more vital, growing Church.

Provide for Immediate Follow-up Teaching

Baptism without follow-up teaching is not only worthless but dangerous. It acts as an inoculation immunizing the converts from experiencing the thrill of a growing faith. Baptized believers who have been neglected for a long period of time are greatly hardened to the message of the Gospel. Adequate follow-up teaching must be given as soon as possible in a form most meaningful to them.

In order to provide such teaching quickly, it will
often be necessary to choose poorly trained laymen who
are recognized leaders of the group being discipled, and
give them on-the-job training as evangelists. It will
usually be necessary to support them financially largely
from Mission funds for some years until the new Church
has grown to a size that self-support is feasible.   To
refuse to underwrite the finances at the beginning of
a group movement, among depressed classes in particular,
sounds a death knell upon the movement. Without the
necessary follow-up teaching, requiring full-time workers, there is little likelihood of a large healthy group
movement sweeping in the majority of the caste.

Pray and Work for Deeper Commitment

Group movements to Christ are usually motivated by a
combination of social and spiritual forces. When baptism
is administered quickly on confession of faith converts
often do not experience the transforming power of the
Lord. They have made an initial commitment that can be
called "conversion" in the sense that they have turned
away from idols and have now pledged allegiance to Jesus
Christ. Conversion, however, should not be considered
the end but the beginning of Christian experience. A
deeper work of the Holy Spirit needs to take place in
their hearts. It is imperative that believers be led on
from their initial stand at baptism, through a sound
biblical teaching program to a series of experiences
that result in regeneration, revitalization and a growing
faith. Until this happens the discipling is incomplete.
Such an experience can happen at baptism, but it is
more likely to come after the convert has received more
biblical instruction, has participated in the fellowship
of worship, and has found God answering his prayers day
by day.

The Sialkot Convention revival of 1904 to 1910
brought many group movement Christians to this experience
of deeper commitment. Their transformed lives gave new
impetus to the movement and sparked the development
of the Home Mission outreach and of a self-supporting
ministry. Such deepening experiences are essential if
a group movement is to result in a vital Church.

Disciple as Homogeneous Units

In the early stages of a group movement, for the sake of effective evangelism among those not yet won to Christ, it is essential that two divergent castes or tribes not be integrated into one Christian congregation or church organization. Allow each to grow and develop separately following its own indigenous patterns of worship, witness, fellowship, and government. Integration will prove a serious barrier to winning non-Christian relatives of the same caste, and thereby prevent the Gospel from crossing the natural bridges used by God to further His Kingdom. The purpose of such a policy is not to foster caste and class prejudice, but to utilize caste channels as a means of winning as many as possible to the Lord. We can trust the Holy Spirit to gradually break down these barriers as they become mature Christians. As they are drawn closer to the Lord, they will be drawn close to one another. But to force this kind of close fellowship in the early stages can do irreparable harm and result in a stunted group movement.

As a corollary to this point it is important to reiterate the discovery that in the history of the Indian subcontinent no Mission has been successful in discipling large numbers from two different castes at the same time in the same area, as far as we know. Each Mission or Church would be wise to limit its efforts to one caste or tribe. If more than one are discipled, then each should have its separate team of workers, separate services of worship and separate church organization. Comity divisions should be made according to caste or tribe, not by geographical boundaries. Since there are at least thirty different potentially responsive Scheduled Castes in Pakistan today, there should be plenty of scope for many different denominations to work among them without interfering with one another. God grant that precious time and energy may not be spent in unprofitable competition among us, but that each new Church or Mission may be led to unmanned fields that are ripe for harvest.

Much of the secret of the success of the U.P. Mission
in working with the Chuhras was their readiness to adapt
to the ways of the people they wanted to win. The
language of the elite and the literate, Urdu, gave way
to the mother tongue, Punjabi, understood and loved in
the most remote villages of the Punjab. Psalms were
adapted to indigenous tunes that grated on the ears of
the missionaries, but were nevertheless substituted for
translations of English hymns so dear to them with their
connotations of home. These Psalms in Punjabi tunes
and language have enriched the worship of the Church of
the Punjab immeasurably. Stress on literature and
intellectual theological debate changed to an emphasis
on rote memory of the Scriptures, more suited to the
illiterate Chuhras. Without adaptations of this kind,
the movement would not have grown to such proportions.

Today a similar approach is needed. A fluent command
of the mother tongue of the group to be won is one of
the best keys to their evangelism. Anthropological
studies give invaluable insights into the world view,
religious concepts, and power structure of a society.
Those structures and traditions that are not anti-Christian can be left to provide stability and continuity to
the emerging Church, and enable people to become Christians with a minimum of dislocation. Other practices
that are distinctly anti-Christian should be replaced
by functional substitutes that will meet the same
psychological and social needs in a way consistent with
the Christian faith. Such adaptations need to be done
by the indigenous leaders themselves, but can be stimulated by the missionaries. Wise use of these insights
can do much to help a movement develop and grow.

Gear to Large Growth--
"Attempt Great Things for God."

Christian Missions have never been psychologically
or structurally prepared for large group movements. We
feel overwhelmed and embarrassed when one or two thousand
conversions take place in a single year. Yet, the

command of Jesus is to disciple all nations, tribes and peoples. Since that is such a staggering task, we may confine our goals to discipling just the responsive castes and groups in the world. Even that would require a major revolution in mission thinking and strategy.

If all the Missions in Pakistan would determine to give priority to the evangelization of the Scheduled Castes (comprising less than one per cent of the population), with the goal of winning them to Jesus Christ by the year A.D. 2000, they would have to be prepared to handle over 50,000 converts annually to keep up with the population increase. Faith staggers at such a proposition, and yet winning the Scheduled Castes is only scratching the surface of the job to be done.

Will we insist on clinging to our traditional unfruitful methods while millions who are prepared to respond in belief are left without the message of salvation? Or do we have the courage to say with Carey, "Attempt great things for God and expect great things of God."? The King of Kings and Lord of Lords who gave us the command, "Go ... and disciple all nations," accompanied it with just as overwhelming a promise, that makes possible the completion of the task, when He said, "I have been given all authority in heaven and earth ... and be sure of this-- that I am with you always, even to the end of the world."

APPENDIX

A Brief Comparative Study
of Other Churches in Pakistan

A BRIEF COMPARATIVE STUDY OF OTHER CHURCHES IN PAKISTAN

The following study of other Churches in Pakistan is not
intended to be comprehensive in any respect. The growth
of each Church deserves careful analysis, but only a few
major facts about each are included here. The writer
hopes that the very inadequacy of this treatment of these
Churches and the Missions that founded them will stimulate others to produce a thorough study of each one,
for invaluable lessons can be learned from the past that
can sharpen our vision for the present and the future.
Outstanding men of faith are found among both the national
leaders and missionaries in these Churches. We wish we
could dwell on each one, but the purpose of this study
is to point out major policies and procedures and analyze
their effect upon church growth and development. This
is not done from a desire to criticize the work of others.
One has only to read the records of these forerunners in
Mission to be inspired with deep admiration and profound
respect for their consecrated prayerful service. Historical perspective and the advantage of hindsight, however,
enable us to diagnose faulty policies and unproductive
procedures that should be avoided if our present witness
in Pakistan is to be effective.

Figure 23 is a map showing the comity areas of twelve
of the major denominations in Pakistan. Most of these
work within a limited geographical area. The Anglican
Church, however, has widely scattered stations. The
Roman Catholics, Pentecostals, and Brethren are the
largest communions that do not observe comity boundaries,
and are found throughout the land. The large cities of
Karachi, Lahore, Rawalpindi, Islamabad, Hyderabad, Multan
and Peshawar are not restricted to comity but open to
all Churches.

The Roman Catholic Church is the largest Christian communion in Pakistan, including approximately 40 per cent of the Christian population. The Protestants are divided into many different Churches. We will study those that have had the most significance historically in Pakistan.

THE CHURCH OF PAKISTAN

The largest Protestant Church in Pakistan today is the Church of Pakistan formed in November 1970 from a union of the Anglican Church, the Methodist Church of Pakistan, the Sialkot Church Council and the Pakistan Lutheran Church. Their total Christian community numbers approximately 216,000, with 58,370 communicant members. As this is a recent union and each member Church has a distinct history and character, we will study each Church separately in order of the size of their Christian community.

The Anglican Church

Missions: The Church Missionary Society
            The Australian and New Zealand Church
               Missionary Society
            The Society for the Propagation of
               the Gospel

Anglican work in what is now Pakistan began in Karachi in 1850. The work spread to Peshawar (1854), Multan (1856), Hyderabad (1856), Narowal (1859), Sukkur, (1867), Clarkabad (1873) and Quetta (1886), making it the most widespread of all the Missions, having stations throughout the country.

Efforts Among High Castes (1850-1885)

The first 35 years of mission effort in the Anglican Church are characterized by (1) urban evangelism with stress on the distribution of gospel portions; and (2) a strong emphasis upon Christian institutions. Schools

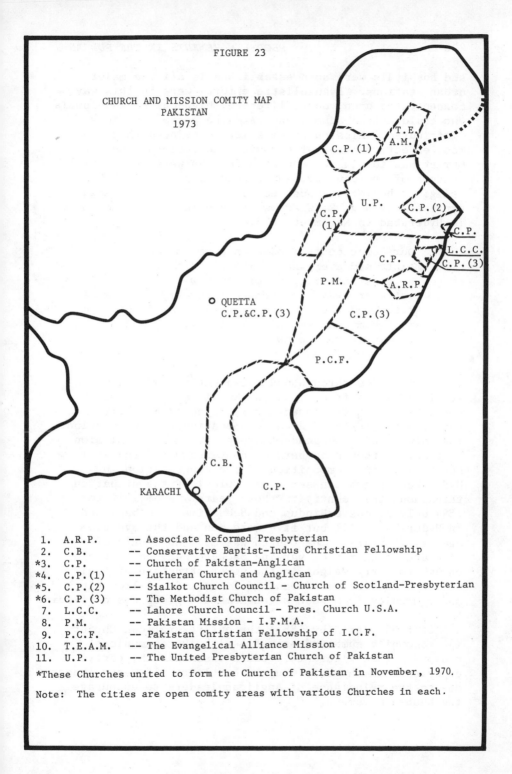

FIGURE 23

CHURCH AND MISSION COMITY MAP
PAKISTAN
1973

T.E
A.M.

C.P.(1)

U.P.

C.P.(2)

C.P.
(1)

C.P.

L.C.C.

C.P.(3)

C.P.

P.M.

A.R.P.

○ QUETTA
C.P.&C.P.(3)

C.P.(3)

P.C.F.

C.B.

KARACHI ○

C.P.

1.	A.R.P.	-- Associate Reformed Presbyterian
2.	C.B.	-- Conservative Baptist-Indus Christian Fellowship
*3.	C.P.	-- Church of Pakistan-Anglican
*4.	C.P.(1)	-- Lutheran Church and Anglican
*5.	C.P.(2)	-- Sialkot Church Council - Church of Scotland-Presbyterian
*6.	C.P.(3)	-- The Methodist Church of Pakistan
7.	L.C.C.	-- Lahore Church Council - Pres. Church U.S.A.
8.	P.M.	-- Pakistan Mission - I.F.M.A.
9.	P.C.F.	-- Pakistan Christian Fellowship of I.C.F.
10.	T.E.A.M.	-- The Evangelical Alliance Mission
11.	U.P.	-- The United Presbyterian Church of Pakistan

*These Churches united to form the Church of Pakistan in November, 1970.

Note: The cities are open comity areas with various Churches in each.

and hospitals were soon established in all the major
urban stations. Evangelistic efforts were in this way
concentrated upon young, literate, high-caste individuals
who could attend school and read the gospel portions
distributed. Mission leaders were convinced that the
most effective means of bringing the whole of India to
Christ was to win the educated few who were the natural
leaders of the country, and to undermine their old
religious beliefs through education. This is clearly
expressed by Rev. R. Clark who wrote in the CMS Log Book
in Hyderabad in November 1883:

> "Our large central mission schools must be
> maintained everywhere with efficiency.
> The constant dripping of Truth will at
> last wear away the stones of bigotry and
> error, and the whole structure of Hinduism
> and Mohammadanism will ultimately, in God's
> own time, crumble away." (under the date
> Nov. 16-20, 1883)

Missionaries through dedicated patient effort won a
few individuals from among the Muslim and caste Hindu
populations. Most converts were rejected by their
families and suffered great dislocation and persecution.
They clustered in dependent groups around each mission
station. Although numbers of converts were greater in
the Punjab, the composition of the congregation in
Hyderabad, Sindh can serve as typical of the situation
throughout the country in those years. From 1875 to
1894 only 12 caste Hindus and 8 Muslims were baptized
in Hyderabad. All but five were men and the average
age was 25 years. The Church was made up mostly of
literate young men of varying backgrounds, not yet old
enough to carry weight in the power structure of their
society. To create a meaningful Christian fellowship
and community from such a conglomerate group was difficult.

After 35 years (by 1885) the entire Anglican Christian community numbered only 511 with 196 communicant
members. (See Figure 24.) This resembles the early
experience of the U.P. Church, but lasted 15 years longer,
due to the reluctance of Anglican leaders to encourage
the Chuhra movement.

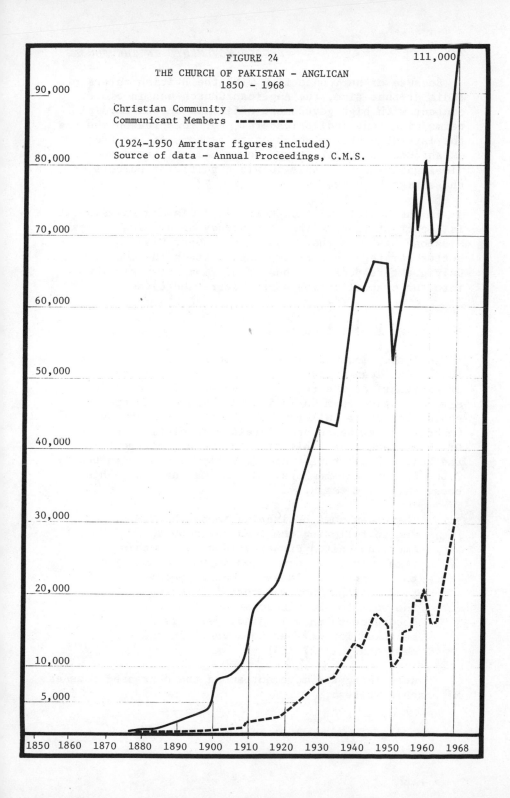

FIGURE 24
THE CHURCH OF PAKISTAN - ANGLICAN
1850 - 1968

Christian Community ———————
Communicant Members ----------

(1924-1950 Amritsar figures included)
Source of data - Annual Proceedings, C.M.S.

111,000

Because of her connection with the British rulers of
India at that time, the Anglican Church was in close
contact with high government officials and on cordial
terms with many Indian leaders. For this reason she has
the largest number of high-caste members of any Protestant Church in Pakistan. Nevertheless, Anglican
missionaries were unable to win significant numbers of
these high born people.

In the history of the Church in India and Pakistan it
is important to note that the steady assumption of most
Missions has been that winning the upper classes is
better strategy than attempting to reach the lower.
Only great response has pushed Mission after Mission
into the evangelization of the depressed classes.

The Chuhra Movement Begins

The group movement among the Chuhras did not begin
in the Anglican Church until 1885 when Dr. Wietbrecht
of Amritsar, at the request of several Chuhra leaders,
agreed to give them Christian teaching and to open a
school for their children. In October of 1885 fourteen
Chuhras in Fatehgarh near Batala were baptized by
Dr. Wietbrecht. By this time the Chuhra movement in
the United Presbyterian area was flourishing with nearly
2,000 communicant members. Mr. R. Maconachie in his
book, *Rowland Bateman,* says:

> There was some hesitation among the C.M.S.
> men in following the lead given by the
> American United Presbyterians who by this
> time were fully committed to work among
> the "depressed classes"; but it became
> realized that God was certainly bringing
> the work to all missionaries, and in
> obedience to this leading, measures must
> be taken for deliberate advance in the
> new path. (1917:101)

In describing the movement among the depressed classes
Maconachie writes:

> ... the most important feature of Punjab
> church history ... (has been) ... the
> gradual drawing of the outcaste classes
> to Christianity ... There were considerable
> searchings of heart among those who led
> missionary policy as to whether it could
> wisely be encouraged or not. We had to
> learn that a movement, assuredly social in
> some degree as to its motive, might through
> the operation of the Holy Ghost prove to
> be earnestly religious also in its develop-
> ment. (1917:99,16)

In 1886 the Church Council made the decision that the
Chuhras would be received into the Church without dis-
tinction, but that they should abstain from eating
carrion and the leavings of others, and should not marry
non-Christian Chuhras. This last requirement was impractical at this stage, for the Chuhra Christian
community was not yet large enough to provide an adequate
scope for making marriage arrangements. It probably was
not strictly enforced.

Some argued that baptizing Chuhras would prevent the
higher castes from responding, but Maconachie states:

> ... on the contrary, the spectacle of the
> changes, physical, intellectual, and moral,
> wrought by conversion to Christianity among
> the "pariahs" has in many places stimulated
> religious inquiry among "caste" neighbors.
> (1917:100-101)

A problem arose over comity boundaries with the U.P.
Mission in the area of Narowal. This was settled after
considerable controversy by transferring a large number
of Chuhra Christians from the U.P. Church to the
Anglican, thereby catapaulting the Anglican Church into
Chuhra work almost against her wishes. The report of
this given in the 1889-1890 Annual Proceedings states:

> A large number of Christians, about 1,150,
> found in seventy-five villages, have been
> transferred to the care of the Society by

the missionaries of the U.P.'s as they
belong to the district of Narowal. Mr.
Bateman has found the charge of these
uninstructed converts a very heavy one.
Fourteen schools are included in the
transfer. (122)

Commenting on these newly-acquired Christians and
what he describes as "indiscriminant baptism," he writes:

When we received these people, together
with a certificate of their baptism,
there were not five in a hundred of
them who knew anything distinctively
Christian, though several hundreds of
them were registered as communicants.
Many would tell you that they had
become Christians *"mukti de waste"*
(to obtain salvation), but if you asked
them what *"mukti"* (salvation) meant,
they could give you no answer at all.
(Annual Proceedings 1889-1890:121)

Eugene Stock, the famous Anglican historian, commenting
on this transfer says:

Why had such people professed to become
Christians at all? Simply because to
them it was a rise in the social scale.
Despised as the Christians were by
the Hindus and Mohammadans, the Chuhras
as such were still more despised ...
Even the catechists who were transferred proved to be useless or worse,
and every one of them had to be dis-
charged. (Vol. III 1899:495)

It is interesting to see Eugene Stock taken in by
this common missiological error. The supposition that
the highly subsidized, paternalistic, hot-house care,
which a Mission can give to a few one-by-one converts
who dribble into a well staffed mission station, is
normal and healthy, is one of the most pernicious and
damaging errors.

The U.P.'s, faced with the practical problem of providing follow-up teaching for thousands of converts,
hired poorly trained catechists on the theory that the
little they could teach was better than nothing. The
Anglicans had not yet faced the problem of shepherding
great numbers with inadequate personnel, for they had
not yet fully entered into the Chuhra movement. They
maintained a high standard of education and training
for their catechists and were appalled at the quality
of Chuhra leaders acquired from the U.P.'s. Even by
1920 there were only 24 Indian pastors serving the
Anglican Church in all of the area now included in
Pakistan. The only other Church officers mentioned are
279 "lay agents"--probably corresponding to "elders"
in the U.P. Church. This lack of personnel greatly
hindered them from taking full advantage of the responsive spirit among the Chuhras. This is brought out by
Rev. W.P. Hares in his report to the C.M.S. Mission in
1910:

> Many more persons would have been baptized
> had there been a larger staff of workers,
> but the size of some of the districts,
> coupled with the widespread nature of the
> movement toward Christianity, made it
> impossible to examine all who had been
> prepared by the village teachers for
> baptism. (*CMS Annual Proceedings* 1910-
> 1911:144)

The Anglicans did not expect such numbers and were
distraught when they received them. Most mission effort
is geared to slow growth. When a fast growing movement
takes place, it is suspect and not wanted, as it upsets
the customary way of discipling converts.

Could Missions in Pakistan gear for one million
converts a year? To win Pakistan in the conceivable
future, more than a million baptisms would have to be
performed each year. We find it difficult to think in
terms like that!

Strict Requirements

The Anglicans maintained strict standards for
baptism and communicant membership. Baptism was administered only after catechists had given the people
extensive teaching. Rev. W.P. Hares tells of the procedure followed in 1910:

> Every adult before baptism has two, three
> or four personal interviews with the
> missionary who examines him as to his
> knowledge of the fundamentals of Christ-
> ianity. (*CMS Annual Proceedings* 1910-
> 1911:144)

The Anglicans were also cautious about making baptized
believers into full communicant members. Although 1,150
baptized Christians had been received from the U.P.
Church, there was no substantial rise in communicants
recorded at Narowal. In 1889 Narowal listed 32 communicants; in 1893 there were 73; in 1900 the number had
dropped to 50; and by 1913 the Christian community in
Narowal district consisted of 1,986 adults in training
for baptism, 3,784 baptized members, and only 223
communicant members. (See Figure 24 and note the wide
disparity that has continued to exist between the number
of Christian community and the number of communicant
members.) These figures reveal the rigid standards they
had for both baptism and communicant membership. In this
way they kept large numbers of people on the fringes of
the Church, denied the privileges of full membership.
One cannot help but wonder if this is not a case when
"we magnify His strictness with a zeal He would not own."

The following passage from the *CMS Annual Proceedings*
of 1913-1914 reveals an awareness of the danger of having
too rigid requirements for baptism:

> The danger seems two-fold. It arises
> from haste and its opposite, delay.
> Haste will give us an ignorant, ill-
> taught Church, unable to read the
> Bible, only half weaned from idolatry,
> a prey to superstition, and a real

> stumbling block to future progress among
> the caste people. On the other hand the
> fact that thousands more than the various
> Missions could account for enrolled them-
> selves as Christians in the census of
> 1911, shows that there is a passion behind
> the movement which it is beyond the power
> of the Missions to check. Delay is there-
> fore even more dangerous than haste, for
> it means not ill-taught, but absolutely
> untaught, and merely self-styled Christ-
> ians, and delay spells opportunity for
> the Arya Samaj and the Mohammadans. (110)

The Chuhras were so eager to align themselves with
Christianity, they were declaring themselves Christians
even without teaching or baptism. In 1911 the Anglicans
had a Christian community of 16,191 in the Punjab alone,
but in the Punjab Census Report for that year 22,924
declared themselves to be Anglicans, a difference of
6,733. The Church was forced to think and plan in terms
of greater numbers and speed than it had done up to
this time.

In 1972 a similar situation developed in Kenya and is
reported in the *Kenya Churches Handbook* edited by the
Anglican missionary David Barrett. In government
statistics an extra 1,260,000 people professed to be
Roman Catholics, and 185,000 to be Anglicans who are
unknown to those Churches and not on their rolls. Why?
The *Kenya Churches Handbook* says:

> The explanation arises directly from the
> fact that both the Catholic Church and
> the other Western churches in Kenya are
> still expanding at the phenomenal rate of
> 5 per cent per year.... But as with most
> Western churches in Africa, the Catholic
> Church requires of its converts a long
> period under instruction in the catechu-
> menate, varying from one to four years;
> with similar figures for the Anglicans ...
> In practice ... the average intending
> Christian, whether Catholic or Protestant,
> takes between five to ten years to reach

> the point of baptism... The fact that it
> may take them up to ten years before
> baptism is probably less their fault
> than that of the churches, whose ponderous
> machinery of initiation cannot let in
> fast enough those who ask for instruction
> and baptism.   (1973:175)

What a tragedy that ecclesiastical red tape is responsible
for keeping thousands and even millions outside of the
Church who are eager to be included!

Migrations

In the 1890's missionaries and pastors followed the
migrations of Christians to the new canal colonies.
Clarkabad was started as a colony of Christians near
Lahore in 1868, and the Christian villages of Montgomery-
wala and Isa Nagri (Batemanabad) were opened in the new
canal area of Jhang. In 1900 Rev. Rowland Bateman
writes concerning the Christians in these new settlements:

> Nearly half of these Christians are from
> the neighborhood of Narowal; many of
> them have been baptized by the U.P.
> missionaries and know hardly anything,
> but are willing and eager to be taught ...
> there are about 1700. (*CMS Annual
> Proceedings* 1889-1890:116)

In this passage Bateman points out one great value of
baptizing people upon simple confession of faith even
without much knowledge of Christian truth, for taking this
step eliminates their prejudice against Christianity and
makes them eager to learn what they can about their new
faith.

The Chuhras continued to migrate until by 1930
there were Chuhra congregations in all the major cities
under the care of the Anglicans. The movement reached
its height from 1905 to 1930, but growth continued after
that at a slower rate. Since World War II the Anglicans

have had to retrench due to lack of funds. They have
turned over various less productive areas to new Missions
that have come into Pakistan since Partition.

Many outstanding leaders have emerged from the ranks
of the Anglican Church through the years. Bishop Chandu
Ray became their first Pakistani bishop in 1963, followed
by Bishop Inayat in 1968. The strongly autocratic nature
of their church government has given stability to the
Church, so that they lost only a few pastors and congregations to the McIntire schism. However, it has hindered
the development of responsible trained laymen. Local
congregations lack the vital leadership seen among the
U.P. elders.

At the time of merger into the Church of Pakistan in
1970, the Christian community of the Anglican Church
numbered approximately 111,000 while her communicant
membership totalled 30,000.

Scheduled Caste Movements

The Anglican Church in the province of Sindh has in
recent years contacted pockets of responsive people from
several of the Scheduled Castes. Figure 25 shows when
baptisms have taken place through the years in the seven
tribes that have yielded the most converts. This chart
evidences both their winnability, and the erratic way
in which they have been evangelized. In spite of these
spasmodic and limited evangelistic efforts among them,
the Scheduled Castes have proved to be the most responsive segment of society in Pakistan today. There have
been a number of baptisms in the following groups:

The Meghwars. In 1925 in Jhimpur near Karachi three
Meghwar men were baptized. A small school and church
were built for them in Mirpur Batoro. Evangelist Hira
Lal worked among them until his death in the 1940's.
Baptisms were performed from time to time until 1947,
totalling 176 people. At the death of Evangelist Hira
Lal the work was interrupted, and only a handful of
Meghwar Christians can be found today. Two or three
have been baptized in recent years.

The Bajanias. From 1939 to 1941 Christ Church, Karachi,
under the leadership of Rev. C. Haskell and Miss Langdale-
Smith, conducted an evangelistic outreach among the
Bajanias or minstrel caste. Evangelist Kara was employed
to work among them and 516 were baptized. Rev. Haskell
was then transferred, the Arya Samaj reform Hindu movement exerted pressure on the group, and finally at
Partition in 1947 many migrated to India. No Christian
from this tribe has been found in Sindh in recent years.

The Vagaris. Christ Church, Karachi, also spearheaded
the outreach to Vagaris living in the Chenesar area
north of Karachi. There were intermittent baptisms from
1937 to 1957, with a total of 126. Again, lack of
follow-up teaching prevented this movement from developing.
For years no work was done among them. Then in 1973
contact was renewed and promises to prove fruitful.

The Kutchi Kohlis. The Bajania leader, Kara, visited a
group of Kutchi Kohlis in 1942 in his profession as a
minstrel. After exhausting his usual repertoire of
ballads and songs, he sang some Christian hymns. This
attracted the interest of the headman of the village,
Bejal, who demanded to know the meaning of these new
songs. Bejal had repudiated idolatry some time previous
to this, and found a message in those Christian hymns
that filled the empty place in his heart. He walked with
Kara the 25 miles to Matli to receive more teaching,
and to ask someone to come to their village to prepare
them for baptism. After some months of teaching, the
great day came when they were ready for baptism. Mr.
Kenneth Gregory gives this revealing account of their
baptismal service in his book, *Stretching Out Continually:*

> Mr. Carson, who had suffered much from
> nominal Christians, indicated that he
> could only baptise the adults, while the
> young children should wait till they
> could understand. There was an immediate
> reaction, "We could not bear to be
> separated from them, if we became Christ-
> ians, and they remained Hindus. If you

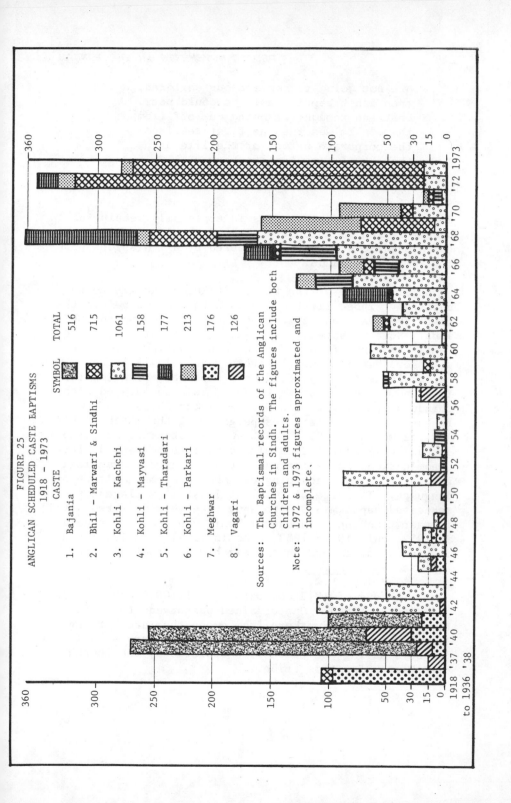

FIGURE 25
ANGLICAN SCHEDULED CASTE EAPTISMS
1918 – 1973

	CASTE	SYMBOL	TOTAL
1.	Bajania		516
2.	Bhil – Marwari & Sindhi		715
3.	Kohli – Kachchi		1061
4.	Kohli – Mayvasi		158
5.	Kohli – Tharadari		177
6.	Kohli – Parkari		213
7.	Meghwar		176
8.	Vagari		126

Sources: The Baptismal records of the Anglican
Churches in Sindh. The figures include both
children and adults.

Note: 1972 & 1973 figures approximated and
incomplete.

are not going to baptise our children,
then don't baptise us! We could not
bear the thought of being cut off from
them." It was then he first realized
the corporate nature of the life and
thought of many Eastern, especially
tribal people. So he obliged! (1972:
110)

Baptizing whole family units is especially meaningful to
people living in a society with a cohesive family structure,
and should be seriously considered by all Missions working in Eastern lands.

Bejal was one of the first 110 Kutchi Kohlis to be
baptized. Those first converts were brought before the
caste tribunal and severely censured for becoming Christians. Some recanted, but Bejal and most of his extended
family remained firm. The movement continued to grow
with some baptisms nearly every year. In 1951 the
second largest group of 75 were baptized, bringing the
total number of baptisms to 294. This encouraged Bishop
Chandu Ray to invite the West Pakistan Christian Council
to have an evangelistic campaign among the Kutchi Kohlis
for one month in 1952. Eighteen Pakistani workers (mostly Punjabis) and sixteen missionaries from many different
denominations participated in the campaign. Practically
none of them knew anything of Kohli customs, culture or
language. In spite of this, at least 14 villages
requested baptism. Sad to say, they were deferred until
further teaching. No Kutchi Kohli baptisms are recorded
in 1952; only 19 in 1953; none in 1954; 9 in 1955; and
it wasn't until 1958 that a sizable group of 51 were
baptized--six years later!

By the end of 1973 approximately 1,100 Kutchi Kohlis
had been baptized. One ordained pastor and three full-
time evangelistic workers from among them are working
to win their own people. One village primary school
for boys having one teacher is operated by the Church
of Pakistan for this tribe.

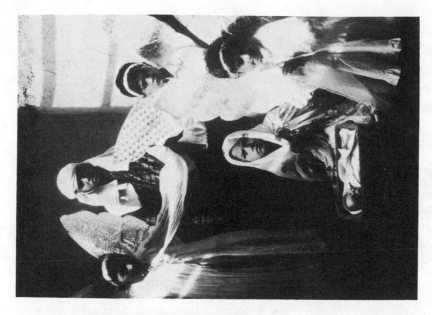

Kohli School Boys Enact the Birth
of Jesus for the First Time

Stringed Instrument Used by the
Scheduled Castes for Worship

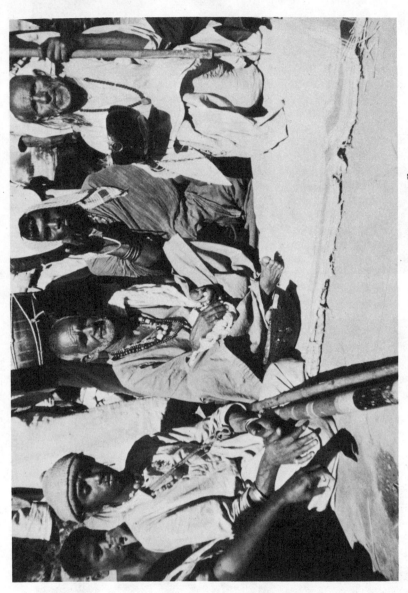

Non-Christian Fakirs or "Holy Men"

The Mayvasi Kohlis. The first three Mayvasi Kohli baptisms took place in 1952 in the Mirpur Khas district. From 1965 to 1968 when the Rev. Joseph Memmon worked full-time in tribal evangelism, significant growth took place. The total number of baptized believers by December 1973 was approximately 160. One evangelist is now employed to work among them, but due to ill health, he cannot work full time and progress is slow.

The Bhils. The first Bhil was baptized in 1918, but no movement started at that time. In 1959 four Dhatki speaking Bhils were baptized in Mirpur Khas. Then from 1968 to 1969 a group of 64 Sindhi speaking Bhils were baptized in the Badin area. In 1971 an influential man of the Dhatki speaking Bhils had cataracts removed at the Christian Caravan Hospital near Mirpur Khas. He heard the Gospel, believed, and returning home convinced his seven sons and other relatives to embrace Christianity. After receiving further teaching from the Bhil evangelist, 200 were baptized in May 1972 followed by another 100 in November. In 1973 an additional 400 were baptized in the same district, bringing the total of Bhil believers in the C.M.S. area to approximately 800. Three Bhil evangelists are employed by the Church of Pakistan to work among this responsive group.

The Parkari Kohlis. In 1898 the catechist, Laxman Hari, was sent to Tando Mohammed Khan to work among the 10 Kohlis (probably Parkari Kohlis) enrolled as catechumens. The following year a school was opened there in a further attempt to reach the Kohlis. However, there is no record of any baptisms among them until 1962 when twelve Parkari Kohlis were baptized in the Badin area. Although Roman Catholics are concentrating especially upon this tribe, there have been approximately 250 Protestant (Anglican) baptisms. Two full-time evangelists from the tribe work among them.

The Tharadari Kohlis. In 1964 there were 40 baptisms among the Tharadari Kohlis in the Mirpur Khas-Umerkot area. Four years later 96 more took place. At present

there are approximately 177 baptized believers, but no
evangelist to work among this responsive tribe.

Summary. From these brief reviews of evangelistic work
among the Scheduled Castes in Sindh, it is evident that
since 1900 many group movements to Christ have been
possible. Some have begun and died out completely.
Some have been arrested before they had a chance to
develop. Others have steadily grown in spite of receiving minimal attention over the years, but have not borne
the abundant harvest they promise to produce. All have
been neglected because of missionary involvement in less
productive areas of service and the persistent theory
that work among the low castes is not as strategic as
efforts among the high-born.

   Bishop Chandu Ray while in office in Karachi did
much to spark interest in tribal evangelism and to provide workers for it. In the last couple of years Bishop
A. Rudwin has given the work new impetus by taking
definite steps to give it greater priority. In 1972 he
appointed the Rev. Bashir Jiwan as Rural Dean for Hyderabad district with special responsibility for encouraging
evangelism among the Scheduled Castes. He has requested
new missionaries for this work and provided for the
training and employment of seven new catechists from
among the tribes, each to work with his own caste group.
In this way a foundation is being laid for greater growth
in the future. God is again giving the Church an oppor-
unity to disciple these responsive castes.

The Methodist Church of Pakistan

*Mission: The United Methodist Church of the
           U.S.A. (formerly the Methodist
           Episcopal Church)*

   Methodist missionary work was established in Karachi
in 1873, in Quetta in 1874, and in Lahore in 1880 as a
ministry to English speaking communities of Anglo-

Indians and Non-conformist British army and civil
personnel. This aspect of the work continued until 1900
when it was turned over to the British Wesleyan Methodist
Church.

In the meantime, the Chuhra movement had gained
recognition as a bonafide work of God. The Methodist
Bishop, Thoburn, in 1896 heartily endorsed the group
conversion method and urged the Methodist Church to
concentrate their efforts on the Chuhras. This is
reported by Copplestone in his book, *Twentieth-Century
Perspectives,* as follows:

> ... Thoburn and his mass-movement leaders
> were actively capitalizing, in 1896, upon
> a discovery ... that transformed the
> apparent obstacle of caste into an advantage
> frequently embarrassing in its opportunities.
> They had found that to convert a family
> rather than an individual could readily
> start a chain reaction of conversions ...
> The impulse to move towards Christianity
> could be transmitted from one family to
> another within that group. ... Since
> there were no artificial barriers within
> the caste group, sometimes an entire local
> caste group would enter the Christian
> community by virtue of a group decision.
> This pattern of "mass" conversion conserved
> the immediate social relationships of the
> individual convert, and by utilizing them
> as lines of infiltration within the caste
> walls, the missionaries often immensely
> speeded up the evangelizing process. (1973:
> 788-789)

Freed from responsibility for the English speaking
congregations in 1900, Methodist missionaries threw
themselves whole heartedly into Chuhra evangelism. They
believed in immediate on-the-spot baptism as soon as
confession of faith was made. This is better than too
much delay, but can result in only a superficial

commitment based on the impulse of the moment, rather
than a carefully weighed decision made after consultation
with the family and clan. A Methodist missionary, Rev.
Thomas, wrote concerning their policy and the reasons
for it as follows:

> ... when the work is well begun in one or
> two places, about all the workers need to
> do is to respond to invitations (to go and
> baptize) and they will soon find that they
> have more work than they can possibly look
> after ... I know some think our work is
> "kucha" [not well done] and that we go too
> fast, but ... looking at it from my point
> of view, golden opportunities are being
> neglected and millions of souls are going
> to destruction which might be saved if there
> was not quite so much theorizing and if all
> would step out boldly on the promises of
> God and trust Him to save those who are so
> willing to accept Christ and be baptized
> in His name. The King's business demands
> haste and I believe it is God's will that
> these people should speedily be brought
> into the light. (Reports and Letters to
> the Board of Foreign Missions of the
> Presbyterian Church U.S.A. Vol. 164-32,
> 1906:3,4)

For this reason the Church grew from a community of
1200 in 1902 to 15,000 by 1915. (See Figure 26.) When
it became the Indus River Conference in November 1924,
it numbered over 40,000 in its Christian community.
(The figures up to this point include the statistics for
the eastern portion of the Punjab that is now part of
India.)

In 1927 the Arya Samaj pressured Christian Chuhras
in the Lahore area to join them, and in 1930 Sikh
persecution was severe. Only a few families recanted
in spite of inadequate pastoral care due to lack of
workers and an emphasis on becoming self-supporting
Unfortunately the Church never did achieve a fully self-
supporting ministry.

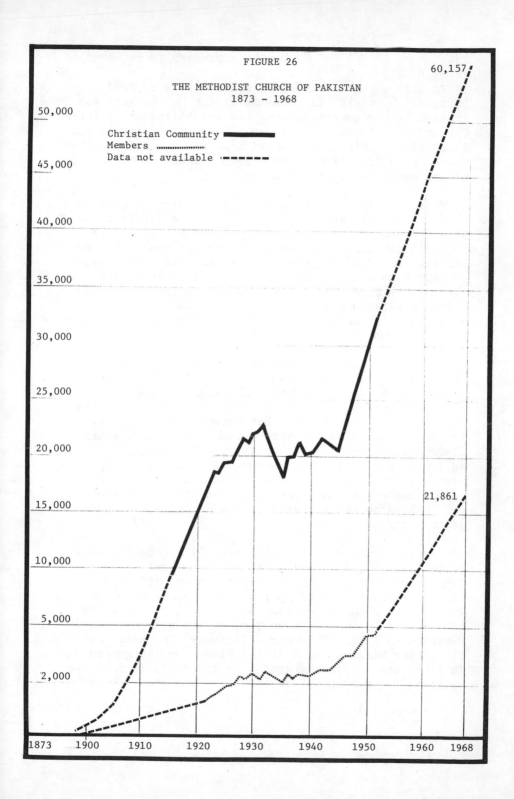

FIGURE 26

THE METHODIST CHURCH OF PAKISTAN
1873 - 1968

Christian Community
Members
Data not available

60,157

21,861

In 1930 a plot of about 25 square miles of land irrigated by newly built canals in the Multan area was granted by the government for the establishment of four Christian villages. Since Rev. Stuntz was instrumental in obtaining this land, one village was named Stuntzabad. These Christian villages have been the source of many of the Methodist Church leaders today.

Partition in 1947 cut the Methodist Mission area in two, with the larger portion in India. A fairly large Christian community migrated from the Methodist area to India to join relatives there and perhaps to follow the Sikh and Hindu landlords they had served for many years. Some went by train and a party of about 400 crossed the border near Bahawalnagar on foot. This is the only sizable migration of Christians to India at Partition that we have discovered in the records of any of the Churches.

At the same time a large group of *Mazhabi* Sikhs of Chuhra background, left behind by the outgoing Sikh community, besieged the Mission asking for baptism. They were motivated largely by a desire for safety from the anti-Sikh and Hindu riots that took place that year. The Mission refused to baptize them under those emergency circumstances, but gave them instruction, and the following year, in 1948, they baptized 2,500 non-Christians. It is significant that these people chose to become members of the tiny Christian minority rather than taking on the religion of the majority community at that time.

Institutional work was not strongly stressed in the early days of the Methodist Mission, but gradually gained importance as the Chuhra movement tapered off. The Mission operated several primary and secondary schools, including the Lucie Harrison High School for Girls in Lahore. These were nationalized by the government of Pakistan in 1972. They ran a Teachers' Training Institute for men in Raiwind until it was closed by the government in 1965, and they cooperated with other Missions in two colleges and a hospital in Lahore.

By the time of Partition all the Chuhras in the Methodist area were either won to Christ or had joined some other faith. The majority community proving resistant, evangelistic outreach waned, and increasing emphasis was placed on education and building up the Church. The Methodists have operated on the same basic assumptions that have motivated most Missions in recent years. They believe that (1) the indigenous Church is the most effective agency for evangelism in a Muslim land; (2) The Church can be effective only if spiritually revived and thoroughly educated; and (3) Missionary effort should therefore be concentrated on literacy for adults, schools from primary level to professional training, and means for deepening the spiritual life of nominal Christians in the Church. These are worthy goals, and have been realized to some extent in that the Church has many educated, Bible reading, spiritually minded members. But as we have already demonstrated in the study of the U.P. Church, these goals are based on false assumptions; therefore have not borne the hoped-for fruit of a revived growing Church, able to win many non-Christians to Christ. The steep angle of the line in Figure 26 from 1950 to 1968 gives the impression that the Methodist Church is growing rapidly. This is deceiving and should be compared with Figure 40, a semi-logarithmic graph that shows the rate of growth in comparison with population growth. This reveals that the rate of increase in the Methodist Church since 1950 is not quite equal to that of the population as a whole. Therefore the rise in Figure 26 must be due almost entirely to biological growth.

At the time of the merger to form the Church of Pakistan in 1970, the Methodist Christian community totaled 60,157, with 21,861 communicant members, 87 ordained pastors, and 112 unordained evangelists. (See Figure 26.)

The Sialkot Church Council

Mission: The Church of Scotland (Presbyterian)

Rev. & Mrs. Thomas Hunter were sent by the Church of Scotland to found a mission among the Sikhs. They arrived in Sialkot early in 1857 after a few months of

service in Bombay. On July 9th, 1857, during the Sepoy
Mutiny they were murdered as they were fleeing their
home for the shelter of the fort at Sialkot. This
tragic loss delayed the witness of the Church of Scotland
until two couples were sent to Sialkot in 1860.

The Mission followed the same pattern of evangelism
used by the U.P. Church in the early days. Urdu
messages were preached in the bazaar, Christian literature
translated and distributed, and schools opened for non-
Christians. They aimed for individual, one-by-one
decisions, using methods that won a few literate, urban
men from the upper castes, extracted from their family
and society. This faced the Mission with the perplexing
problem of providing homes, jobs, wives, and a worshipping
fellowship for converts from a conglomeration of backgrounds.

Soon the work centered upon institutions. As early
as 1869 when they had only 41 communicant members in
the Church, they were committed to 7 boys' schools,
3 girls' schools, and two orphanages. By 1885 there
were 170 baptized Christians, 10 Indian catechists and
10 schools with a total of 1,610 students, but only
two missionary families to supervise it all, the
Youngsons and McCheyne Pattersons. Evangelistic work
inevitably took second place.

The Chuhra Movement

The Church of Scotland was slow to become involved
in the Chuhra group movement. It was not until 1885 that
they baptized their first group of five men. These men had
been contacted some months previously in their village
of Amoutrah. They were inclined toward Christianity
from the first because they had Christian relatives in
another part of the district, probably U.P.'s. Dr.
Youngson made the original contact and then sent his
catechist, Natthu Mall, several times to give them
further teaching. Five of the men one day walked 14
miles to Sialkot to be baptized.

It is evident that the Church of Scotland lacked understanding of group movements and their potential for evangelism, otherwise they would have cordially welcomed this movement much earlier. The first baptisms in their Church took place twelve years after the beginning of the Chuhra work in the U.P. Church, in spite of the fact that both Missions had their headquarters in Sialkot where Ditt was baptized in 1873. By this time the U.P. Church had over 2,100 communicant members, mostly Chuhras.

There is no indication in the records that the missionaries of the Church of Scotland actively opposed the inclusion of Chuhras into the Church as some other Missions did. Probably they were so busy looking after their institutions and so confident that the school approach to the high caste was right, that they simply did not take time to pursue the open door of opportunity in Chuhra evangelism. They didn't feel it was particularly strategic. Living in close proximity to the growing movement among the U.P.'s they gradually became convinced of its worth so that once the movement got started in their area in 1885, it made rapid progress. By 1890 the total number of baptized Christians had jumped to 2,132; by 1895 it was 3,883; and the next decade brought the number up to 5,277 by 1905. (See Figure 27.) Dr. Youngson took great interest in the Chuhras and made a detailed study of them and their religion that was later published.

The Church of Scotland was responsible for the area north of Sialkot toward Jammu and Chamba. Although these mountainous regions made up the largest geographical portion of their mission area, the great majority of their church members eventually came from Sialkot where the movement among the Chuhras was concentrated. Both Sialkot and Gujrat district had many Chuhras, but the ones around Sialkot were more responsive. Most of the Chuhras in Gujrat district had already become *Musallis*, the name given to Chuhras who adopted the Muslim faith. The *Census Report* for 1911 shows only 1,197 Chuhras listed as Hindus in the Gujrat area, while 33,674 were *Musallis*. The Census Report states that only 463 in Gujrat were Christians, in contrast to the 46,267 in Sialkot district.

In 1886, the year following the baptism of the first Chuhras, the Church of Scotland opened nine village primary schools to educate the children of Chuhras who up to this time had been barred from attending school. The Boys' Boarding School at Daska was opened in July, 1886, to give higher training to the most promising students from the villages. That same year a training school for catechists and lay-readers was opened in anticipation of the need for a large increase in village evangelists. Village schools continued to multiply as the movement grew. Out of Sialkot City High School, established in 1889 primarily for non-Christians, grew Murray College, founded in 1909. Christians number less than ten per cent of the student body of the college, for few are able to obtain a college degree. Nevertheless, mission schools continued to play an important role in training Christian leaders until they were nationalized by the government of Pakistan in 1972.

The Church Strengthened

McCheyne Patterson was one of the founders of the Sialkot Convention, along with John "Praying" Hyde of the American Presbyterian Mission. These two men spent days in prayer prior to the Convention of 1904 at which time revival came to many denominations in the Punjab. The Church of Scotland, centered right in Sialkot, was especially blessed by the revival years from 1904 to 1910. By the end of that time her baptized Christian community totaled approximately 8,000.

Near the turn of the century a hospital was opened for women at Gujrat and one for men at Jalalpur Jattan. God has used these to spark several conversions from among non-Christians. A canal colony in Sheikhupura District was granted to the Christians connected with the Church of Scotland in 1900. The village established was called Youngsonabad and has produced many leaders.

In 1904 the Punjab Mission of the Church of Scotland joined with other Presbyterian Churches of India to become the Union Presbyterian Church of India. Dr. Youngson was the first moderator. Twenty years later,

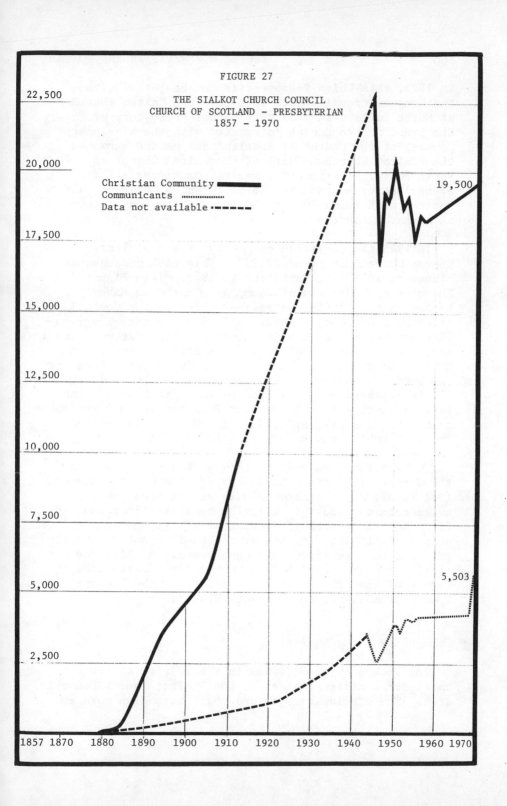

FIGURE 27

THE SIALKOT CHURCH COUNCIL
CHURCH OF SCOTLAND - PRESBYTERIAN
1857 - 1970

in 1924, this Union Presbyterian Church joined with
the Congregational Church to become the United Church
of North India. In 1953 the Sialkot Presbytery of
the Synod of the Punjab integrated with the Missionary
Council of the Church of Scotland and became known as
the Sialkot Church Council of the United Church of
North India. Its function was to administer all the
evangelistic, educational (except Murray College), and
medical work formerly done by the Mission, and to act
as a church court.

In 1946 the Christian community of the Sialkot
Church Council numbered 22,970. This took a downward
plunge to 16,277 at Partition in 1947. (See Figure 27)
The mission districts of Jammu and Chamba in Kashmir
became part of India, entailing a loss to the Council
of about 2,000 Christians. In 1948 the entire congregation of twenty families in Bhimber in Azad Kashmir were
massacred by Pathan raiders. In addition, Christians
have migrated from Sialkot District in large numbers for
the border areas have been torn by war and ravaged by
floods repeatedly. Many fled to India at Partition; more
have moved to cities throughout Pakistan to seek employment. For example, by 1955 over 700 from the Sialkot
Church Council area had settled in Karachi.

The gap that has existed through the years between
the number of baptized believers and communicant members
(See Figure 27) indicates unduly strict membership requirements or laxity in bringing believers from the
first important step of baptism to the second crucial
step of full participation at the Lord's table. Happily
this has been remedied in recent years. By 1974 the
total community of 17,500, a very healthy ratio, the
result of special efforts on the part of the present
Bishop of Sialkot, the Rt. Rev. W.G. Young.

Evangelism Among Muslims

The Chuhra movement waned in the 1930's, as few
unaligned Chuhras remained in the Sialkot Church Council
area. The missionaries turned their attention more and

more to Muslim evangelism. During World War II and two
or three years following Partition, few Muslims were won.
The Christians were afraid to carry on an active witness
as they were unsure of their status in the new Muslim
state. The Constitution of the newly formed country of
Pakistan guaranteed all religions the right to practice
and to propagate their faith. This was immensely reassuring to the Christians and enabled them to witness
more boldly.

A combination of factors produced a decade of unusual
response among Muslims from 1954 to 1964. Severe
riots between two Muslim sects, the Ahmadiyyas and the
Sunnis, caused great consternation and disillusionment
in the majority community. Part of that period was
characterized by instability in the government and
political upheaval. Several times disastrous floods
devastated the Sialkot area. These all contributed to
making Muslims more receptive to the Gospel. One missionary in Sialkot recorded the baptisms of fifty-three Muslim
converts during that period. Thirty-five of these were
men, mostly young, urban, and educated; nine were women
and nine children. As usual they were ostracized from
their families and dependent for their support until
they could obtain jobs. The Christian community set up
a fund for the care of converts, and took part in the
evangelistic effort in this way. Barkat Khan, a teacher
in the Sialkot Boys' High School, became deeply interested in Muslim evangelism and is still active in
writing, printing and distributing literature geared to
Muslims. Many others helped too.

The fact that Christians are unusually encouraged by
fifty Muslim converts from one district in a decade
(even though some of them later recanted) is an indication of how resistant that community still is at present.
Since the 1965 war with India, when Christians were
persecuted especially in border areas such as Sialkot,
there have been almost no converts from the majority
community in the Sialkot Church Council area. Significant
church growth from the Muslim community is unlikely until
some means can be devised of winning responsive segments
of them in whole family units.

Evangelism Among Scheduled Castes

The Sialkot Church Council has placed more emphasis
than most Churches in the Punjab upon outreach to the
Scheduled Castes located in their district. Groups of
Balmikis have been sought out, taught and baptized in
Kharian, Head Rasul, Mandi Bahauddin, Khewra and
Gharibwal, totaling thirty or forty families. The
Church in Mandi Bahauddin runs a nursery school for
about 20 Balmiki children. Local pastors have taken
the initiative in this effort in most cases.

At the Sialkot Convention in 1957 a semi-nomadic
group of depressed class people from Wazirabad, called
the Gagare, came to a U.P. missionary asking for Christian teaching. They were referred to the Church of Scotland, as Wazirabad is in their comity area. This sparked
a new evangelistic outreach by the U.P. Church to relatives of the Wazirabad Gagare living in Gujranwala city.
(See pages 206-207.) However, the Sialkot Church Council
did not seem to take advantage of the opportunity in
Wazirabad until 1961 when the first baptisms from among
the Gagare of that area are recorded. Since that time
the movement has grown until now a total of about forty
families of Gagare have been baptized in Wazirabad and
Sialkot districts. This is the largest group of Gagare
Christians in Pakistan. A full-time worker was assigned
to minister to them, but he did not continue in it long.
Due to deep-seated prejudice against them, the Gagare
have not been able to integrate happily into local church
fellowships but have their own worshipping communities.

A leader of the Gagare, Sain Chamba, claims that
there are 200 more families in the Sialkot area who are
ripe for evangelism. Several thousand live throughout
the Punjab with large concentrations in Lyallpur and
Sahiwal districts. As yet there is no evangelist from
among their own number. This opportunity for considerable
church growth has not been adequately pursued by any
Church in Pakistan, but the Sialkot Church Council has
pointed the way and demonstrated that the Gagare can be
won in significant numbers by family units.

When the Sialkot Church Council merged to become the Sialkot Diocese of the Church of Pakistan in 1970, her Christian community totaled 17,500 with 5,503 communicant members. (See Figure 27.)

The Pakistan Lutheran Church

Missions: *The Danish Pathan Mission*
                 The Finnish Missionary Society
                 The Norwegian Mission to Moslems
                 The Society-in-Aid of the P.L.C.
                   (Denmark)
                 The World Mission Prayer League
                   (U.S.A. and Canada)

The first representatives of the Lutheran Church were women sent by the Danish Pathan Mission to Mardan in the Northwest Frontier Province in 1903 to open a hospital. (See Figure 23). Their purpose was to evangelize the rugged independent Afghan-Pathan tribespeople who for years resisted British conquest, and later distinguished themselves by their skill and courage while serving in the British army. The Lutherans have found these people rocky soil in which to plant the Word. Not only do they resist conversion, but in their zealous opposition to Christian teaching they have dotted the Frontier with the graves of several missionary and Pathan martyrs.

The Danish Pathan Mission gained its first male member when Jens Christiansen married one of their nurses in 1926. He teamed up with a Pathan convert, Rev. A. Taib, who was baptized in 1928. Together they itinerated in the villages, prepared Christian literature, revised the Pushto New Testament, and established Mardan the only Pushto speaking congregation found in Pakistan today.

Few Pathans confessed their faith in Jesus Christ. The Church only began to grow when Punjabi Christians migrated to the Frontier to work as laborers or sweepers. Groups of Balmiki sweepers were also won in several places, but hundreds of these remain to be reached. The Pakistan Lutheran Church officially came into being in 1955.

In 1946 the Anglican Church invited the World Mission
Prayer League to take over the work in Dera Ismail Khan,
Tank, and Risalpur. Other Lutheran groups came to reinforce the work: The Norwegian Mission to Moslems sent out
one couple in 1959; The Finnish Missionary Society began
sending workers in 1960 and have become the largest Lutheran Mission working in Pakistan; and the Society-in-Aid of
the Pakistan Lutheran Church which was formed in Denmark in
1962 following a tragic split in the Danish Pathan Mission.

The Lutherans have opened several reading rooms to provide non-Christians with Christian literature. They erperi-
mented with a traveling library of tracts and Gospels along
with famous Pushto literature in order to establish rapport
with intellectual Pathan leaders. This has had to be abandoned for lack of workers.

Recent Lutheran work has been carried on primarily through
institutions. The hospital at Tank, acquired from the C.M.S.
in 1958, provides an evangelistic opportunity to witness to
non-Christian patients and their relatives. Several primary
schools that cater only to the Christian community teach an
excellent, carefully-prepared Bible curriculum. In Dera
Ismail Khan a Bible Training Institute was opened in the
mid 1960's, with an industrial department attached, with the
purpose of training Christian laymen well grounded in the
Scriptures, and "tent-making" pastors who support themselves
at secular jobs in order to minister in areas that cannot
afford to support a pastor.

According to the latest figures available in the *World
Christian Handbook* of 1968, the Pakistan Lutheran Church
has a Christian community of 1,700, with 500 communicant
members. In 1970 she joined with others to become the
Church of Pakistan.

The Lahore Church Council

Mission: *The Presbyterian Church in the U.S.A.*
          (now part of The United Presbyterian
          Church in the U.S.A.)

As early as 1835 the famous American Presbyterian
pioneer missionary, John Lowrie, was invited by the
ruler of the Punjab, Maharajah Ranjit Singh, to visit

Lahore. The Maharajah urged him to open a school to
teach English to Sikh children, sons of the ruling class.
He even offered 2,183 rupees toward the project in 1844.
Lowrie refused, however, because the Maharajah would not
agree to allow Christian teaching in the school. It is
interesting to note that 15 years later the Presbyterians
opened their first school in Lahore in the former palace,
Rang Mahal, after the fall of the Sikh regime.

It was not until the British annexed the Punjab in
1849 that regular mission work could be established there.
John Newton and Charles Forman of the American Presbyterian
Mission (hereafter referred to as the A.P. Mission) founded
the first mission station in the area now called Pakistan
by settling in Lahore. Outstations were Shahdara and
Sharakpur located northwest of Lahore adjoining the
U.P. Mission area. In 1856 Rawalpindi was occupied as
a main station. Murree, a hill station in the Himalayas,
was visited each year from Rawalpindi--an arduous climb
by horse cart, taking two to three days. Both Rawalpindi
and Murree were turned over to the United Presbyterian
Mission in 1891.

Kasur, thirty miles southeast of Lahore, was period-
ically visited by Presbyterian missionaries from 1883 on,
but was occupied by the Zenana Bible and Medical Mission
(now called the Bible and Medical Missionary Fellowship)
in 1893. It became a sub-station of the A.P. Mission in
1900, and later proved to be the most fruitful center for
church growth in that Mission.

Early Evangelistic Efforts

The A.P. Mission stressed two primary means of reaching people for Jesus Christ--preaching and education.
Both were strongly evangelistic in character in the
early years of mission work. Convinced that winning the
upper classes was the best strategy in the overwhelming
task of bringing all of India to the Lord, the missionaries aimed both the proclamation and education primarily
at the intellectual literates.

Evangelistic preaching was used a great deal at the
beginning of the work mostly in the cities, but also in
rural areas. Each missionary was expected to spend a
part of every cold season in itinerant preaching in
villages, unless prevented by ill-health or unusually
pressing duties on the station. A printing press in
Ludhiana printed thousands of tracts and books that were
widely distributed during these itinerations.

For forty years the Mission carried on <u>daily</u> preaching
in the bazaar and on the streets. The results were
distressingly slim. At the end of 20 years of work,
by 1869, the communicant membership totaled 44 (35 in
the Lahore area; 9 in Rawalpindi). (See Figure 28.)
In 1889, after forty years of work, the whole Christian
community numbered only 346 with 139 communicant members.
In spite of great zeal and amazing persistence in pro-
claiming the Gospel, the results were insignificant.
What was wrong?

If all the Missions surrounding the Lahore-Kasur area
had similar results, the blame could perhaps be laid
squarely on the resistant soil in which the Word was
being planted. The fact that the U.P. Mission, adjoining
the A.P. Mission to the north, had by 1889 a communicant
membership of 6,600, indicates that not all the soil in
the area was hard. Lack of results cannot always be
blamed on rocky soil. The sower also has a responsibility
to see that the seed falls mostly in fertile productive
ground. Otherwise his Master is not likely to be pleased
with his work.

The A.P. Mission, in accordance with the pattern
followed by most of the other established Missions of
that day, was aiming at high caste literate people. The
converts that dribbled in one-by-one congregated in
clusters of houses near the mission station and were
dependent upon the missionaries. The pattern is tragically
familiar, but lasted longer than in most other Missions.
The first group of adult baptisms recorded was 58 in 1891.
It took forty-eight years to bring the Christian community
up to 1,000.

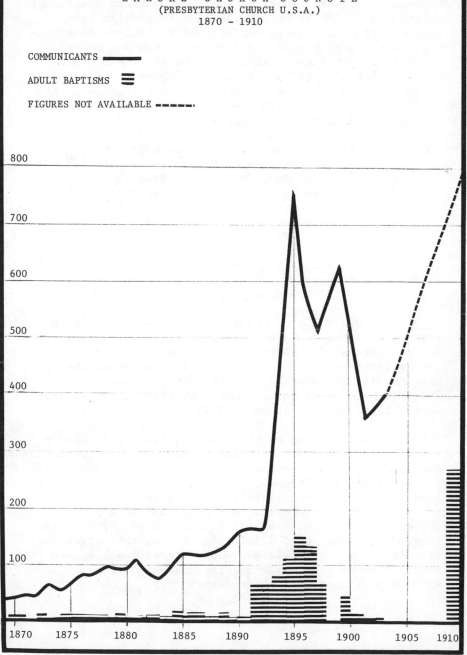

FIGURE 28

L A H O R E   C H U R C H   C O U N C I L
(PRESBYTERIAN CHURCH U.S.A.)
1870 – 1910

COMMUNICANTS ▬▬

ADULT BAPTISMS ☰

FIGURES NOT AVAILABLE ▬ ▬ ▬

The second approach was called "evangelistic education."
An anglo-vernacular school was founded for non-Christian
high-caste boys in Lahore as soon as the first missionaries
arrived in 1849. It became the Rang Mahal High School.
Forman Christian college was started in 1865 as an exten-
sion to the High School. By 1886 the work had expanded
to include twenty branches of Rang Mahal High School,
with a total of 1,675 students. The emphasis upon
educational work gradually outweighed all other aspects
of the ministry. This is clearly revealed by a report
to the General Assembly in 1929:

> The faith which the Mission has in Christ-
> ian education as a means to the spread of
> the Kingdom of God, and the building up of
> His Church is reflected in its investment
> of life and money. Leaving out of consid-
> eration the foreign staff, out of a total
> budget of Rs. 253,729, Rs. 121,000 or more
> than 47 per cent of the total was invested
> in education as compared with Rs. 81,252
> for purely evangelistic agencies, and
> Rs. 8,863 for medical work. (II Part:117)

By the 1890's the U.P. Mission was spending a large
percentage of their budget to pay simple Chuhra evangelistic workers to shepherd the thousands of Chuhras
coming into the Church. During that same period the
A.P. Mission was pouring the greatest part of their
budget into schools in the hope that they too would produce a large harvest of souls. Was this hope realized?

The avowed purpose of these schools was to influence
students to accept Jesus Christ as Savior. The curriculum
included compulsory courses in Bible and Christian ethics;
daily worship was attended by all; and each staff member
keenly felt his responsibility to witness to individual
students with the intent of bringing them to a personal
decision for Christ. In addition, the staff of the Rang
Mahal High School held a daily service on the street outside the school for all who would listen. Nobody can
accuse them of being half-hearted in their evangelistic
efforts, but what were the results?

Mr. John Newton in summarizing the outcome of these extensive efforts says:

> After all that has been said about the
> success of these Mission schools, it must
> be acknowledged that they have shown very
> small results in the way of direct con-
> versions. (1886:30,31)

In spite of the dedicated teaching and witness they received, few students had the courage to openly declare their faith in Christ. Unaccustomed to making a major decision apart from their family and clan; unable in their immaturity to face the social pressure and ostracism that such a decision would demand, the students were in no position to change from their old faith to a new one. The few who did were too young to be able to influence their families to do likewise. They were usually pressured into recanting, or else thrown out of their homes. When an occasional baptism of a student occurred, it caused such a furor in the community that the school was forced to close down for a time.

Although the prominent missionary, John Newton, had admitted as early as 1886 that education was ineffective as a means of the evangelization of non-Christians, the A.P. Mission persisted in its heavy stress on institutional work. Orphanages, girls' schools, and medical work were added to the institutional burden, requiring ever increasing numbers of missionary personnel, so that evangelism was gradually squeezed out. Nearly forty-five years of missionary work had passed before the A.P. Church took up the challenge of reaching the responsive Chuhras.

The Chuhra Movement

In 1886 a few Chuhras were baptized by Dr. Forman, who regarded their responsiveness as a great opportunity for the Gospel. There is no indication of strong opposition in the A.P. Mission to the inclusion of the depressed classes as was true of some other Missions. On the other hand, no special effort was made at that stage to leave their unproductive methods and concentrate deliberately on the responsive Chuhras.

The number of adult baptisms up through 1890 totaled
133. It was not until 1891 that any sizable number of
adult baptisms appear in the records. The Chuhra
communities of Manihala and Soga, two towns between
Lahore and Kasur, had received teaching for some time.
In 1891 twenty adults from Manihala and 36 adults from
Soga were baptized by Dr. Forman. These made up 56
of the 58 baptisms recorded for that year, and mark the
real start of the Chuhra movement in the A.P. Church.

For several years following, there was a steady rise
in adult baptisms as can been seen by 64 baptisms in
1892; 112 in 1894; and 132 in 1896. (See Figure 28 for
details of each year.) The movement gave promise of
greatly increasing growth, yet surprisingly from 1897
to 1906 there were only an average of about 30 adult
baptisms a year. In contrast, the first few years of
the 20th century brought an average of nearly 1,000
baptized believers each year into the adjacent U.P.
Church. (See Figure 39.) Why this disparity?

There are three basic reasons for lack of growth
that can be found in the A.P. records. First, most of
the missionaries at that time were located in Lahore
and had responsibilities in the various institutions.
They were faithful in daily preaching, but because of
their institutional duties, they naturally concentrated
more and more on urban evangelism. Most of the responsive
Chuhras were rural in those days. Only one missionary
man was assigned full time to rural work. He lived in
Lahore but his territory included all the area between
Lahore and Kasur, 30 miles away. Kasur did not even
become a sub-station of the A.P. Mission until 1900;
and not a full station in its own right until 1912. The
only missionary living outside of Lahore all those years
was Miss Thiede who lived in the small town of Wagah,
16 miles east of Lahore.

The report of the Punjab Mission to the General Assembly
in the U.S.A. in 1893 expresses the realization of the
importance of the Chuhra movement and the necessity of

building a mission center in a more rural area in order
to take advantage of it. Concerning the work among
Chuhras Miss Thiede wrote:

> There is among them a wide-spread desire
> for better things and a feeling that these
> better things will be found in Christianity.
> There is a seeking after God, and a remark-
> able interest in hearing of the love of God
> as manifested through His Son our Saviour.
> A large number have been admitted by us to
> baptism, and still larger numbers are seek-
> ing admission thus into the Church of Christ
> on earth. ... There is at present great
> need of a village mission in connection
> with the Lahore station. It is impossible
> to properly carry on the work already begun--
> much less to enlarge it--until a mission
> bungalow is built in the very midst of the
> district itself. (*General Assembly Minutes*
> (1893:82,84)

It was not until 1912 that the Mission followed Miss
Thiede's suggestion to build a mission center in the
midst of the Chuhra work. They chose Kasur. The "large
number" of baptisms referred to above amounted to a
total of only 202. Yet for a Mission accustomed to the
slow one-by-one extraction method, even this was overwhelming. Few Missions are geared to handle numbers of
converts in proportion to the avowed goal of discipling
the nations for Jesus Christ.

Second, there was a lack of emphasis upon winning
Chuhras even among rural workers. The idea was to
preach to all without discrimination, but work through
the high castes whenever possible as a key to winning
all castes. *The President's Report on the Work of the
Punjab Mission* even as late as 1907 contains this report
concerning Kasur:

> In the villages, all classes are reached
> by the public preaching of the Gospel.
> The practice of the preachers in this
> district is to go first of all to the higher
> classes and afterward to the lower.(1907:122)

It took years of unproductive service to convince missionaries of the value of giving priority to responsive
peoples.

The third reason for such slow growth from 1897 to
1906 lay in the prevalent philosophy that a great deal of
pre-baptismal teaching needs to be done, and too many new
candidates for baptism should not be taken on until
sufficient care has been given to those already converted.
This position is forcefully argued by Rev. Gould in a
letter to the Secretary of the Board in the U.S.A. Robert
E. Speer, as late as 1906:

> As for the low caste people ... we could
> easily have hundreds of baptisms in a very
> short space of time if we but followed the
> policy of our Methodist brothers! They make
> willingness the test, rather than fitness.
> Our way is to teach first and when the
> candidate seems intelligently and earnestly
> ready, we administer baptism. This of course
> shuts out a large number who apply for baptism
> only because they have the hope that as Christ-
> ians they will be freed from the disagreeable
> *begar* (compulsory labor), or will receive a
> grant of land and the missionary's help in all
> law cases. (Official Letters to the Board
> Vol. 164-32, 1906:3)

In answer to the argument that Chuhras were coming only
for worldly motives, Miss Thiede pointed out that although
the motives were often not spiritual in nature, it is the
responsibility of the Christian worker to transform them
into spiritual motives by the way he instructs inquirers.

The above strategy was geared to slow growth, to the
hot-house rearing of the occasional convert, such as
they had experienced up to this time. It could not be
adjusted to handle hundreds of converts such as they could
have had in those days. In 1895 the *Sixtieth Annual Report*
makes this statement:

> There have been this year altogether 157
> baptisms, including children. These all are
> Chuhras ... Added to those baptized of former
> years, the total is 495 ... Many more could
> have been baptized, and there are several
> villages at present time desirous of being
> taught, preliminary to receiving baptism,
> but until more workers are available to
> continue the work, they must be deferred. (48)

Obviously a total of less than 500 baptized members was so
unexpected and unusual, the Mission didn't know how to
handle it except by holding back on evangelism. Not only
did they stop searching for lost sheep, they refused to
open the door to those asking to come in!

The President's Report on the Work of the Punjab Mission
in 1907 marked the beginning of a new era in A.P. Mission
work. This report was the result of a year of careful
study that the President of the Mission was assigned to do.
He made the following excellent recommendations.

1) Transfer all available missionaries into rural evangelism. Educationalists, even college professors, were
included in this detailed list of workers to be transferred.

2) Organize a definite congregation, or church, wherever
possible, with a committee responsible for maintaining
regular worship. Elders should be appointed and trained
as soon as possible to take over the work of this committee.

3) Require every paid evangelistic worker to run a secular
school for two hours a day five days a week in addition to
his pastoral work. Classes are to be for Christians to
enable them to read their Bible and grow in faith.

4) Place special emphasis on winning the responsive
Chuhras and Chamars.

Although only some of the suggested personnel were
transferred from educational work to village evangelistic
work, nevertheless, the Church began to grow as efforts
were increasingly concentrated upon the Chuhras. Peak
growth came during the decade of 1911 to 1921 and centered
around Kasur in particular. (See Figure 29.)

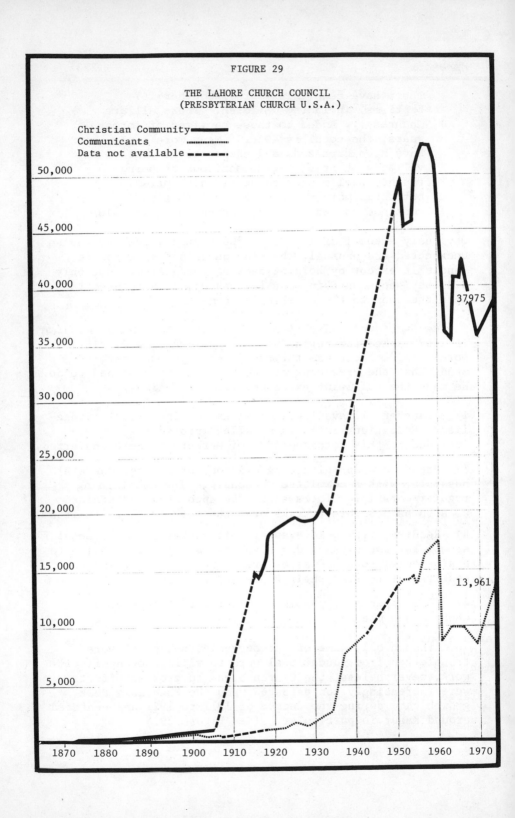

FIGURE 29

THE LAHORE CHURCH COUNCIL
(PRESBYTERIAN CHURCH U.S.A.)

Christian Community ———
Communicants ....
Data not available — — —

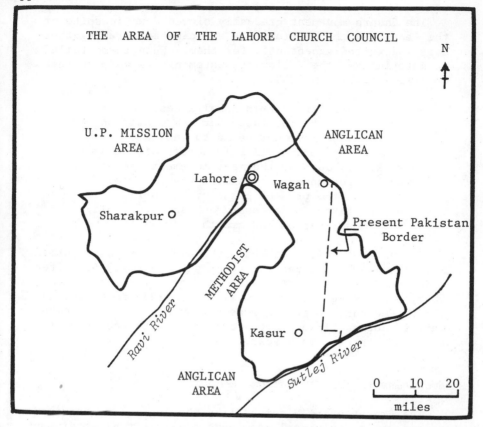

THE AREA OF THE LAHORE CHURCH COUNCIL

N

U.P. MISSION AREA

ANGLICAN AREA

Lahore   Wagah

Sharakpur O

METHODIST AREA

Present Pakistan Border

Ravi River

Kasur O

ANGLICAN AREA

Sutlej River

0   10   20
miles

By 1925 baptized Christians totaled 19,000; 12,000 of these or 63 per cent, lived in Kasur district. They had only 1,067 communicant members. Compare these figures with the Methodist Church who occupied an adjoining area half the size of the A.P. Mission area (see map above) and turned their full attention to evangelizing nationals only in 1900, over fifty years after the start of the Presbyterian work. In 1925 the Methodists had a baptized community in the Lahore area alone of over 21,000 with a communicant membership of 4,000. (See Figure 39.) Even at the peak of her development the A.P. Mission fell short of the growth potential of her situation. Institutional work continued to require a large proportion of mission personnel and budget, and too much stress on "quality" in converts made her hesitant to baptize people when they were ready and eager for baptism.

The Chuhra movement gradually slowed down in spite of
the fact that the missionaries anticipated more ingatherings and waited expectantly for them. When these failed
to materialize, the following statement was made to the
General Assembly in 1930:

> As we consider work in rural areas, we are
> impressed with the fact that the cessation
> of the mass movement seems to indicate
> a permanent change in this aspect of the
> work. ... Just as the mass movement seemed
> to be spontaneous and almost unavoidable,
> no doubt the present phase of the work
> may be taken as necessary and an opportunity
> for consolidation and growth. (97)

In spite of this statement, the A.P. Mission performed
more than 200 adult baptisms each year up to 1935. After
that the Church only grew at a rate of 1-1/2 per cent a
year, increasing slowly from 21,000 in 1935 to 38,000 in
1972. Few adult baptisms were performed, and the growth
rate is not sufficient even to keep up with the rate of
biological growth each year.

Requirements for Communicant Membership

The Presbyterian Mission, like the Anglicans, required
considerable Scriptural knowledge and spiritual attainment
before allowing baptized converts to be full communicant
members of the Church. Arthur Brown in his book, *One
Hundred Years*, mentions the results of this policy:

> As a result, almost everywhere in our
> districts there is a vast disproportion
> between probationers or baptized Christ-
> ians and full church members. (1936:647)

This is also discussed in the *Report on Study of Work*
in 1938 as follows:

> Partly due to standards set up for entrance
> into full Church membership, but more
> because of the physical difficulty of

arranging for instruction and reception
of members in the hundreds of scattered
villages, the percentage of communicant
members is distressingly small. In 1925
the number was 3,527, [This includes
the numbers for all of the Punjab, even
those portions now part of India.] or
11 per cent of the total baptized
community; in 1931 it was 5,322 or
13 per cent. At present there are 6,793
communicants, representing 16-1/2 per
cent of the total enrolled group of
Christians. (2)

In 1970 the communicant membership of the Lahore Church
Council was 37 per cent of her Christian community--a
much more healthy ratio.

The line in Figure 28 showing communicant membership
rises steeply from 1892 to 1894 to a peak of over 750,
then makes a sudden drop to 515 in 1897 followed by
another downward plunge to 360 in 1902. Nothing in the
records studied indicate the reason for this. We can only
conjecture that rolls were drastically purged or that the
term "communicant" was reinterpreted to satisfy stricter
requirements. This needs further study.

A similar abrupt drop in statistics both in the Christian community and in communicant membership is found in
Figure 29 for the years 1959 to 1961. For some years
prior to this drop statistics had been poorly kept from
incomplete records supplemented by estimate and conjecture.
These were felt to be considerably overdrawn, so were
pared down in 1961 to more nearly represent the true
situation. A concern for keeping careful statistics is
important in order to make accurate analyses of progress
in church growth. Early missionaries were faithful in
this, but the figures given in recent years in most church
records have been fluctuating and unreliable.

Self-Government and Self-Support

The Presbyterian Church organized its first Synod in
1901 as an integral part of the U.S.A. Church. This did
not last long, for in 1904 they joined other Presbyterian
and Reformed Churches in India to form the Union Presbyterian Church of India. From this time on she was
administratively separate from the Presbyterian Church
in the U.S.A. In this aspect they were nearly half a
century in advance of most other Missions. However, Brown
writing in 1936 makes this comment as to the actual extent
to which the Church was self-governing:

> Technically, therefore, self-government
> has been achieved since the Church is
> ecclesiastically independent. But self-
> government can hardly be deemed complete
> as long as missions composed of foreigners
> retain much of the real authority, including
> control of the purse upon which a large
> part of the work depends. The transfer of
> power from Mission to Church is an accepted
> policy and is being gradually developed,
> but fulfillment is yet in the future.
> (1936:654-655)

In 1924, as a result of further unions, the Presbyterian
Church in the Punjab became the Lahore Presbytery of the
United Church of North India. In 1951 the Lahore Presbytery was integrated with the Presbyterian Mission, and was
called the Lahore Church Council of the United Church of
North India. This Council was responsible for the
administration of all the evangelistic, educational, and
medical work formerly done by the Mission. This name has
continued even after official connection with the United
Church of North India was broken off in the 1960's, due
to increasing difficulty of communication between India
and Pakistan.

Although the Presbyterian Church in the U.S.A. and the
United Presbyterian Church of North America united to
form the United Presbyterian Church in the U.S.A. in 1958,
their two independent "daughter" Churches, the Lahore

Church Council and the United Presbyterian Church in
Pakistan, have not united, but still function as separate
communions. Both are completely self-governing, not only
in theory but in practice, with missionaries taking almost
no part in the decision making processes. Both have had
serious problems with factionalism in recent years, and
have lost a number of pastors and congregations to the
McIntire schism.

The development of self-support has lagged far behind.
For a viable self-supporting congregation, the Christian
community needs to be sufficiently large and compact that
one man can serve them and receive enough support on
which to live. Only in the cities of Kasur and Lahore
were there large enough communities of Christians to make
this possible. By 1930 out of 29 organized congregations,
only two were self-supporting. By 1945 although there
were 8,500 communicant members and 28 organized churches,
still only three of them were self-supporting. The goal
of self-support was only realized in recent years when
all subsidy from the U.S.A. was gradually cut off on a
sliding scale.

At Partition most of the Presbyterian Mission area
remained in India. Only Lahore and Kasur were left on
the Pakistan side of the border. Kasur is so near the
border with India that it suffered much during the wars
of 1965 and 1971. Presbyterian missionaries have not
been allowed to reside there since the 1965 war. There
is no Presbyterian missionary in Lahore at present who is
in full time evangelism or work with the Church. All
are connected with some institution or social organization
or are in administrative positions in the Mission. The
former mission schools have been under Christian Pakistani
administration and management for some years, but were
nationalized by the government in 1972.

It appears that God is allowing the doors to close on
traditional types of missionary service, both in work with
the Church and in educational institutions. This should
free personnel and budget for new evangelistic opportunities
in Pakistan that could open up many exciting possibilities
for church growth in the future.

The Salvation Army

The Salvation Army began work in the Punjab in 1883 by
establishing a station in Lahore. Soon they had evangelistic workers in a variety of areas in the Punjab. The
Chuhra movement was getting under way at that time in the
Sialkot-Zafarwal area. Salvation Army policy in every
country was to help the poor, so they didn't fall into
the trap of attempting to win the high castes, but geared
immediately into Chuhra evangelism. By 1896 they had a
center in Gurdaspur from which they made itinerations
into the group movement districts. Growth was steady but
slow until about 1906 when their Christian community
suddenly rose rapidly at a rate of nearly 1,000 members
a year. This spectacular growth was due to their policy
of accepting members with a minimum of delay, and their
promptness in following the migrations of the Chuhras
to the new canal colonies at the turn of the century.
They made their headquarters for the Bar area in Jhang,
and colonized a Christian village called Shanti Nagar
near Khanewal in 1916. They found the Chuhras of the
canal colonies unusually responsive because they were
dislocated from their old familiar cultural patterns
and social ties. For this reason the Church grew steadily
until the Chuhra movement waned in the 1930's.

It is interesting to note how God used General Booth,
the founder of the Salvation Army, to spark a revival among
pastors in the Anglican and U.P. Churches in 1896. This
eventually led to the Sialkot Convention revivals of 1904
to 1910 that brought blessing to many parts of India.
(See pages 127-139 for more details of this revival.)

Evangelism was the primary thrust of the Salvation Army
but they also opened small primary schools for Christian
children and village clinics in various centers. In 1910
they opened a weaving factory to employ the men and boys
of a criminal tribe called the Pakhiwara. They also
established centers to teach the poor various methods of
agriculture, weaving and embroidery, and silk production.

In early years the Salvation Army were considered intruders by the established Churches, for they did not observe comity. In recent years, however, they have become members of the Pakistan Christian Council and a much happier spirit of mutual respect and cooperation has developed. The report from the field for 1967 claims a total Christian community of 31,071, and in 1973 they had 21 missionaries. (See Figure 38.)

The Associate Reformed Presbyterian Church

The Associate Reformed Presbyterian Church of the U.S.A. (hereafter called the A.R.P. Church) sent out Miss Minnie Alexander in 1906 to work with the United Presbyterian Mission in anticipation of opening a field of their own. In 1910 she was joined by Rev. and Mrs. Ranson. After they had done language study under the supervision of the U.P.'s Dr. Ewing, Chairman of the Committee on Comity, offered them two of the four tehsils of Montgomery District (now called Sahiwal) as a site for their new Mission. Montgomery was a canal colony with great potential, expected to double in size when the new canals opened in 1914.

The U.P.'s urged the A.R.P.'s to occupy this new field speedily before some less desirable Mission bought up the opportunity. An advisory committee of U.P.'s was appointed to help them begin their work. A Methodist missionary who had done some itinerating in the area not only turned over the work to them, but loaned them his evangelistic workers, familiar with the district, until they were able to train men to take their places. The U.P.'s also gave two evangelistic workers to help them begin their work. U.P. missionaries took turns working with them in the early months, and also sent an ordained Indian minister to pastor one of the two churches organized in the first year. The A.R.P.'s have always maintained a close tie with the U.P. Mission.

The Chuhra Movement.

The Ransons and Miss Alexander, having observed the people movement closely in the U.P. area, were convinced of the value of it, and from the start placed their

emphasis upon winning the Chuhras. This saved them many
years of fruitless labor. Some Christians had migrated
to Montgomery to obtain jobs. The *Census Report of 1911*
mentions 471 of them, all but four being Protestants.
These welcomed A.R.P. workers and introduced them to
other Chuhra communities in the area. During the first
year a U.P. evangelist, Peter, succeeded in preparing
for baptism 32 people from one village. That village
was made the first camping site when the missionaries
started itinerating in November 1911. They baptized
another adult and three children; organized a congregation
with 45 members; and chose and ordained two elders and
two deacons. By the end of 1911 Mr. Ranson had baptized
50 people. Two years later there were 589 persons
associated with the A.R.P. Church. (See Figure 30.)
This was an encouraging beginning to the work.

The decade from 1911 to 1921 brought an incredible
number of migrating Chuhras into Montgomery District. The
Census Report of 1911 lists only 471 as Christians. By
1921 there were 41,181 Christians of whom 12,576 claimed
to be Presbyterians. The A.R.P. Church, the only
Presbyterian group in the area, reported only 4,500
people in their Christian community at that time. Either
many baptized U.P.'s or A.P.'s had migrated to the area
and not yet been shepherded by the A.R.P.'s, or thousands
were claiming to be Christian who never had been baptized
or associated with any Church. Their eagerness to be
counted as Presbyterians, however, reveals the great
potential that existed for discipling these dislocated
people.

There were 12,500 Chuhras who claimed to be Presbyterians;
another 13,200 belonging to other Protestant groups not
working in the Montgomery area; plus responsive non-Christian Chuhras, all waiting to be taught. Had the Mission
been prepared to handle large numbers, it could have grown
to phenomenal proportions. Lacking experience and adequate
personnel, they worked hard, expanded as rapidly as they
felt they could, but left the majority of the Chuhra
community untouched.

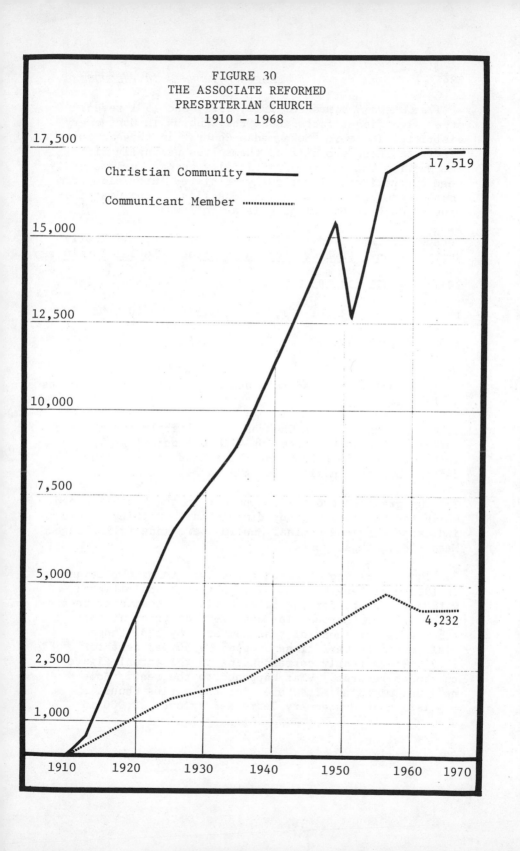

FIGURE 30
THE ASSOCIATE REFORMED
PRESBYTERIAN CHURCH
1910 – 1968

The *Census Reports* for 1911, 1921, and 1931 reveal
other significant facts about the Chuhras in Montgomery
district. The term "Mohammedan Chuhra" in these reports
refers to those who aligned themselves nominally with
the Muslims but had never officially become Muslims or
been circumcised. Those fully initiated into Islam from
among the Chuhras were called "Musallis." The distribution of Chuhras by religion is as follows:

Census Report	Chris-tians	Hindu Chuhras	Sikh Chuhras	Musalli Chuhras	Moham. Chuhras	Yearly Totals
1911	471	11,395	33	18,238	12,404	42,541
1921	41,181	11,001	1,818	44,176	203	98,379
1931	17,245	12,092	547	46,058	14	75,956

The above facts lead to a number of unhappy conclusions
as follows:

1) The number of Hindu Chuhras rose slightly during this
period, not enough to keep up with biological growth.
This indicates that they must have lost some to other
faiths, but not in significant numbers.

2) The greatest growth is apparent in the Musalli group,
while the Mohammedan group diminished to nothing. This
indicates that the nominal Muslims were made full fledged
Musallis in those years.

3) The 41,181 who declared themselves to be Christians
in 1921 must have been to a large extent unaffiliated
with any Church, for the total Christian community recorded by all the Churches in Montgomery district at that
time falls far short of that number. By 1931 those
claiming to be Christians dropped by 56 per cent to
17,245--more nearly corresponding to the actual figures
on church records. What happened to the rest? Some
no doubt migrated elsewhere, for the entire Chuhra
population in Montgomery decreased by over 22,000 in

that decade. However, it is apparent that many who were
eager to call themselves Christians in 1921, had aligned
themselves with some other group by 1931.

A.R.P. Mission records also show a dearth of adult
baptisms from among non-Christians after the first few
years. Overwhelmed by thousands of baptized Christians
transferred from Churches in the north but desperately
needing follow-up teaching, they soon became immersed
in building up the Church, with little time left for
evangelism among non-Christians.

In the ten years from 1901 to 1911, over 8 million
people died in the Punjab from unusually severe epidemics
of cholera and bubonic plague. The attention of the
A.R.P. Mission in its formative years was naturally drawn
to the staggering medical needs of the country. In
June 1911, a small dispensary for women and children was
opened in Montgomery. By 1917 this was expanded to
become the Nancy Fullwood Memorial Hospital that has
operated ever since, primarily for women.

Village schools were established in several centers
and have been important in developing Christian leadership.
A boarding school for Christian girls was opened in
Montgomery to enable village girls to get an education.
In 1916 two canal colony villages were settled by Christ-
ians. One was named Ransonabad. Two more were settled
in 1924. Out of these villages have come many of the
A.R.P. church leaders.

The A.R.P. Mission, because of the limited size of its
field and its relatively small Christian community, has
been unusually successful in carrying on an effective
follow-up teaching program for their Church. Their people
are well taught, but the Church is not growing. The
latest figures show a Christian community of 17,519 with
4,232 communicant members. (See Figure 30.) This is an
increase of only approximately 2,000 in Christian community
since Partition in 1947--not enough to keep up with
biological growth. Factionalism has been an increasing

problem as the Church has become independent of the
Mission. The McIntire schism carried off some of their
pastors and congregations. However, they have evidenced
greater stability than found in the U.P. Church and the
Lahore Church Council.

Scheduled Caste Opportunities

During the early years of the Mission, Chamars (leather
workers related to the Meg caste in the U.P. area)
revealed great interest in the Gospel. In the *Report on
Study of Work Central Board of the Punjab Mission Area*
the following reference is made to this depressed class:

> The Chamars particularly are an encouraging
> group. They are more wide-awake than the
> Chuhras, have higher moral standards, more
> diversified occupations and more economic
> resources. But these very differences
> may make difficult their turning to Christ-
> ianity in groups. The break with the old
> brotherhood in the matter of eating and
> marriage will be greater than in the case
> of Chuhras. In fact, the few who have
> become Christians say that they cannot stay
> in the villages among their own people.
> If this is so, then no mass-movement is
> possible, for that presupposes for most the
> ability to stay in the same place and
> occupation as formerly. (1938:6)

Had a missionary or national worker been assigned to work
exclusively with the Chamars to enable them to become
Christians without having to integrate with the predominately Chuhra Church, it is possible that a sizable
movement could have developed among them. However, it
is undoubtedly true that the factors mentioned above
made them more conservative and difficult to win.

Since 1970 a subcaste of the Chamars, called Meghwars,
have shown a definite interest in the Christian faith.
These live in the Liaqatpur area of Bahawalpur. Two adult
literacy workers and one evangelist have been sent from
the A.R.P. Church to work among them. Punjabi Christians

in Sahiwal help finance this outreach and some have taken
part in brief evangelistic trips among them. Unfortunately
only 13 of these Meghwars have been baptized as yet, but
several families are ready for baptism. It is important to
create as large an initial fellowship of believers as
possible so that they form a social unit able to resist
ostracism and persecution.

The work among the Meghwars has been hindered by the
interested response of two other Scheduled Castes in that
area: the Bavaris and a Bhil group known as "Thori."
These live interspersed with the Meghwars but are considered lower on the caste scale. Workers attempting to
evangelize several groups simultaneously have found that
this creates serious barriers to the spread of the Gospel.

The religious leader of another Scheduled Caste group
known as the Gagare claims that the largest group of
Gagare in Pakistan are in the Sahiwal district. They
have proved responsive in other areas and should be contacted in Sahiwal as well.

Sound church growth principles need to be studied and
applied to this situation to prevent these movements
from being stunted, and to enable potentially responsive
people to be discipled.

The Pentecostal Churches

*(The Full Gospel Assemblies, The Pakistan
Assemblies of God, The United Pentecostal
Church in Pakistan, etc.)*

*Missions: The Scandinavian Free Mission,
The Orebro Mission of Sweden,
The British Assemblies of God, etc.*

There are many different Pentecostal Churches in
Pakistan. Some of these are connected with a Mission;
others are entirely indigenous.

The Scandinavian Free Mission began work in Pakistan
in 1943, and was joined in 1960 by another Scandinavian
Pentecostal group, the Orebro Mission of Sweden.   Their
main emphasis is on evangelistic outreach to nominal
3rd and 4th generation Christians, though they have some
efforts among Muslims as well. They sponsor frequent
spiritual life conventions in a variety of centers,
featuring evangelists from many different parts of the
world. Their healing services attract many non-Christians.
Some have been healed and have publicly testified to the
fact. This undoubtedly has had an impact on the Muslim
community, but has not yet resulted in any significant
number of baptisms from among them.

These Missions have avoided establishing large medical
or educational institutions, but have put stress on adult
literacy by financing many adult literacy teachers in
village and city centers. They operated some small
primary schools for Christian children until the government of Pakistan nationalized most private schools in
the Punjab in 1972. They still have a number of small
clinics, a hostel for village children to study in government schools in Lyallpur, and a child care center. They
also run a Bible School in Lahore for training evangelistic workers and ordained pastors. They stress spiritual qualifications rather than academic standards for
their pastors. These are paid largely from foreign funds
and little progress has been made toward a self-supporting
ministry.

For many years the Pentecostals have conducted a
refresher course for pastors and workers for a month during
harvest season when little pastoral work can be done in
rural congregations because of the long working hours of
the people. This is a helpful way to provide needed
spiritual refreshment and pastoral training each year.

The British Assemblies of God have one missionary
couple working in Hyderabad, Sindh. They have a bookroom
as an evangelistic outreach, and a small church fellowship. A larger group in the Punjab, known as the Pakistan
Assemblies of God, are not connected with any Mission but
have indigenous leadership.

The United Pentecostal Church in Pakistan, who baptize in the name of Jesus only, have five missionary workers in Lahore, and small scattered congregations of Punjabi Christians. They employ several Pakistani evangelists.

Since the Pentecostals arrived after the Chuhra movement was over, and because they do not observe comity, their growth has been almost entirely by transfer from other Churches, but it is undeniable that often this is accompanied by a real conversion experience or a deepening of commitment.

In 1968 the Pentecostals had a Christian community of 6,892 of whom 2,318 were communicant members. Their missionary personnel has been enlarging rapidly reaching a total of 25 in 1973. (See Figure 38.) They have been especially plagued by factionalism. In some urban areas several different Pentecostal denominations have sprung up, each with a tiny following of people. If the attention of these Churches could be focused on the evangelization of non-Christian responsive people, their preoccupation with minor differences among themselves would disappear and the Church could expand not only by biological and transfer growth, but by bringing in many who do not now bear the name of Christian.

The Pakistan Mission of International Foreign Missions Association

The Pakistan Mission came to Pakistan in 1954 from the U.S.A. and accepted responsibility for the work in Muzaffargarh and Dera Ghazi Khan districts previously manned by the C.M.S. (See Figure 23.) It is a non church-related faith Mission, evangelical and non-sectarian in character, affiliated with the International Foreign Missions Association.

Located in a strongly Muslim area, the Church consists primarily of colonies of Punjabi sweeper Christians who have migrated in search of employment, along with some farm laborers living in the canal colonies in that area.

This has provided the Mission with a Christian community
of nearly 2,000. Due to rigid requirements for membership, they have only 220 communicant members, slightly
over ten per cent. The Mission has concentrated on
evangelistic work avoiding the establishment of institutions.

Evangelistic prospects do not seem promising in the
Pakistan Mission area. Two ladies for some years have
carried on an unusual Bible teaching ministry among
rural non-Christian women through running a small clinic.
Lives have been changed, but severe persecution resulted
when some converts openly confessed their faith. There
have been few baptisms from among the Muslims. The
Census Report of 1961 lists only 300 Scheduled Caste
people in that area. So until some responsive segment
of Muslim society can be found that will turn to Christ
in family units, little church growth can be expected.

The Pakistan Christian Fellowship of
The International Christian Fellowship
(formerly The Ceylon and India General Mission)

The Pakistan Christian Fellowship entered Pakistan in
1955 at the invitation of the Anglican Church, to take
charge of mission work in the Rahim Yar Khan district and
a portion of Bahawalpur. It is a non-sectarian, evangelical faith Mission, with workers from a variety of
countries. They fell heir to some small groups of
Punjabi Christians who had migrated to the canal colonies
in that district. A Christian village has also been
colonized and is under their care. Much-needed teaching
and pastoring of these groups have absorbed the attention
of many of their mission workers. They now have a
Christian community of 1,750 of whom 400 are communicant
members. (See Figure 31.)

Since 1965 the Pakistan Christian Fellowship have
taken an active part in reaching a Scheduled Caste, the
Marwari-speaking Bhils (usually called Marwaris in that
area.) They cooperate closely with the Conservative
Baptists in a joint committee for reaching this tribe,
known as the Marwari Christian Fellowship Committee.

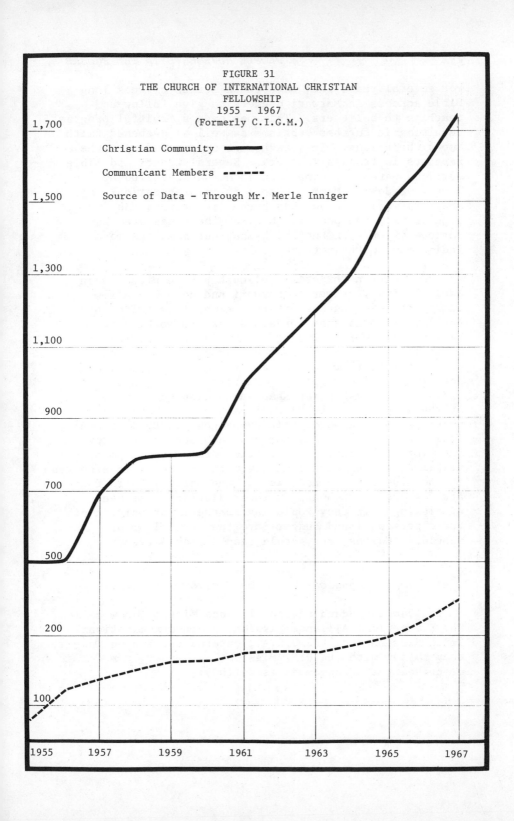

FIGURE 31
THE CHURCH OF INTERNATIONAL CHRISTIAN
FELLOWSHIP
1955 - 1967
(Formerly C.I.G.M.)

Christian Community ━━━━━

Communicant Members ▬ ▬ ▬ ▬

Source of Data - Through Mr. Merle Inniger

1,700

1,500

1,300

1,100

900

700

500

200

100

1955   1957   1959   1961   1963   1965   1967

For several years they have run a series of week long
Bible schools in Marwari centers to give follow-up
teaching to believers. This has been a fruitful program
resulting in further baptisms as well as deepened faith
among Christians. They have also cooperated with the
Baptists in translation work. Several tracts and Bible
portions have been completed in Marwari, including the
Gospel of John. Mark's Gospel is in preparation. A
small Marwari hymnbook has been mimeographed and is
popular with the people. Many of the songs are translations of Urdu or Punjabi hymns, but some are more
indigenous to their tribe.

The Pakistan Christian Fellowship have prepared an
adult literacy primer in Marwari and have had a few
campaigns to encourage literacy among them. They have
two full time national ordained pastors working in
Marwari Bhil work. One of them is a Marwari, the other
a Punjabi. One of the most encouraging aspects of
their work is that they have involved the Punjabi Christians in tribal evangelism. Members of the Punjabi congregations in Rahim Yar Khan and Sadiqabad provide much
of the support of the Marwari pastor, and take part
voluntarily in evangelistic campaigns and Bible schools.
This has provided a healthy outreach opportunity for
the Punjabi Church. As yet this work among responsive
tribal people has not been given the priority it deserves
in the Mission. In addition to the Marwari Bhils there
are responsive Meghwars in their district that need
discipling. If they would invest the major portion of
their personnel and budget into the evangelism of
Scheduled Castes, they could reap a rich harvest.

The Evangelical Alliance Mission (T.E.A.M.)

In 1946 the Scandinavian Alliance Mission, now called
The Evangelical Alliance Mission, a non-denominational
faith Mission from the U.S.A., entered the Punjab in
cooperation with the U.P. Mission. *A Century for Christ*
describes the arrangement as follows:

... (T.E.A.M.) designated its newly appointed personnel to work in our mission stations
and institutions with a view to acquiring
eventually an area themselves in which they
could work independently and particularly
for the evangelization of Muslims. (1955:43)

In 1949 T.E.A.M. was given the Hazara district north
of Taxila in the Northwest Frontier Province. Campbellpur
was added in 1957. T.E.A.M. was to concentrate on Muslim
evangelism with the understanding that the existing U.P.
congregations in those centers would remain a part of the
Rawalpindi Presbytery of the U.P. Church. In recent years
factionalism in the U.P. Church has made this arrangement
untenable. T.E.A.M. has established worshipping fellowships apart from the U.P.'s both in Abbottabad and
Campbellpur in an effort to counteract the demoralizing
effects of the McIntire schism on the Christian community,
and to provide much needed Christian nurture. They now
have several congregations with a total Christian community
of 600, of whom 160 are communicant members. In 1973
forty-five foreign missionaries were connected with this
Mission. (See Figure 38.)

The Mission School in Abbottabad was inherited from
the U.P.'s when T.E.A.M. took over the area. When the
government required mission schools to teach Islam
to all Muslim students, T.E.A.M. determined to change
the school into a co-educational institution just for
Christians. In this way they have been able to keep a
strong Christian witness in the school with the purpose
of producing dedicated leaders for the future Church. As
schools in the Frontier Province have not been nationalized, this school is still operating under mission management.

Although quite a few T.E.A.M. missionaries are involved
in work with the Church, evangelism among non-Christians
has been the focal point of T.E.A.M.'s ministry from the
start. A good percentage of their large Mission have been
dedicated Muslim evangelists, sensitive to cross-cultural
aspects of evangelism and skilled in both Urdu and Hindko
(the local language of Hazara district). They have made
extensive tours throughout the area in an effort to present
the Gospel message to as many as possible. Book stores

and reading rooms have been established in Rawalpindi,
Murree, Abbottabad and at the hospital in Qalanderabad
to provide interested Muslims with Christian literature
and an opportunity to ask questions in private. These
have been among the most successful of their kind in
Pakistan in terms of amount of literature sold, but few
converts have been won.

Bach Hospital in Qalanderabad was opened early in
their ministry as another means of outreach to the
resistant community around. The evangelistic program of
this hospital has been excellent. Not only are daily
preaching and teaching given to patients and their
relatives in several languages, but evangelistic teams
have used these contacts to establish a witness in the
home villages of many interested patients. Yet in spite
of all this faithful consecrated effort, by 1969 the
result of twenty years' work in terms of Muslim converts
was 22!

Why have the results been so few? Is there any hope
of a greater harvest in the future? What can be done to
overcome the traditional resistance of the Muslim
community? These questions have been haunting all who
are engaged in Muslim evangelism in Pakistan.

There is no easy answer. Yet church growth principles
provide some clues that should be pursued in the development of a new approach to Muslims. Probably the most
important clue lies in realizing that the Muslim community
is not uniformly resistant. Certain classes of society,
certain hill tribes, or certain occupational groups may
prove far more responsive than others. One hill tribe
in the T.E.A.M. area has yielded several families of
Christians who are still at liberty to visit their
relatives without ostracism. This tribe may be fertile
ground for sowing the Word. Such groups should be
sought out and approached in a way that results in entire
extended families coming to the Lord as a social unit.
Only then will there be hope of cracking the wall of
resistance now so evident in the Muslim community in
Pakistan. (See pages 201-203 for further insights into
this problem.)

The Indus Christian Fellowship

Mission: *The Conservative Baptist Foreign
Mission Society*

The Conservative Baptist Mission from the U.S.A.
started work in upper Sindh on the western side of the
Indus River in 1954, at the invitation of the Anglican
Church, formerly responsible for that district. Since
the people of the area are predominately Muslim, the
Mission concentrated particularly on their evangelization.
Christian literature, tracts and Gospels, were prepared
in both Urdu and Sindhi and widely distributed. Christian teams visited cattle fairs and religious festivals
to sell and distribute literature. The Mission organized
the Sindhi branch of the Pakistan Bible Correspondence
School offering courses in Sindhi, Urdu and English.
Enrollment in the Correspondence School has steadily
increased and it has been the means God has used to draw
several key men to Himself who have proved valuable in
the work.

All Conservative Baptist missionaries are expected to
learn both the national language of Pakistan, Urdu, and
the provincial language, Sindhi. Half of the Mission
studied Sindhi as their first language. These concentrated
largely on evangelism among non-Christians. The other
half learned Urdu as their first language. These became
concerned for scattered pockets of Punjabi Christian
sweepers and farm laborers who had migrated to the area.
The Punjabis form the nucleus of small congregations
worshipping in Urdu and Punjabi. Non-Christian Sindhi-
speaking converts have been unable to integrate happily
into these culturally and linguistically different fellowships. This has proved a hindrance in winning non-Christians. From 1954 to 1965 a total of 31 adults were baptized,
a large majority coming from the Punjabi community.

A Scheduled Caste group of circus performers and
entertainers, called the Bazigars, showed considerable
interest in the Gospel prior to 1965. The Mission contacted them a few times but made no concentrated effort

to win them. During the war with India in 1965 they became
Muslims. A few from the Bagari caste have been baptized
but no movement has developed among them as yet.

In 1965 an influential Marwari-speaking Bhil, named
Dom Ji Philip, found the assurance of salvation and new
life through Bible Correspondence courses. He asked for
a man to come to this home village near Ghotki and teach
his family. The Conservative Baptists sent their only
national evangelist to teach them for a week. He returned
enthusiastic about the way his message had been received
by the Marwari Bhils. That year ten Marwaris were
baptized.

In a paper entitled *The Marwaris,* Mr. Ray Buker, who
was assigned by the Conservative Baptists to concentrate on,
Marwari evangelism reports, "By the end of 1966 several
hundred Marwaris had professed to accept Christ as
their personal Savior, and a total of thirty-two had
been baptized." (1969:6) Why were only 32 baptized out
of so many avowed believers? Too long a probation period
preceding baptism is one of the most effective ways of
stunting the growth of a group movement.

The greatest increase in baptisms in the Mission came
from 1967 to 1969. A total of 225 people were baptized
in those three years; 140 of them or over 50 per cent
were Marwaris. (See Figure 32). Receptivity among the
tribes was heightened by the 1965 and 1971 wars with
India. Being Hindu in orientation, the Scheduled Castes
feel insecure in a Muslim nation and fear a sudden turn
of public opinion against them. This makes them more
open to becoming Christians. God has used this natural
instinct for safety as a means of drawing them to Himself.

Unfortunately Mr. Buker had to return to the U.S.A.
in 1969, and no missionary was free to give this work full
time until it was assigned to Mr. Winters in 1971. In
the meantime, Dom Ji fell dangerously ill and was preserved to the ministry only by the miraculous grace of
God. Growth was slow during 1970 and 1971, but since
1972 baptisms have increased more rapidly. By the end
of 1972 a total of approximately 240 Marwari Bhils had
been baptized by the Conservative Baptists. This con-
stitutes nearly 60 per cent of their total of 415 baptisms.

A Marwari Bhil Baptism

Evangelist Dom J; Philip (right) Shares God's Word
with an Elder of the Marwari-Bhil Tribe

Nomadic Tribe Receiving Christian Teaching

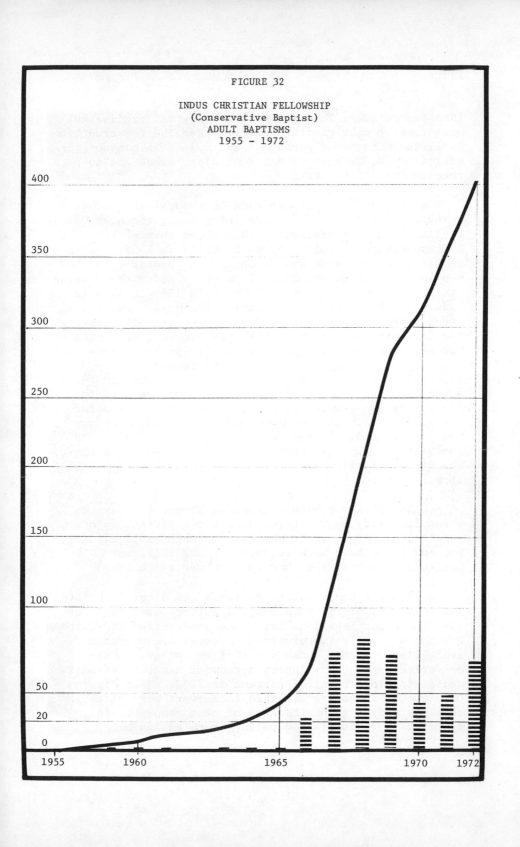

FIGURE 32

INDUS CHRISTIAN FELLOWSHIP
(Conservative Baptist)
ADULT BAPTISMS
1955 – 1972

(See Figure 32.)   This movement shows great promise but
must receive much greater priority from the Conservative
Baptists in terms of personnel and budget if many of the
estimated 20,000 Marwari Bhils of upper Sindh are to be
reached for Jesus Christ.

A short lived effort was made to evangelize the Od
tribe in Dadu district. A promising young educated Od,
Ranjah, became interested in the Gospel through the Bible
Correspondence School. He was baptized in 1959. Seven
of his relatives were won to Christ and baptized in 1968.
Ranjah was made an evangelistic worker under the Mission
and Mr. and Mrs. Winters were sent in 1969 to live in
Dadu and encourage this movement. The next three years
seven more of Ranjah's relatives were baptized, bringing
the total to 15. As yet Ranjah has proved ineffective so
far as an evangelist to his own tribe, probably because he
is young while they respect age; he is more highly
educated than most of his tribe; and he is married to
a Punjabi girl. He has many gifts and may be used in
the future as he matures, or some more effective older
man may be won, in answer to prayer, who can lead many
Ods to the Lord. At the end of 1970 Ranjah opened his
own business but has continued as a volunteer evangelist.
The Winters family were transferred into Marwari Bhil
work.

Medical work has been carried on from early days as
a supplementary means of reaching the resistant majority
population. At first it was done through small clinics,
but now these have been replaced by the Shikarpur
Christian Hospital that has been in use since 1971.

In 1972 the Conservative Baptists had a total Christian community of 794 with 396 communicant members. They
have three congregations and three unorganized worshipping
groups; with only two ordained pastors, one unordained
evangelistic worker, and 8 part-time workers. Conservative Baptist missionary personnel has been steadily
decreasing to a total of sixteen in 1973. (See Figure 38
Only two of these are assigned to Marwari work although
this has proved to be the area of most response. A
common fallacy in mission policy is to assign the

most workers to people who are difficult to win, in the
hope that greater numbers will help to "storm the fort,"
and batter down the walls, so they can be won. Such a
policy results in responsive fields being unharvested
due to a shortage of reapers, while unripe fields receive
many workers but remain unproductive because they are not
yet ready to yield their harvest. A wiser principle is
to follow the example of a plantation owner who concen-
trates his workers in the fields that are ready for
reaping, leaving only a few to tend the unripe areas
to keep him informed as to when they too will be ready
for harvest. It is urgent that the Mission recognize
and take seriously the responsiveness of the Marwari
Bhil group and speedily reinforce its outreach to them
in order to win them while there is an open door.

The Brethren Churches

*Mission: The Brethren Missionary Fellowship
            (including several Brethren groups)*

It is difficult to discover accurate facts about the
Brethren Churches because they lack a central organization
and don't keep statistics.

The Plymouth Brethren have had work in India since
1836, but must have entered the Punjab sometime around
1890. From the start they have not observed comity
boundaries, so their congregations are located all over
Pakistan. The largest groups, however, are in Multan,
Lahore, Rawalpindi, and Kohat. One of the main thrusts
of their work is to convert nominal Christians. Their
congregations have grown largely by transfer growth from
both Protestant and Roman Catholic Churches. They have
an estimated number of 50 assemblies or congregations in
Pakistan, a Christian community of about 11,000, and
approximately 2,000 communicant members. Most of their
pastors are not formally trained in a Bible School or
Seminary; nor do they work full-time at the ministry,
but support themselves with a secular job and do their
church work outside of work hours. In spite of this,
they have often proved more successful than the more
highly trained, full-time pastors of other denominations.

Perhaps this is because they live more nearly on the same level as their congregation and take on this ministry not as a profession but voluntarily. All congregations are self-supporting.

The missionaries of the Brethren Missionary Fellowship come from a variety of sending groups, but work cooperatively on the field in a loosely organized Brethren Fellowship. In 1973 there were 23 missionaries in all the Brethren groups combined. (See Figure 38.)

In addition to their work among Christians, the Brethren have attempted to win non-Christians by running clinics and bookrooms, and by distributing Christian literature. They spearheaded the establishment of a Christian publishing house, the Masihi Isha'at Khana, in Lahore, that publishes many Christian books each year in Urdu and English. This has been a great service to the whole Church.

In 1904 a son was born to devout Hindu parents in the Punjab who for certain family reasons dedicated him to the Sikh religion, giving him the name Bakht Singh Chabre. In 1926 his father sent him to London to study mechanical engineering. During the next few years he had repeated contacts with Christians both in England and Canada where his study of the New Testament led him to faith in Christ. He was baptized in 1932 in the Broadway West Baptist Church in Vancouver.

The following year Bakht Singh returned to India where he gradually became an outstanding evangelist. He was first licensed by the Anglican Church and worked for four years in Karachi with the C.M.S. missionary, the Rev. Haskell, in developing cottage Bible Study groups and enriching the spiritual life of the congregation. Later he left the Anglican Church and worked independently. Although he was never officially associated with the Brethren Churches, he has been classified with them because of the independent nature of his ministry and his stress on believer's baptism. He has been greatly used

as a convention speaker all over the Indian subcontinent,
to bring many nominal Christians to a vital faith. At
Partition he chose to remain in India with headquarters
in Madras where he has continued to be a source of
blessing to many.

The Afghan Border Crusade

The Afghan Border Crusade (called the A.B.C.) was
founded in the Northwest Frontier Province by Mr. Jack
Ringer in 1944. He was no stranger to the Frontier, but
had served there first in the British army and later
under the Central Asia Mission from 1938 to 1940. When
the Central Asia Mission withdrew from the Frontier to
concentrate upon Kashmir, Mr. Ringer established the
A.B.C. Mission to carry on the work. The A.B.C. is an
international, inter-denominational faith Mission with
the primary goal of evangelizing the Pathans of the
Frontier.

Their primary evangelist from the start has been a
Punjabi raised in the Frontier who speaks Pushto fluently,
but is nevertheless not a Pathan. This may have proved
an additional stumbling block to the already formidable
barrier of ingrained anti-Christian prejudice among the
Pathans. Only a few Pathans have been baptized and some
of them did not remain faithful. However, a small
Church known as "The Evangelical Free Church" has been
established among Punjabi Christians who have migrated
to the Frontier. Sixty-six families make up the
Christian community of the A.B.C. Mission. Over half of
them live in Mardan where the headquarters of the Mission
is located; others are in Peshawar, Kohat and Nowshera.
Oghi has been an outstation with a medical clinic for
many years.

The A.B.C. Mission had six missionaries in 1973.
(See Figure 38.) One of their most effective ministries
has been among Christian airforce officers stationed in

the frontier. Bible study and fellowship groups have
brought many of these keen young men into a vital
relationship with Jesus Christ and sent them out to serve
zealously in the fellowship of other denominations.

Worldwide Evangelization Crusade

The Worldwide Evangelization Crusade (known as W.E.C.)
first sent workers to the Northwest Frontier Province in
1935. Mr. Rex Bavington with four others came to Haripur
in Hazara district to help the Ashby sisters. These
amazing women had done independent pioneer work witnessing in the Haripur and Kashmir areas since 1913. In
1919 they purchased a sixteen acre farm to provide a
source of income for their Mission, and to give non-
Christian inquirers and new converts a place to live and
work in Christian fellowship. At the height of the project there were 60 or 70 at the farm, both men and women,
but no records are available of the number of people won
to Christ by this method. The periodical prayer bulletin
they sent out mentions an occasional convert from Islam
or Hinduism, but the project was increasingly plagued
by insincere inquirers looking for a soft place to live
with all expenses paid.

W.E.C. took over this Haripur farm for a time and used
it as a base for their work. They ran a hostel for
Christian children in Abbottabad, and opened primary
schools in a number of centers in Kashmir as well as in
Abbottabad and Muzzafarabad, the present capital of
Azad Kashmir. Later W.E.C. returned the farm to the
Ashbys who sold parts of it and willed the remainder to
one of the faithful converts who had taken the name of
John Ashby. He still lives there as a Christian, but
most of his family have married Muslims and left the
faith. Efforts at the colonization of converts have
almost invariably ended in sorrow like this. They do
not produce a growing witnessing Christian fellowship.

W.E.C. has established stations in Peshawar and
Quetta. Their Christian community in Peshawar consists
of 20 families. One or two families live in Abbottabad
and vicinity; while a small group gather in Quetta.
These are made up largely of Punjabi Christians who
have migrated to these areas.

The Seventh Day Adventists

Dr. Mann, the first missionary of the Seventh Day
Adventist Mission (called the S.D.A.) opened work in
Gujranwala in 1913. He was soon joined by others. They
arrived at the height of the Chuhra movement to Christ.
From 1909 to 1912 the U.P.'s in whose comity area the
S.D.A.'s settled, were baptizing an average of 3,000
people a year. The years following their arrival
correspond with World War I, when baptisms fell to just
over 1,000 a year--still a large number. (See Figure 12.)
Although Gujranwala was in the midst of this tremendous
growth, the S.D.A.'s recorded their first baptism in
1917, after four years of effort.

In 1916 land was purchased in the city of Chuhar
Khana in the canal colony of Sheikhupura. A center was
soon established in Lahore as well. The Sheikhupura
canal colony area was one of the most responsive to the
Gospel because the Chuhras who migrated there were
dislocated from their former familiar surroundings and
open to change. According to the census reports
Khangah Dogran Tehsil (the county in which Chuhar Khana
was located) had 10,000 Christians in 1911. By 1921
there were 18,000 Christians and 25,000 Hindu Chuhras,
the group most open to conversion. The potential for
church growth either by transfer or by conversion was
unlimited. The S.D.A. Church was situated directly in
the center of all this potential, yet she progressed
at such a slow rate that thirty years later, by 1943,
her communicant membership totaled 245--an average of
8 people a year! (See Figure 33.) What was the reason?

The cause of such slow growth cannot be blamed upon
any lack of dedicated spiritual leadership on the part
of the S.D.A. missionaries, nor upon their doctrines.
The answer probably lies in the approach they used to
evangelism. All over the world the S.D.A.'s are famous
for their Christian literature, Bible study courses, and
publications on science and health. These emphases
they transferred to India. Working largely in English
(though later they did develop Urdu literature too),
they set up the Voice of Prophecy Bible Correspondence
School, prepared Sabbath School materials and published
a health magazine. These were utilized only by a few
elite English-speaking people who were not responsive
to the Gospel. It left untouched the illiterate rural
Chuhra population who were turning to Christ by the
thousands all around them.

From the start the S.D.A. work was strongly oriented
toward institutions. They established schools, mostly
in English medium; and operated trade schools connected
with a variety of factories that manufacture vanilla,
puffed wheat, peanut-butter, and other products. In
1947 work was established in Karachi. A large hospital
was built that has a nurses' training school connected
with it. Dental clinics are found both in Karachi and
Rawalpindi. These cater largely to the foreign community
and high class Pakistanis. This approach netted them
only a small elite Christian community, most of whom
speak beautiful English, are skilled in selling literature,
and quite Western in manner.

After 1943 S.D.A. growth rate increased. By 1953 her
communicant membership was nearly 1,200; by 1963 it was
about 2,180; in 1971 it peaked at 2,875; but by 1972 it
had fallen to 2,518. (It is quite likely that the
sudden peak shown in Figure 33 from 1967 to 1971 is a
statistical error.)

Why was the S.D.A. Church growing steadily though not
spectacularly at a time when the Chuhra movement was
over and most other Churches in the area had leveled
off or were declining in growth? Again the answer

FIGURE 33

THE SEVENTH DAY ADVENTIST CHURCH

1913 – 1972

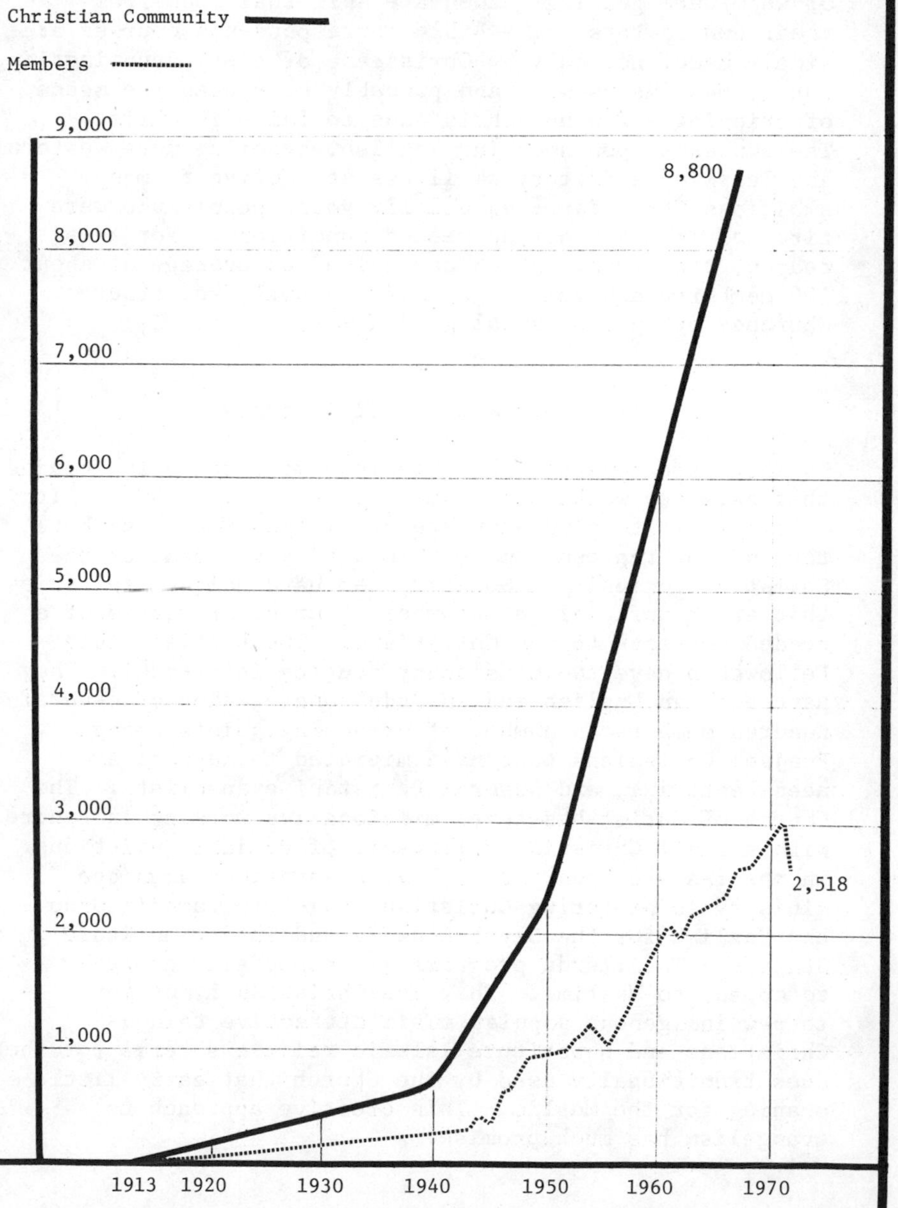

Christian Community ━━━━━

Members ⋯⋯⋯⋯⋯⋯

probably lies in the characteristic methods used by the
S.D.A. Church.   Their Bible Correspondence Courses and
excellent Sabbath School materials appealed to the 3rd
and 4th generation Christians in other Churches, many
of whom were getting inadequate spiritual food from
their own pastors.   The Bible correspondence courses are
widely used, not only by Christians of every denomination,
but by Muslims as well and probably have been the means
of bringing a few non-Christians to faith in Christ.
The emphasis upon speaking English, becoming more Western,
and learning a factory skill was attractive to many
ambitious Christians, especially young people who were
tired of living under depressed conditions.   For this
reason, the S.D.A. Church has gained an average of about
100 members each year by transfer growth from other
Churches or by biological growth.

Missions With Small Churches

There are several other Missions more recently founded
that have few workers and small church fellowships.   It
is difficult to find accurate statistics for these but
they do not represent more than a tiny per cent of the
Christian community.   Some of them have unique ministries
that are beneficial to the whole Church, or represent a
needed outreach to non-Christians.   The Baptist Bible
Fellowship have two missionary couples in Karachi.   They
have both an English and an Urdu congregation of several
hundred members; a number of preaching points among
Punjabi Christians that have migrated to Karachi and
need pastoring, and several Pakistani evangelists.   The
Church of Christ has three missionaries working in Lahore
with a small Christian fellowship of Punjabi Christians.
In the last few years they have spearheaded a unique
ministry in preparing Christian radio programs in Urdu
and English for the Seychelles Island Christian Radio
Station.   Their Urdu programs are especially geared
to appeal to Muslims.   They use Christian hymns set
to new indigenous popular music attractive to non-
Christians and substitute Islamic religious terms for the
ones traditionally used by the Church that carry little
meaning for the Muslim.   This creative approach to
evangelism has much promise.

Helping or Service Missions

There are a number of helping or service Missions that
have a policy of not establishing their own Churches
but of strengthening the existing Churches in their
areas. Some of the larger ones are mentioned below in
greater detail:

The Bible and Medical Missionary Fellowship
(formerly the Zenana Bible and Medical Mission)

The Zenana Bible and Medical Mission was established
in England for the purpose of sending women missionaries
not to establish a Church overseas, but to help in the
educational, medical, and evangelistic work already
founded by other Missions. They began work in the Punjab
in the 1890's, and for the most part assist in a variety
of institutions run by others. In the 1950's they began
sending men missionaries as well, so changed their name
to the Bible and Medical Missionary Fellowship. In
1973 they had 23 missionaries working in Pakistan. (See
Figure 38.) Only the following two institutions in
Pakistan are their own:

1) Kinnaird High School for Girls in Lahore is a boarding
school primarily for Christians, with a good Bible teaching program. It has been used to bring many nominal
Christian girls to a vital faith.

2) The Christian Caravan Hospital in the Hyderabad
district of Sindh is particularly significant to our
study, for it is contributing actively to evangelistic
efforts among the rural people of Sindh. The C.C.H., a
movable hospital made up of trailers and pre-fabricated
houses, was started in 1960 by Dr. Jock Anderson. It
moves every three to five years and locates in areas
where medical facilities are inadequate. People flock
to the hospital from a great variety of tribes and ethnic
groups found in that area of Sindh. Located in the
heart of the recent movements among the Scheduled Caste
tribes, it is playing a significant role in sowing the

Seed among responsive peoples. The hospital has been
used to bring a number of individuals to confess Christ
in baptism. Recently it sparked off the conversion of
a sizable group of Bhils from the Mirpur Khas area.
(See page 248 for details of this event.) This hospital
can be greatly used by God in the future, especially
if the staff will concentrate their efforts on the
Scheduled Castes who are open to the Gospel in an unusual
way at this time.

The Reformed Churches of the Netherlands

When the door closed to work in Indonesia during the
1950's, the Reformed Churches of the Netherlands offered
to send missionaries to help any Mission that requested
their aid.   They have been used in a great variety of
capacities working in cooperation with many different
Churches as staff members of hospitals, colleges,
technical schools, and the Christian Study Centre. They
also operated a social work project for refugees. In
1973 there were 11 missionaries from this group in
Pakistan.

The United Fellowship for Christian Service
(formerly the Women's Union Missionary Society)

The Women's Union Missionary Society of America
established work in Multan in 1956, taking charge of a
women's hospital at the request of the Anglican Church
who did not have the personnel to man it. Recently
they too have begun to include men into the Mission and
so have changed their name to the United Fellowship for
Christian Service. They had 8 workers in Pakistan in
1973. (See Figure 38.) They have a strong evangelistic ministry at the hospital in connection with
their medical work. They also offer a training course
in midwifery and place abandoned or orphan children
into Christian homes for adoption.

Miscellaneous Groups

The fellowship of Evangelical Baptist Churches in
Canada have one couple in Karachi who have an unusual
ministry of personal witness and literature distribution
to Muslims and Parsis. The Christian Literature Crusade
have one couple who run a bookstore in Karachi and
concentrate on literature distribution. The Child
Evangelism Crusade for Christ International has three
workers in Lahore who produce and promote a variety of
visual aids for teaching children. They also train local
congregations in ways of evangelizing children. The
Mennonite Central Committee provides short-term young
men to help with agricultural projects in various centers.
In 1973 there were two working in Multan district. The
Kherwara Mission of Denmark has one couple living in
Mirpur Khas, Sindh, in charge of a hostel for Christian
boys, largely from tribal backgrounds.

In addition to these there are four couples working
independently. Three of these work in the Northwest
Frontier concentrating on Pathan evangelism through
preaching, medicine, literature distribution, and
visitation. The fourth couple live in Pasrur and run
a Christian home for poor children.

The Roman Catholic Church

The earliest record of Christian witness in the area
of India occupied now by Pakistan was in the Moghul period
from 1579 to 1581. Portuguese Jesuit missionaries were
established in the courts of Akbar and Jahangir. They were
given a pension and allowed to build a church in Lahore.
When Shah Jahan came to power he dismissed the missionaries and tore down the church. No Christian community
in Pakistan dates from that period.

In Sindh Fr. Louis Francis of the Carmelite order
arrived in Thatta on the Indus River in 1613. He built
a church and a small monastery there in 1618, and during
his ministry baptized several Hindus and Muslims. The

Augustinians also set up work in Thatta a little later.
Anti-Portuguese feeling gradually built up until the
Augustinians felt forced to leave in 1655. The
Carmelites abandoned Thatta in 1672. There is no trace
of these Missions today.

Roman Catholic mission work was re-established in
Sindh in 1842 by the Carmelites after the conquest of
Sindh by the British. Returning as chaplains to the
British troops, they also established a center for
Indians in Hyderabad, and opened a school in Karachi,
now famous as the St. Patrick's School.

In 1852 the Carmelites were replaced in Sindh by the
Jesuits who continued the work until 1935 when the Dutch
Franciscans took over. Most missionary effort in the early
days was geared to reach the Goans, South Indians, Anglo-
Indians and Europeans, not the local population. In the
1860's, however, some Sindhi converts are mentioned in
their records, who had become a problem because they
did not come as family units but as single individuals
and were not able to form a meaningful Christian fellowship. The Rt. Rev. Alcuin van Miltenburg comments:

> They [Sindhi converts] had not been able
> to form their own community as they had
> either not been able to convert their
> families, or their wives had died child-
> less, or they had married into and had
> been absorbed into non-Sindhi Catholic
> families, so that there existed no Sindhi
> Catholic community, be it ever so small.
> (1947:26)

In the Punjab a Roman Catholic priest established
residence in Lahore in 1852. By 1880 this had expanded
to include a missionary center and an orphanage for
girls. As early as 1853 there was a Roman Catholic
priest in Sialkot. By 1889 it was an important mission
center with six missionaries. They wrote of "numerous
conversions," probably from among the Chuhras, as the
movement was well under way in the U.P. Church in Sialkot
district by then.

In 1892 the Bishop purchased 175 acres and colonized Mariabad in the Chenab Canal Colony. They later expanded this to 700 acres. Other Christian villages were colonized in various canal areas as time went on. From 1892 Catholics vigorously extended their work throughout the canal colonies, concentrating on the Chuhras, and finding them responsive.

The Roman Catholic Church was strategically located in relation to the Chuhra movement. They had a strong station in Sialkot when the Chuhra movement was first growing, from 1884 through 1910. Then they expanded throughout the canal colonies where the largest accessions from the Chuhras took place from 1905 to 1915. (See Figure 18.)

Growth from 1901-1931

Being one of the first Missions in the Punjab in the 1850's, the Catholics had ample time to analyze the situation and take full advantage of the responsiveness of the depressed classes. Official Roman Catholic statistics for the early part of the 20th century were not available to the author. However, the *Census Reports* for 1901, 1911, 1921 and 1931 reveal a surprising slowness in growth in comparison with Protestant groups in the early years of the Chuhra movement. (See Figure 34.)

In 1901 eighty-four percent of all conversions to Christ in the Punjab took place in Gujranwala, Sialkot, and Lyallpur districts. The Roman Catholics had a Christian community of only 1,252 in these three districts, and an estimated total of 1,500 for the whole Punjab. By 1911 this number had grown to 6,741 for those three districts, and a total of 8,022 for the whole Punjab. This seems like an encouraging increase in one decade, but when compared below with the Protestant figures for 1911. it becomes dwarfed.

	Divisions of the Punjab	Roman Catholics	Protestants
1911	Lahore Division	4,063	87,356
	Rawalpindi Division	404	10,087
	Multan Division	3,544	32,974
	Bahawalpur Division	11	35
	Totals	8,022	121,452

The Roman Catholic Church comprised only six per cent of the whole Christian population of the Punjab in 1911.

A comparison of the figures in the 1921 Census Report is also revealing as follows:

	Divisions of the Punjab	Roman Catholics	Protestants
1921	Lahore Division	13,192	152,400
	Rawalpindi Division	3,067	16,711
	Multan Division	15,378	57,195
	Bahawalpur Division	12	94
	Totals:	31,649	226,400

During that one decade the Roman Catholic Church increased rapidly at an annual growth rate of 14-1/2 per cent or 23,615 people. Seen by itself this is outstanding growth, but when compared to the Protestants who increased over 4 times that amount or by 104,948 persons during the same period, it isn't so impressive. The Roman Catholic Church still had only 12.4 per cent of the Christian population of the Punjab.

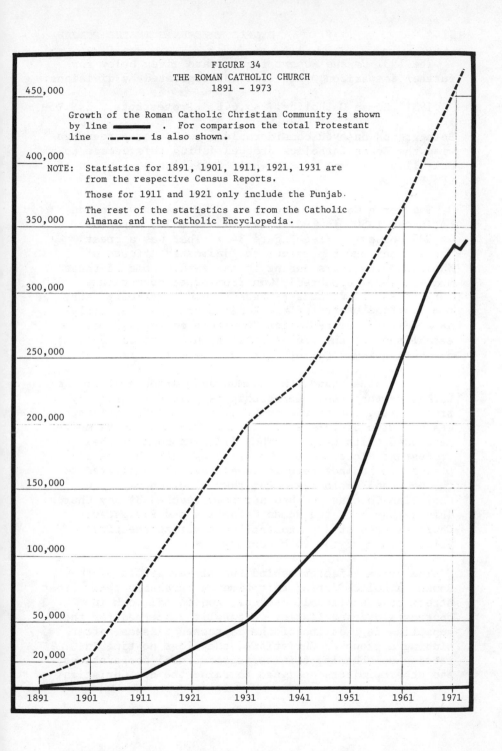

FIGURE 34
THE ROMAN CATHOLIC CHURCH
1891 - 1973

Growth of the Roman Catholic Christian Community is shown
by line ━━━━ . For comparison the total Protestant
line ┅┅┅┅ is also shown.

NOTE: Statistics for 1891, 1901, 1911, 1921, 1931 are
       from the respective Census Reports.

       Those for 1911 and 1921 only include the Punjab.

       The rest of the statistics are from the Catholic
       Almanac and the Catholic Encyclopedia.

450,000
400,000
350,000
300,000
250,000
200,000
150,000
100,000
50,000
20,000

1891   1901   1911   1921   1931   1941   1951   1961   1971

The 1931 *Census Report* figures are given below for
further comparison, this time not separated by divisions.

1931 Roman Catholics: 45,641   Protestants: 349,659

Both groups enjoyed considerable growth, but percentage-
wise the Roman Catholics dropped during this decade to
only 11.5 per cent of the whole Christian population of
the Punjab.

The Roman Catholic Church in 30 years grew from an
estimated 1,500 in 1901 to 45,641 in 1931, more than
44,000 persons. (See Figure 34.) That was a great
achievement and represents the dedicated efforts of
hundreds of workers during those years. Some of these
members were undoubtedly won from other communions,
for Protestant records repeatedly and vigorously decry
the "encroachments" of the Roman Catholics. As early
as 1888 the "Inter-Mission Committee on Popery" was
established by the Protestants in an effort to
counteract Roman Catholic activities.

On the other hand, the common accusation against the
Catholics that their membership is gained entirely by
proselytism, not by the conversion of non-Christians,
was not true of this early period when the Chuhra movement was at its height. They did find some of the
Protestant "lost sheep" who were neglected by their
pastors or had not been followed when they migrated to
the new canal colonies. But they also won many non-
Christian Chuhras who had not been reached by any Church.
This is why both the Roman Catholics and Protestant
Churches grew at a phenomenal rate during the first
thirty years of the 20th century.

The primary factor behind the slower growth of the
Roman Catholics during this time was probably their great
stress on educational, medical, and social work in
contrast to evangelistic. Naturally concerned for the
appalling degradation of the depressed classes, after
winning a group of Christians, they lost no time in
setting up schools, clinics, agricultural cooperatives,
and other projects designed to raise the new Christian

community out of its poverty and illiteracy to a
position of respect in society. This was a worthy
and necessary effort, but it occupied so much of the
time and strength of the majority of missionary personnel,
that as much stress could not be given to evangelism as
Protestant Missions gave. Roman Catholics always seemed
to have adequate personnel and financial resources to
build up an elaborate network of institutions. The
more limited resources in Protestant Missions of both
money and personnel has no doubt been a blessing in
disguise, preventing them from investing so heavily in
institutions, and spurring them on to develop indigenous
leadership at a faster rate.

Growth from 1931-1972

The next figures available for the Roman Catholic
Church are found in *The Catholic Encyclopedia,* published
in 1950 and probably represent their statistics for
1949.   These are not only for the Punjab, but for the
whole of (West) Pakistan. Compared to the Protestants
they are as follows:

   1949   Roman Catholics: 123,164   Protestants: 351,205

During this period the Roman Catholics made a significant gain in percentage, now comprising 25 per cent of
the total Christian population. As the Chuhra movement
waned, the Protestant Churches stopped increasing except
by biological growth. The Roman Catholics, however,
were just starting into the era of their greatest
expansion. From 1950 to 1972 the Church almost tripled
in size, and made great gains on the Protestants as is
seen by the comparative figures below:

   1972   Roman Catholics: 341,231 Protestants: 545,501

At present count, therefore, the Roman Catholic Church
comprises 38.5 per cent of the total Christian population of Pakistan.

Why has the Roman Catholic Church made such spectacular growth since the end of the Chuhra movement? Where are her new members coming from?

Since the 1930's there have been no significant gains from non-Christians in any Church, except for a few years immediately following Partition when some pockets of Scheduled Caste people became Christians who previously were unaligned or only nominally attached to Hindu or Sikh communities that fled to India. Since 1950 most of the major Protestant denominations have not been able to keep up to their biological growth rate, so are actually declining, even though their numbers continue slowly to increase. The sharp rise in the membership of the Roman Catholic Church during this period evidently comes from winning to her ranks thousands of former Protestants.

How has the Roman Catholic Church been able to win such a large number of Protestants? Several factors have contributed to this significant number of transfers. They are discussed below:

1) *Relief Supplies*. Partition in 1947 left the Christian community financially poor and economically insecure, because many of their Hindu and Sikh landlords had fled the country. Severe floods devastated the Punjab in 1950, 1954, 1955 and 1959, destroying the homes and crops of thousands of Christians. Church World Service and Catholic relief organizations poured in badly needed supplies. When the emergency situation was over, Church World Service diminished its supplies and later discontinued them altogether because of the greed, jealousy, and factionalism they produced in the Church. The Catholic Church continued to receive massive relief supplies. These were distributed to Catholic school children and church members. In order to be eligible to receive regular relief goods, thousands of nominal Protestants became members of the Roman Catholic Church.

2) Number of Foreign Personnel. By the late 1950's the
major Protestant Missions in Pakistan were steadily
diminishing in missionary personnel. The recruits sent
out in large numbers after World War I were retiring
and not being replaced because of lack of funds in the
home Church, coupled with a policy of "working oneself
out of a job"--i.e. training a national replacement.
Evangelistic workers were withdrawn from work with the
Church to cover shortages of staff in mission institutions.
The Church was left to struggle along with a minimum
of encouragement and teaching.

In the meantime, Roman Catholic foreign personnel was
steadily increasing. They started many new schools for
villagers and for urban Christian sweeper communities.
They provided services in education, medicine, and
agriculture that the Christian community appreciated.
As Protestant institutions decreased, Roman Catholic
work increased, naturally attracting many Christians
to transfer their membership.

3) Factionalism. As the various Protestant national
Churches won independence from their "mother" Churches,
factionalism increased. Pastors became more and more
involved in party struggles and neglected to feed their
flock. Roman Catholic priests regularly toured the
villages on their motorcycles, and provided encouragement
and worship opportunities to many neglected Protestant
congregations. As Protestant leaders vied for positions
of power in their church courts, the Roman Catholics
were busy winning the people to their church.

These seem to be the major reasons for the progress
made by the Roman Catholic Church from 1931 when she had
only 11.5 per cent of the Christian population, to 1972
when she had become 38.5 per cent of the total, with
341,231 in her Christian community.

Movement Among Scheduled Castes in Sindh

Early work in Sindh concentrated upon the Goans,
South Indians, Anglo-Indians and Europeans. Then by
1935 over a thousand Punjabi Chuhras migrated from the

Punjab and were baptized in Karachi, primarily in the
Lyari Slaughter House quarter. In Hyderabad 95 Punjabi
sweepers were baptized during the same period. From
1940 to 1946 large groups of Punjabi sweepers were
baptized in Sukkur and form the majority of the congregation there.

In 1936 some Bhils showed an interest in the Gospel
in Nawabshah. A priest took up residence there and
built a hospital, a school, and a church. An agricultural project and a fair price provision shop were
established but failed. The first Bhils were baptized
in December 1941, followed by several family groups.
After six years of effort, permanent homes for 24
families of Bhils were provided by the Roman Catholics.
It is sad to note that at Partition time in 1947 these
Bhils fled to India and since then no further effort
has been made by the Roman Catholics among the non-
Christian Bhils remaining in the Nawabshah area.

In 1944 the first group of Kohlis was baptized near
Matli. By 1947 there were two villages with small mud
chapels, and a second group had been baptized. At Matli
a boarding school was started to educate both Kohli
and Punjabi children. By 1970 approximately 5,000 Kohlis
of the Parkari group in the Matli area, and 500 Kutchi
Kohlis in the Nawabshah and Mirpur Khas areas had been
baptized.

At a meeting in Mirpur Khas in 1967 the Catholics
set up a plan for the complete Christianization of the
Parkari Kohli tribe. Their plan includes land settlement, education, religious and vocational training and
social uplift. They have already trained 23 Parkari
Kohli catechists and established their circuits. They
have four or five priests working full time with this
tribe who have learned the language and customs of
the people. Much of this program has not yet been
implemented, however, due to lack of personnel and
funds.

Characteristics of Roman Catholic Work

There are a number of characteristics of the Roman
Catholic missionary effort in Pakistan that have signif-
icantly affected the growth and development of her Church.

Foreign Leadership. Protestant Missions have made it a
policy to develop indigenous leadership able to administer
and manage institutions as well as pastor and govern
their own Church. They stress democratic procedures in
making decisions so that nationals can learn by doing.
In recent years almost all Protestant institutions have
been under the management of Pakistani staff.

The Roman Catholics follow a different policy in
their work. They have maintained foreign leadership in
the Church and in her institutions. The number of
Roman Catholic foreign workers in Pakistan today is
greater than (possibly nearly double) the combined number
of all Protestant missionaries in the land. (See
Figure 38.) They have trained a few Pakistani priests
and nuns, largely Goans. They have paid catechists
working as local pastors, carefully supervised by a
foreign priest. This autocratic form of church government is more efficient, with less money and time spent on
committee meetings or discipline cases. Catechists
are required to keep accurate records and to maintain a
program of regular worship among the people in their
charge. Also Roman Catholic priests and nuns can give
themselves more fully to their work because they have
no family responsibilities that necessarily take up the
time of most Protestant missionaries.

Although the policy of foreign control is more
efficient and fruitful at present, it is short sighted.
If foreign missionaries should be expelled from Pakistan,
the Roman Catholic Church would be bereft of most of
her capable leadership, and left weak in everything but
numbers.

In recent years the Roman Catholics have taken steps
to remedy this situation. They have established and
expanded seminaries for training Pakistani priests. A
Minor Seminary was started in Lahore in 1951. The
Regional Major Seminary was in Lahore, then in Quetta,
but was shifted to beautiful new facilities in Karachi
in 1958. It offers a six year course and is beginning
to provide the Church with better trained national leadership. The Archbishop in Karachi and the Bishop of
Hyderabad Diocese are both Pakistanis of Goan descent.
Goans are citizens of Pakistan but speak English and
have a distinct culture of their own. Truly indigenous
leadership needs to be further developed, both priests
and laymen.

No Effort to Win Muslims. It seems to be a policy of
the Roman Catholic Church not to attempt to convert or
baptize Muslims. In their schools they have never
required non-Christians to take any catechetical training
or Bible study. In their hospitals they have no
evangelists to visit non-Christian patients or hold
general meetings in the wards with the purpose of giving
Christian teaching. It is a pity that the outstanding
example they set in attitudes and actions, and the good
will engendered through their excellent educational and
medical facilities are not used to bring people to
Jesus Christ. They have unlimited opportunities in
their institutions to make a clear witness in high places,
but these are not utilized.

Stress on Institutions. The great majority of Roman
Catholic missionary personnel and budget have gone into
educational and medical institutions. They have two
general types of institutions: (1) Schools and hospitals
that cater to the wealthy and influential and charge
heavy fees for their services. These have adequate
foreign personnel, beautiful buildings, and the latest
equipment. Schools of this kind offer a European type
education that appeals to officers in government circles.
Their hospitals are attractive to influential people
because of their excellent facilities and loving service.

This gives the Roman Catholics a greater security in the country, for people of position are loathe to do away with their institutions. When privately owned schools were nationalized by the government of Pakistan in 1972, some of the best Roman Catholic English-medium schools were exempted.

(2) In addition to the high calibre institutions for wealthy non-Christians, the Roman Catholics have numerous small indigenous-type schools and village dispensaries catering largely to Christians. These give their services at nominal prices to all Christians, and have helped to develop a more literate Church.

A Changing Atmosphere. Sweeping changes have come into the Roman Catholic Church in recent years. Their attitude towards Protestants is much more cordial than before, and on several occasions they have urged joint projects in the way of schools and church buildings in areas where the Christian community is mixed Catholic and Protestant. Most of these projects have not yet materialized, but a cooperative spirit is developing.

In order to be less offensive to Muslims, the Catholics have removed images from many of their churches now, and some church buildings are patterned after mosques. Liturgy has been translated from Latin into Urdu, and they are beginning to sing many Urdu and Punjabi hymns learned from the Protestants. Bible reading by laymen is encouraged, and great strides have been taken in adult literacy in cooperation with the Adult Basic Education Centre, until recently a totally Protestant organization. These are encouraging signs that in the future we can spend less time opposing one another, and concentrate together on the overwhelming task of winning the non-Christians to faith in Jesus Christ.

Summary

An overall view of the statistics of the Christian Church in Pakistan can be seen in Figures 35 and 36. The Roman Catholic Church is by far the largest single Church having a community of approximately 341,000 or

nearly 39 per cent of the whole Christian population.
The United Presbyterian Church was the largest Protestant
communion until 1970 when the Church of Pakistan was
formed from a merger of the Anglican, Methodist, Sialkot
Church Council and Lutheran Churches. These Churches
have a combined Christian community of 216,000 or 25
per cent of the total number of Christians. The U.P.
Church is close behind with 21 per cent and a community
of 187,000. All other denominations have a much smaller
constituency.

Figure 37 gives the exact number of Christian community
and of communicant members in each Church according to
the latest statistics available. The final column projects these official figures to 1972 on the basis of
the national population growth rate. The total number
of Christians at that time was approximately 878,000
or 1.36 per cent of the entire population of Pakistan.

Figures 39 and 40 compare the way the Protestant
Churches have grown from 1885 to the present. The U.P.
Church was not only much larger than the others, but
started to grow much sooner because they were the first
to accept the Chuhra movement as a bonafide work of God.
They had a Christian community of 10,000 before the
others had scarcely begun to grow. Figure 39 shows a
steep rise in growth during the last five years for all
Churches. This appears encouraging but is actually
deceiving because simple biological growth on a large
base adds up to many people. Figure 40 must be compared
in order to get the true picture. The top line of
Figure 40 shows the population growth rate for all of
Pakistan. The total Protestant growth rate is shown
just below, revealing the unhappy fact that Protestant
Churches are not even keeping up to their biological
growth rate. In other words, far from reaching out to
draw in many non-Christians, they are declining, unable
even to hold the children of present members in the
Protestant fold.

The steep climb shown from 1970 to 1973 on the U.P.
Church line is due to inaccurate statistics and does
not represent any actual growth. The only Protestant
group growing at a faster rate than population growth

is the Seventh Day Adventist Church who are gaining
members by transfer from other Christian communities.

Figure 41 compares the rate of growth of the Roman
Catholic and Protestant Churches to the national growth
rate. The Protestants increased greatly up to 1930 and
since then have not kept up with their biological growth
rate. The Roman Catholics grew very slowly up to 1900
but have increased steadily ever since, far exceeding
the rate of biological growth. The entire Christian
community, however, is rising at approximately the same
rate as the total population, another indication that
the increase in the Roman Catholic Church comes primarily as transfer growth from the Protestant Churches
with no significant progress being made by either group
in discipling the non-Christian population.

Figure 38 gives a list of the Missionary Societies
or Agencies with personnel in Pakistan. We have been
unable to find accurate statistics for the Roman Catholic
foreign personnel because their records combine both
foreign and national workers. Our estimate is that they
number at least 800, more than one and a half times the
number of Protestant missionaries. The United Presbyterian and The Evangelical Alliance Missions have the
most personnel among the Protestants. The Seventh Day
Adventists may equal them in number, but the records
available to us do not specify how many of their
workers are foreigners.

An analysis of the activities of Protestant missionary
personnel reveals a number of significant points. The
following data is based on the 1973 figures for the
personnel of each Mission. It is impossible to determine
accurately the type of work done by some individuals,
partly because the author is not personally acquainted
with them and their work but primarily because most
missionaries do a little of several different categories
of service. This has been taken into account whenever
possible; for instance, in cases where a missionary spends
half time with the Church and half time in evangelism
among non-Christians, he is given half a count in each
category. In spite of inaccuracies, this summary clearly
shows what work is being given priority in Pakistan today.

There were about 485 Protestant missionaries connected with all the Missions in Pakistan in 1973. (See Figure 38.) Of these, 262 belong to Missions established in Pakistan before World War II. The remaining 223, or nearly half, are members of new Missions, starting work in Pakistan following 1943. Forty-six missionaries are listed under the Seventh Day Adventist Mission. Since the author is not acquainted with the details of their work, their missionaries have been left out of the percentages given below. It is probable, however, that the S.D.A.'s do not take much active part in Muslim or tribal evangelism, but concentrate on education, medicine, literature, social work, and building up the Church.

Protestant missionaries (excluding the S.D.A.'s) give the majority of their time to the following activities.

TYPE OF WORK	PERCENTAGE OF MISSIONARIES
1. Building up the Church -- pastors, Bible School and Seminary professors, literacy, student work and college chaplains.	42 %
2. Medicine -- administrative and medical work in hospitals, clinics, or leper asylums.	22 %
3. Education -- schools (excluding Bible schools and Seminaries), colleges, and Murree Christian School for missionaries' children.	16 %
4. Muslim Evangelism -- evangelists, Bible Correspondence Schools, Christian Study Centre, radio ministry.	10 %
5. Administration of Mission Societies	4 %
6. Social Work, Agriculture, and Miscellaneous	3 %
7. Work Among Scheduled Castes	3 %

In spite of the large percentage of missionaries working directly or indirectly with the Church, Protestant Churches in Pakistan are not even keeping up with their biological growth rate.

Over forty per cent of the missionaries are in institutional or administrative posts that require a full working day devoted to the technical aspects of their work. Opportunities for witness and evangelism must be consciously sought on the job or after hours. These institutions perform many important and needed functions, but results in terms of baptized converts are negligible.

An equivalent of fifty full-time workers' efforts are going into Muslim evangelism, with an annual total of a score of baptized believers at the very most.

The Census Report for 1961 lists 37,593 Scheduled Caste people in the Punjab and 378,766 in Sindh. (See Figure 42.) Projected to 1973 at the annual population growth rate for Pakistan of 3.3 per cent, the total number of Scheduled Caste people in the country would have been 585,200. Wherever these census figures for the Scheduled Castes have been checked they have been found to be considerably lower than the actual number of people. Therefore we estimate that the number of Scheduled Caste people almost equal the Christian population in Pakistan.

Baptisms have been taking place among the Scheduled Caste tribal people on an average of 300 to 500 a year in recent years, in spite of the fact that at present only 14 missionaries are active in this work, and most of them have been in it for only a few years. If hundreds of tribal people have been won when all of the Missions in Pakistan combined have put only 3 per cent of their missionary staff and a fraction of their budget into this effort, what could happen if these and other

responsive segments of society were given <u>priority</u>
<u>status</u> in the work of most Missions? Then there would
be some hope of seeing church growth in Pakistan on
a scale that would delight the heart of the Good
Shepherd who rejoices with all the angels in heaven
whenever lost sheep are brought into the fold.

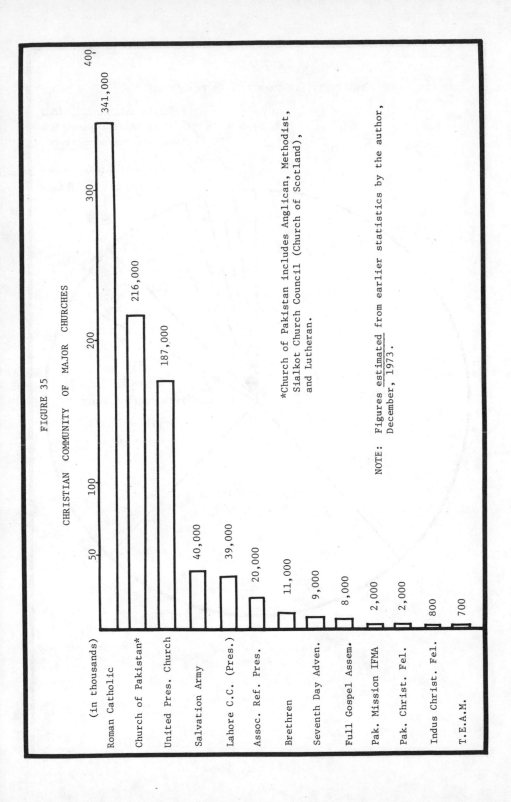

FIGURE 35

CHRISTIAN COMMUNITY OF MAJOR CHURCHES

*Church of Pakistan includes Anglican, Methodist, Sialkot Church Council (Church of Scotland), and Lutheran.

NOTE: Figures estimated from earlier statistics by the author, December, 1973.

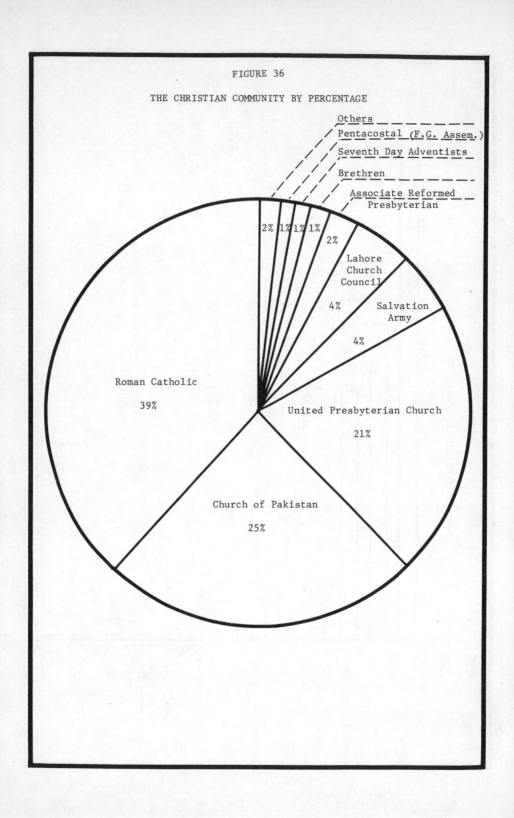

FIGURE 36

THE CHRISTIAN COMMUNITY BY PERCENTAGE

Others

Pentacostal (F.G. Assem.)

Seventh Day Adventists

Brethren

Associate Reformed Presbyterian

2% 1% 1% 1%

2%

Lahore Church Council

Salvation Army

4%

4%

Roman Catholic

39%

United Presbyterian Church

21%

Church of Pakistan

25%

CHURCH STATISTICS   FIGURE 37

Official figures are given below with the year of the data. The estimated community figure for 1972 is projected on the basis of a national growth rate of 3.3% and then the figure rounded off.

NAME OF CHURCH	COMMUNICANTS (Official Data)		COMMUNITY (Official Data)		ESTIMATED COMMUNITY '72
1. Roman Catholic	341,231	(72)	341,231	(72)	341,000
2. Church of Pakistan	58,370	(68)	202,000	(70)	216,000
3. United Presbyterian	53,240	(71)	187,000	(72)	187,000
4. Salvation Army	31,121	(73)	40,422	(72)	40,000
5. Lahore Church Council	13,200	(71)	37,975	(71)	39,000
6. Associate Reformed Pres.	4,232	(68)	17,519	(68)	20,000
7. Brethren	2,000	(68)	10,000	(68)	11,000
8. Seventh Day Adventist	2,518	(72)	8,800	(est)	9,000
9. Full Gospel Assemblies (Pentecostal)	2,318	(68)	6,892	(68)	8,000
10. Pakistan Mission of International Missions	220	(68)	2,000	(68)	2,000
11. Pakistan Christian Fellowship of I.C.F.	400	(67)	1,700	(67)	2,000
12. The Evangelical Alliance Mission	160	(69)	600	(69)	700
13. Conservative Baptist	396	(72)	794	(72)	800
14. World Wide Evangelization Crusade					200
15. Afghan Border Crusade					340
16. Baptist Bible Fellowship					300
17. Southern Baptist			291	(71)	290
TOTAL					877,630

FIGURE 38

MISSIONARY SOCIETIES AND AGENCIES

NAME OF MISSION	YEAR ENTERED	NO. OF MISS. IN 1973
1. Afghan Border Crusade	1944	6
2. Associate Reformed Presbyterian	1906	15
3. Baptist Bible Fellowship	1952	4
4. Baptist Independent	c.1958	2
5. Bible & Medical Missionary Fellowship	c.1893	23
6. Brethren Missionary Fellowship	1892	9
7. British Assemblies of God	c.1960	2
8. Child Evangelism Fellowship	c.1954	3
9. Christian Literature Crusade	1960	2
10. "Christians" (non-denominational)	c.1968	4
11. Church of Christ	c.1960	3
12. Church Missionary Societies:		
United Kingdom	1850	28
New Zealand	1918	14
Australia	1954	2
13. Church of Scotland	1856	12
14. Conservative Baptist	1954	16
15. Danish Pathan Mission (Lutheran)	1903	4
16. Finnish Missionary Society (Lutheran)	1960	21

MISSIONARY SOCIETIES AND AGENCIES (continued)

NAME OF MISSION	ENTERED	NO. OF MISS. IN 1973
17. (German Mission to Lepers)		c.4
18. International Christian Fellowship	1954	19
19. Kherwara Mission (Danish)	1956	2
20. Methodist College in Korea	c.1963	1
21. Murree Christian School	1955	8
22. Norwegian Mission to Moslems	1959	2
23. Pakistan Mission of International Missions Inc.	1955	12
24. PAX Service (Mennonite)	1960	2
25. Reformed Churches of the Netherlands	c.1958	11
26. Salvation Army	1883	21
27. Scandinavian Free Mission	1943	18
28. Service Overseas (German)		11
29. Seventh Day Adventist	1913	46
30. Society-in-Aid of the Pakistan Lutheran Church (Denmark)	1962	4
31. The Evangelical Alliance Mission	1946	45
32. United Fellowship for Christian Service (formerly Women's Union Miss. Soc.)	1956	8
33. United Methodist Church (U.S.A.)	1873	21
34. United Pentecostal Church	c.1969	5

NAME OF MISSION	ENTERED	NO. OF MISS. IN 1973
35. United Presbyterian Church (U.S.A.)	1849	48
36. United Society for the Propagation of the Gospel (Anglican)	c.1900	9
37. World Mission Prayer League (Lutheran)	1946	12
38. Worldwide Evangelization Crusade	1935	4
39. Independent Missionaries		8
	Total	491

ROMAN CATHOLIC WORKERS

These figures include both foreign and national workers. It has been impossible to determine what percentage of them are foreign, but I would estimate the number at 800. (Statistics from the Catholic Almanac 1974)

1.	Priests	229
2.	Men Under Religious Orders	233
3.	Women Under Religious Orders	585
4.	Workers in Schools	231
5.	Workers in Institutions	122
	Total	1,400

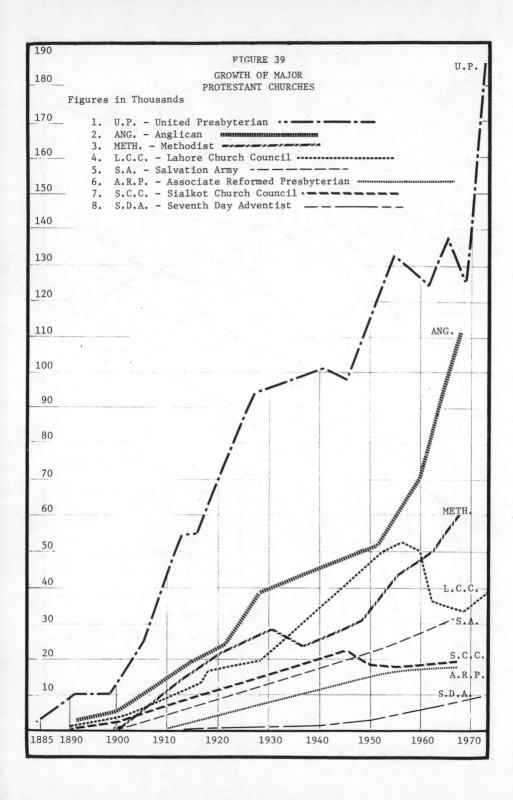

FIGURE 39

GROWTH OF MAJOR
PROTESTANT CHURCHES

Figures in Thousands

1. U.P. – United Presbyterian
2. ANG. – Anglican
3. METH. – Methodist
4. L.C.C. – Lahore Church Council
5. S.A. – Salvation Army
6. A.R.P. – Associate Reformed Presbyterian
7. S.C.C. – Sialkot Church Council
8. S.D.A. – Seventh Day Adventist

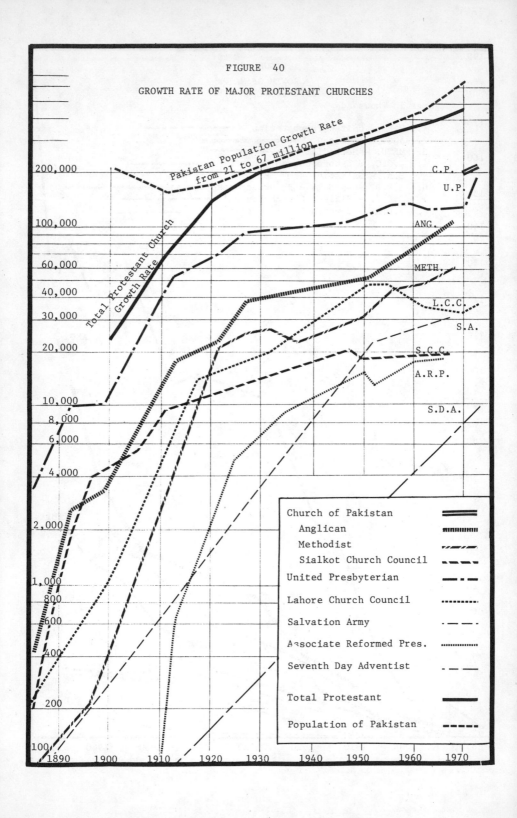

FIGURE 40

GROWTH RATE OF MAJOR PROTESTANT CHURCHES

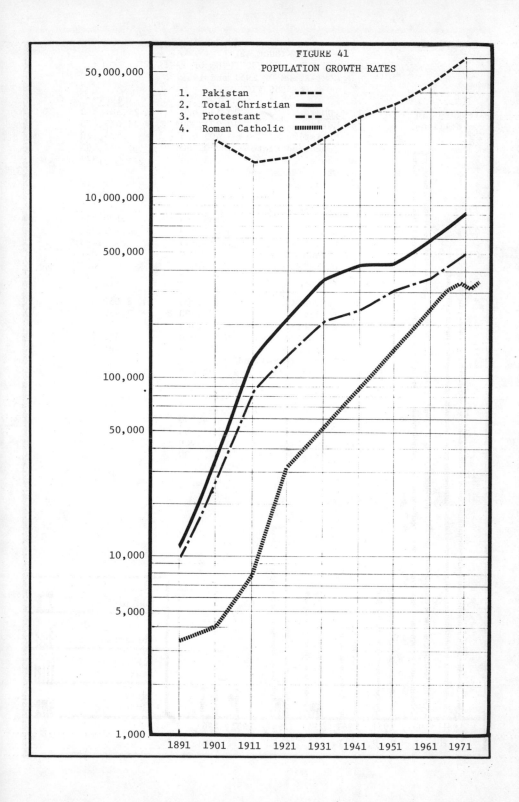

FIGURE 41
POPULATION GROWTH RATES

1. Pakistan   - - - - -
2. Total Christian ━━━━━
3. Protestant   ━·━·━
4. Roman Catholic ▥▥▥▥▥

FIGURE 42
RELIGION IN THE FOUR PROVINCES OF PAKISTAN
A COMPARISON OF 1951 and 1961
CENSUS FIGURES

		1951	1961
1.	PUNJAB	20,637,000	25,581,713
a.	Muslim	20,201,000	25,013,825
b.	Christian	403,000	524,770
c.	Scheduled Caste	30,000	37,593
d.	Caste Hindu	3,000	4,372
e.	Other (Parsi and Buddhist)		1,112
2.	NORTHWEST FRONTIER	5,865,000	4,140,247
a.	Muslim	5,858,000	4,131,087
b.	Christian	4,000	7,463
c.	Scheduled Caste	2,000	812
d.	Caste Hindus	1,000	663
e.	Others	0	79
3.	SINDH	5,748,000	8,559,538
a.	Muslim	5,536,000	7,936,979
b.	Christian	6,000	76,931
c.	Scheduled Caste	325,000	378,766
d.	Caste Hindu	146,000	189,764
e.	Others (Parsi and Buddhist)	7,000	7,098
4.	BALUCHISTAN	1,154,000	1,161,011
a.	Muslim	1,137,000	1,146,352
b.	Christian	4,000	4,720
c.	Scheduled Caste	1,000	840
d.	Caste Hindu	12,000	8,996
e.	Others	80	103

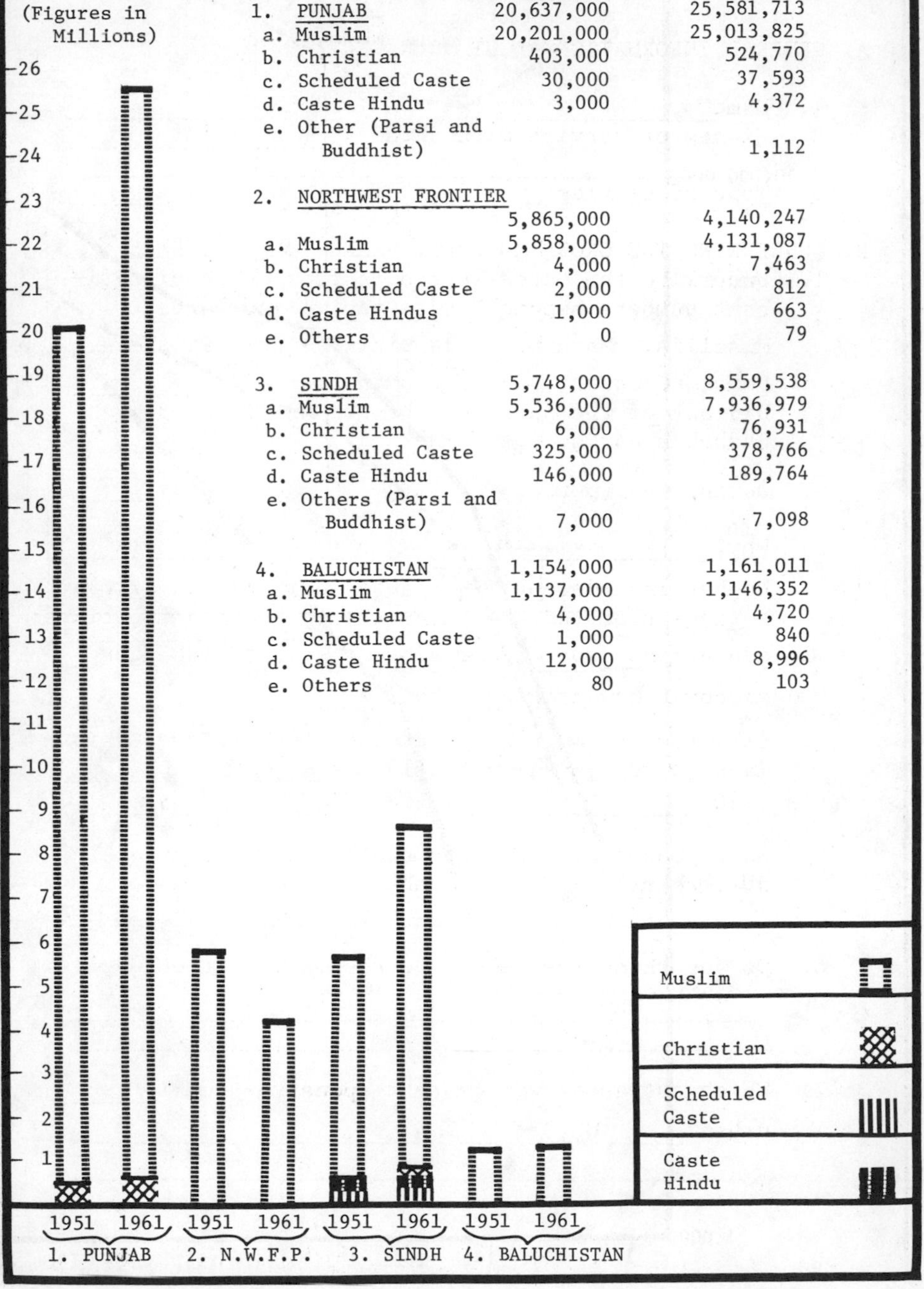

(Figures in Millions)

Legend:
- Muslim
- Christian
- Scheduled Caste
- Caste Hindu

1951 1961   1951 1961   1951 1961   1951 1961
1. PUNJAB   2. N.W.F.P.   3. SINDH   4. BALUCHISTAN

FIGURE 43

QUESTIONNAIRE

A. GENERAL INFORMATION ABOUT YOUR SERVICE

   1.   Name_____ Mission_____

   2.   Places of service with dates_____

       _____

   3.   Type of service_____

B. CONCERNING THE GROUP MOVEMENT AMONG THE OUTCASTES

   1.   Underline the outcaste groups from which significant numbers became Christians in your area:

       Musallis, Mazhabis, Balmikis, Chamars, Megs,

       Doms, Chuhras, Gagare. Any others?_____

   2.   Did any of the outcastes become Musallis or
Mazhabis during your time?_____

       During what period?_____How Many?_____

       Why?_____

   3.   Number in order of importance your opinion of what
motives prompted the outcastes to become Christians:

       education___social standing___spiritual hunger___

       economic advantages___other_____

   4.   Estimate the number of outcastes who become Christians in your area in the 1930's_____

       1940's_____1947 ff._____

   5.   What groups of outcastes are living in your area
at present? (Estimate number)_____

       _____

   6.   Do you think they would be responsive to evangelism?

       _____Why?_____

       _____

   7.   Which outcastes were more responsive--rural?_____

       urban?_____Why?_____

       _____

FIGURE 43 (continued)

C. CONCERNING THE REVIVAL PERIOD, 1904 ff.

1. Were any of the following a part of the Sialkot Convention revival? a. speaking in tongues_____ b. miracles of healing_____ c. other unusual manifestations_____

2. Until what date was the Sialkot Convention a source of <u>unusual</u> revival?_____

D. CONCERNING THE PENTECOSTAL CONTROVERSY IN THE U.P. MISSION IN THE 1920's.

1. What was the main issue?_____

2. How long did it cause tension?_____

3. Did other Missions have such a controversy?_____ Which ones?_____

4. Did nationals also speak in tongues?_____

   Approximately how many?_____

5. Did this result in any split in the national Church?_____

6. Did Synod deal with the problem at all?_____

   If so, how?_____

7. Did the controversy affect the growth of the Church in your opinion?_____

8. How many missionaries left over this issue?_____

9. Has any revival taken place in any portion of the U.P. area since this period?_____Where and when?_____

E. CONCERNING EFFORTS AMONG MUSLIMS, HIGH CASTE HINDUS, SIKHS, etc.

1. How many Muslims_____, High caste Hindus _____, Sikhs_____were baptized in your area during your time of service?

2. Number in order of importance your opinion of what motives prompted them to become Christians: education__, social betterment_____, spiritual hunger____, economic uplift_____, other (specify)

FIGURE 43 (continued)

3. What percentage apostatized? Muslims_____,
   High caste Hindus_____, Sikhs_____

4. What percentage of the outcaste converts apostatized?

   _____

5. What were the major reasons for high class converts
   apostatizing?_____

   _____

6. What were the reasons for outcastes apostatizing?

   _____

7. Do you know any higher caste converts who came as
   families? Explain._____

   _____

8. What methods have you found most successful in
   winning Muslims to Christ?_____

   _____

F. CONCERNING INSTITUTIONAL WORK

1. Do you feel that Christian institutions could be
   run on a self-support basis by Pakistanis?
   Schools (1st-10th)____, Colleges_____, Hospitals
   _____. If so, would they accomplish the
   purpose for which they were established?_____
   Explain_____

2. In the light of the development of government institutions, how necessary do you feel it is for the
   Church to continue operating Christian primary
   schools_____
   secondary schools_____
   colleges_____
   hospitals?_____

3. Do you think that well-run hostels in the cities
   to enable village children to study in city schools
   could adequately replace our boarding schools and
   colleges?_____Why?_____

   _____

4. Do you feel our institutions are important primarily for the uplift of the Christian community?___
   or for outreach to Muslims?_____
   Why?_____

FIGURE 43 (continued)

5. Do you feel they are adequately (enough to justify their existence and budget) fulfilling their purpose at present?_____

G. CONCERNING THE CHURCH AND EVANGELISM

1. Membership figures for the U.P. Church show a sharp rise of approximately 7,000 communicants immediately following Partition. What is the reason--conversion of large numbers of outcastes not wanting to leave Pakistan?_____

_____

Migration of Christians from India?_____
Padding of statistics to get more relief?_____

2. Now that the Church is responsible for its own work and independent of the U.S.A. Church, what do you feel should be the place and work of evangelistic missionaries? List any ideas below.

Bibliography

ADDLETON, Hugh
    1964   Circular Letter, October 1964

ALEXANDER, Mary Jane
    1942   *Voice of Pain*. Moultrie, Georgia, The
                Observer Printers Inc.

ALEXANDER, Minnie
    n.d.   *A.R.P.'s in India*. Charlotte, North
    c. 1912   Carolina, Observer Printing House,

    1951   *The Susquecentennial History of the Associate
                Reformed Presbyterian Church 1903-1951*.
                Chap. II, "Foreign Work Pakistan (India)"
                Clinton, S.C., Presses of Jacob Brothers
                Printers.

ANDERSON, Emma Dean, and CAMPBELL, Mary Jane
    1942   *In the Shadow of the Himalayas*. Philadelphia,
                Judson.

    1945   *The Birth of a Self Support Church in the
                Punjab India*. (no publisher mentioned)

    1945   *A Punjabi Crusader*. San Diego, California
                (no publisher mentioned).

ANDERSON, J.D.C.
    n.d.   *If Any Thirst*. Sandbach, Cheshire, Wright's
    c.1960   Ltd.

ANDERSON, William B., and WATSON, Charles R.
   1909   *Far North in India.* Philadelphia, Board of
               Foreign Missions of the United Presbyterian
               Church of North America.

ASHBY, C.M.
   1929-32   *The Haripur Bulletin,* Vol. I, Aug. 1929;
               July 1930, Dec. 1930; Vol. II, June 1931,
               Sept. 1931; Vol. III, June 1932, Dec.1932.

   1936-40   *Kashmir and Frontier Bulletin.* Dec. 1936,
               June 1938, Oct. 1938, Mar. 1939, June 1939,
               Aug. 1939, Dec. 1939, Oct. 1940.

ASIMI, Alfred Alla-ud-Dean
   1964   "Christian Minority in West Punjab." An
               unpublished Ph.D. dissertation, New York
               University.

BALLANTYNE, Agnes
   1950   *Witnessing in the Punjab.* Pittsburgh,
               Women's General Missionary Society of the
               U.P. Church of North America Literature
               Department.

BARCLAY, Wade C.
   1957   *History of Methodist Missions Part Two, The
               Methodist Episcopal Church 1845-1939 Vol. 3
               Widening Horizons 1845-1895.* New York, The
               Board of Missions of the Methodist Church.

BARRETT, David, ed.
   1973   *Kenya Churches Handbook, The Development of
               Kenya Christianity 1498-1973.* Kisumu, Kenya
               Evangel Publishing House.

BLONDEEL, Emmerich
   1973   "A Short History of the Catholic Diocese at
               Lahore-Part II." *Al Mushir (The Counselor),*
               Vol. XV, Nos. 1-3 Jan.-Mar. 34-40.

BRIGGS, George W.
   1953   *The Doms and Their Near Relations.* Mysore,
               India, Wesley.

BROWN, Arthur J.
   1936   *One Hundred Years.* New York, Revell.

BROWN, Frances E.
   1953   "Evangelistic Ministry – Sindh, *Women's
               Missionary Magazine*. (May) 572.

BUKER, Ray Jr.
   1965   Circular Letter, August 1965.

   n.d.   "The Marwaris." An unpublished study.
   c.1969

CAMPBELL, Earnest Y., ALTER, J.P., and JAI SINGH, Herbert
   1966   *The Church as Christian Community*. London,
               Lutterworth.

CAMPBELL, Mary J.
   1908   *Daughters of India*. Monmouth, Republican
               Atlas Printing Co.

   1918   *The Powerhouse at Pathankot*. Mysore City.
               Wesleyan Mission Press.

A CENTURY FOR CHRIST IN INDIA AND PAKISTAN 1855–1955
   1955   Lahore, W. Pakistan, M.I.K. Press.

CHURCH MISSIONARY SOCIETY OF THE ANGLICAN CHURCH
   1853–   *Annual Proceedings of the Church Missionary
   1950   Society*. 1853, 1855–1865, 1869–1877, 1879,
               1881–1905, 1907–1913, 1921–1950.

   1850–   Log Book, Hyderabad Sindh Mission, 1850–1933
   1933   (handwritten)

   1847–   Baptismal Record Books:
   1973   1. Badin, All Saints Church: 1958–1971
               2. Harperabad: 1921–1967
               3. Hyderabad, St. Phillip's Church: 1875–
                    1969.
               4. Karachi, Christ Church: 1898–1961.
               5. Karachi, Holy Trinity Church: 1847–1852;
                    1954–1970.
               6. Kotri: 1853–1922
               7. Mirpur Khas, St. John's Church: 1951–1971
               8. Sukkur: 1885–1959.
               9. Tando Adam: 1968–1973
             10. Tando Allah Yar, Church of Pakistan:
                    1959–1971.

CHURCH MISSIONARY SOCIETY OF NEW ZEALAND
   1937-47   "Christ Church Monthly News Sheets." Christ
              Church, Karachi, 1937-1947, Ed. by C.
              Haskell, Karachi.

   1953-62   "Sind Newsletter." Mar. 1953; Jan., April,
              June, Sept.-Dec. 1955; Dec. 1956; May, July,
              Oct., Dec. 1957; Aug., Nov. 1958; April,
              July 1959; March, June, Sept., Dec. 1960;
              April, July, Oct. 1961; April, July, Oct.
              1962.

   1963-74   "Sind Newsletter-West Pakistan." Sept.,
              Dec. 1963; Aug., Nov. 1964; March, June,
              Sept. 1965; May, Aug., Nov. 1966; July,
              Dec. 1967; Aug. 1968; April, Sept. 1969;
              June 1970; April 1971; June 1973; April
              1974.

CHURCH OF PAKISTAN
   n.d.   "Statistics of Membership, Workers and
   c.1968   Buildings." For the Church Union Committee,
              Sialkot, Pakistan. (mimeographed.)

CHURCH OF SCOTLAND
   1950-54   *Report of the Foreign Missions Committee
              of the Church of Scotland*. Submitted to
              the General Assembly. 1950-1954.

   1967-70   *The Overseas Council Report*. 1967-1970.
              Edinburgh, Foreign Mission Office.

COMFORT, Richard O.
   1957   *The Village Church in West Pakistan*. Lahore,
              Pakistan. Northern Pakistan Printing and
              Publishing Co.

CONSERVATIVE BAPTIST CHURCH
   1965-72   Baptismal Records of Dom Ji Phillip, 1965-
              1972.

COXILL, H., and GRUBB, Kenneth, ed.
   1952-67   *World Christian Handbook*. 1952, 1957, 1962,
              1967. New York, Abingdon.

COPPLESTONE,   J. Tremayne
1973   *History of Methodist Missions Vol. IV*
            Twentieth Century Perspectives.   New York,
            The Board of Global Ministries, The United
            Methodist Church.

CUNNINGHAM, J.D.
1918   *History of the Sikhs.*   London, Oxford
            University Press.

DAS, Andrew Thakur
1945   *Eminent Christians: Some Eminent Pastors*
            of the Punjab Church.   Lahore, Punjab
            Religious Book Society. (written in Urdu)

DOMMEN, Arthur
1968   "Untouchables of India Still Not Emancipated."
            Los Angeles Times, May 7, 1968.

FOREIGN MISSIONARY JUBILEE
1905   *Convention of the U.P.C.N.A. Fiftieth*
            Anniversary.   Philadelphia, Board of Foreign
            Missions of the U.P.C.N.A.

FOX, Felician
1973-   *The Catholic Alminac.*   Huntington, Indiana,
1974   Our Sunday Visitor, Inc.

FREITAG, Anton
1963   *The Twentieth Century Atlas of the Christian*
            World.   New York, Hawthorn Books, Inc.

GAIT, E.A.
1913   *Census of India 1911, Vol. I, Part I,*
            Calcutta, India, Superintendent Government
            Printing.

GODDARD, Burton, ed.
1967   *The Encyclopedia of Modern Christian Missions.*
            Camden, New Jersey, Thomas Nelson & Sons.

GORDON, Andrew
1886   *Our India Mission.* Philadelphia, Andrew
            Gordon.

GOVERNMENT OF INDIA
1912   *Census of India 1911, Vol. XIV, Punjab,* Parts
I & II. Lahore, Civil and Military Gazette.

1923   *Census of India 1921, Vol. XV, Punjab,and
Delhi,* Parts I & II. Middleton, L. and Jacob,
S.M., Lahore, Civil and Military Gazette.

1933   *Census of India, 1931, Vol. XVII,* Parts I
& II. Khan Ahmad Hasan Khan, Lahore, Civil
and Military Gazette.

GOVERNMENT OF PAKISTAN
1952   *Census of Pakistan 1951, Vol. I,* Aslam
Abdullah Khan, Lahore, Civil and Military
Gazette.

GREGORY, Kenneth
n.d.   *Stretching Out Continually; A History of*
c.1973   *the New Zealand Church Missionary Society
1892-1972.* R.W. Stiles & Co. Ltd.

HARES, W.P.
1927   "The Call From the Land of the Five Rivers."
in H. Whitehead, ed. Lahore, Pakistan.
(no publisher).

HASKELL, Charles W.
1957   *A Sinner in Sind.* Wellington, New Zealand
Wright and Carman, Ltd.

HAUSER, A.
1968   Interview on Brethren Churches in Pakistan.
September 28, 1968.

HEINRICH, John C.
1937   *The Psychology of a Suppressed People.*
London, George Allen and Unwin, Ltd.

HEWAT, Elizabeth
1960   *Vision and Achievement 1796-1956.* London,
Thomas Nelson and Sons.

HEWLETT, S.S.
  1909   *Mass Movements in Indian Evangelization.*
            Mussoorie, India, Mafaselite Printing Works.

HILLMAN, Eugene
  1965   *The Church as Mission.* New York, Herder
            and Herder.

HOLLISTER, John N.
  1956   *The Centenary of the Methodist Church in
            Southern Asia.* Lucknow, India, Lucknow
            Publishing House.

HOPKINS, Thomas J.
  1971   *The Hindu Religious Tradition.* Encino,
            California, Dickenson Publishing Company, Inc.

HULL, Ernest
  1913   "India," *The Catholic Encyclopedia.*
            Vol. VII: New York, the Encyclopedia
            Press Inc.

HUTTON, J.H.
  1963   *Caste in India.* London, Oxford University
            Press.

IBBETSON, Denzil
  1881   *Outlines of Punjab Ethnography - Extracts
            From the Census Report 1881,* Vol. I.,
            Calcutta, Superintendent of Government
            Printing.

IMAMUDIN, S.J.
  1968   *Fida-e-Salib.* Lahore, M.I.K. Press. (written
            in Urdu)

ISAACS, Harold
  1964   *India's Ex-Untouchables.* New York, The
            John Day Co.

KAUL, Harikishan
  1912   *Census of India 1911 Vol. XIV Punjab* Parts
            I & II. Lahore, Civil and Military Gazette.

KHAN, Ahmad Hasan
    1933   *Census of India 1931 Vol. XVII Punjab*
              Parts I & II. Lahore, Civil and Military
              Gazette.

KHAN, Aslam Abdullah
    1962   *Census Report Pakistan 1961, Vols. I & III*
              Lahore, Ilm Printing Press.

LALLEMAND, A.
    1950   "Pakistan," *The Catholic Encyclopedia,*
              Supplement II,Vol. XVIII.

LAMBERT, Richard D.
    1973   "Pakistan," *The Encyclopedia Americana,*
              Vol. 21. New York, Americana Corporation.

LATIMER, C.
    1912   *Census of India 1911 Vol. XIII Northwest*
              Frontier Province. Peshawar.

LEIDEN, Carl
    1973   "Pakistan." *The Encyclopedia Americana*
              1973 Annual. New York, Americana Corp.

LEWIS, Oscar
    1958   *Village Life in Northern India: Studies in*
              a Delhi Village. Urbana, University of
              Illinois.

LOEHLIN, C.H. and HAMILTON, B.L., ed.
    1931   *Self Support in Village Churches of India.*
              Bangalore, India, The Scripture Literature
              Press.

    1966   *The Christian Approach to the Sikh.*
              Edinburgh House Press.

LUCAS, Ed., and DAS, F. Thakur
    1938   *Research Studies in the Economic and Social*
              Environment of the Indian Church. Lahore,
              Northern India Printing and Publishing Co.

MACONACHIE, R.
    1917   *ROWLAND BATEMAN.* London, Church Missionary
              Society.

MANDELBAUM, David G.
  1972   *Society in India Vols. I & II.* Berkeley,
              University of California Press.

MARTIN, E. Josephine
  n.d.   *A Father to the Poor.* (no place) Published
  c.1955   by the descendants of Dr. & Mrs. Samuel
              Martin.

MARTIN, Samuel
  1893   "Second Paper" in *Report of the Third
              Decennial Missionary Conference* 1892-93
              Vol. I. Bombay, Education Society's Steam
              Press.

MASCARENHAS, Louis
  1967   "Pakistan," *The New Catholic Encyclopedia.*
              New York.

McCONNELEE, J.A.
  1909   "The Movement Among the Chuhras of the
              Punjab." in S. Hewlett, ed.

McGAVRAN, Donald A.
  1955   *The Bridges of God.* New York, Friendship
              Press.

  1955   *How Churches Grow.* New York, Friendship
              Press.

  1965   *Church Growth and Christian Mission.*
              New York, Harper and Row Publishers.

  1970   *Understanding Church Growth.* Grand Rapids,
              William B. Eerdmans Publishing Co.

McLEISH, Alexander
  1931   *The Frontier People of India.* London,
              World Dominion Press.

MERCER, Irene C.
  1934   *Seed Corn.* Pittsburgh, Board of Administra-
              tion of the United Presbyterian Church.

METHODIST CHURCH IN THE U.S.A.
1956-59   *Report of the Division of World Mission*
           of the Methodist Church. New York, Board
           of Missions of the Methodist Church 1956-
           1959.

1912-65   Baptismal Records:
           Karachi; Brooks Memorial Church: 1918-1965
           Hyderabad; Methodist Church: 1912-1938

METHODIST EPISCOPAL CHURCH
1922-52   *Minutes of the Indus River Conference 1922-*
           1952. Lucknow, India, Methodist Episcopal
           Church.

METHODIST CHURCH (UNITED METHODIST)
1972   *Project Handbook Overseas Mission of the*
           United Methodist Church. Cincinnati,
           Service Center Board of Missions.

MIDDLETON, L., and JACOB, S.M.
1923   *Census of India 1921 Vol. XV, Punjab and*
           Delhi, Parts I & II. Lahore, Civil and
           Military Gazette.

MILLER, Basil
1943   *Praying Hyde.* Grand Rapids, Michigan,
           Zondervan.

MILLIGAN, Anna B.
1921   *Facts and Folks in Our Fields Abroad*
           Philadelphia, United Presbyterian Board of
           Foreign Missions.

MISSION HANDBOOK
1973   *North American Protestant Ministries*
           Overseas Directory. 10th edition, Monrovia,
           California, MARC.

NANDA, B.R.
1958   *Mahatma Gandhi.* Boston, Beacon Press.

NEILL, Stephen
 1970   *The Story of the Christian Church in India
           and Pakistan.* Grand Rapids, Michigan,
           Eerdmans.

 1971   "Pakistan." *Concise Dictionary of the Christ-
           ian World.* New York.

NEWTON, John, HOLCOMB, H.H., and SEILER, G.W.
 1886   *Historical Sketches of the India Missions of
           the Presbyterian Church in the U.S.A.*
           Allahabad, India, Allahabad Mission Press.

ORR, J. Edwin
 1970   *Evangelical Awakenings in India,* New Delhi,
           National Printing Words.

 1973   *The Flaming Tongue.* Chicago, Moody Press.

PANIKKAR, K.M.
 1963   *The Foundations of New India.* George Allen
           and Urwin Ltd.

PARENT-TEACHERS ASSOCIATION DIRECTORY OF MISSION WORKERS
 1973   Mimeographed by Murree Christian School,
           Jhika Gali, Murree Hills, Pakistan.

PARSHALL, Phillip
 1974   "A Loving Approach to Islam." *Church Growth
           Bulletin,* Vol. X, No. 4:348-349, Pasadena.

PHILLIPS, G.E.
 1913   *The Outcastes' Hope.* Edinburgh, Turnbull
           and Spears.

PICKETT, J. Waskom
 1933   *Christian Mass Movements in India,* New York,
           Abingdon.

 1938   *Christ's Way to India's Heart.* Lucknow,
           Lucknow Publishing House.

PRESBYTERIAN CHURCH IN THE U.S.A.
     1859-   *Minutes of the General Assembly of the*
     1973   *Presbyterian Church in the U.S.A. Part I:*
                 1859, 1860, 1868-87, 1889-97, 1899, 1901-03,
                 1906-20, 1921-36, 1953-55, 1957-73.

     1888-   *Part II:* 1888, 1890-92, 1894, 1896-98, 1903,
     1970   1912, 1915-16, 1921-70.

     1883-   *Annual Reports of the Lodiana Mission of the*
     1931   *Presbyterian Church of the U.S.A.* 1883, 1894,
                 1896, 1907-1911, 1912-1918, 1920-1922, 1923-
                 1931.

     1906   Board of Foreign Missions Correspondence,
                 India. Vol. 164-32:3,4. Punjab, India.
                 (m/f used)

     1907   *The President's Report on the Work of the*
                 Punjab Mission of the Presbyterian Church in
                 the U.S.A. Ludhiana, Ludhiana Mission Steam
                 Press.

     1917-   *Annual Meeting Minutes of the Punjab Mission*
     1935   *of the Presbyterian Church in the U.S.A.,*
                 1917-19, 1931-35.

     1925-   *Minutes of the Joint Committees and Inter-*
     1945   *mediary Boards of the United Church of India*
                 (North) and the Punjab Mission of the
                 Presbyterian Church in the U.S.A. 1925-27,
                 1930-32, 1935, 1945.

     1938   *Report on Study of Work, Central Board of*
                 the Punjab Mission Area, 1938, Lahore,
                 Northern India Printing & Publishing Co.

     1951-   *Annual Meeting Minutes of the Lahore Church*
     1952   *Council,* 1951, 1952. Lahore

PUNJAB CHRISTIAN COUNCIL
     1926   *Proceedings of the Fourteenth Annual Meeting*
                 at Lahore. Mysore, Wesleyan Mission Press.

RALSTON, Benjamin
     1965   Circular Letter, April 1965.

READ, William R.
1965   *New Patterns of Church Growth in Brazil.*
         Grand Rapids, Michigan, Eerdmans Publishing
         Co.

REPORT OF THE THIRD DECENNIAL MISSIONARY CONFERENCE 1892–
1893.
1893   Bombay, Education Society's Steam Press.

REPORT ON STUDY OF WORK.
1938   Lahore, Northern India Printing & Publishing
         Co.

RINGER, Jack
1970   Interview concerning the Afghan Border
         Crusade.

ROSE, Horace A.
1911   *A Glossary of Tribes and Castes of the Punjab
         and Northwest Frontier Province.* Vols.I & II.,
         Lahore, Civil and Military Gazette Press.

ROSS, Edith W.
1953   "Evangelistic Ministry - Lyallpur and Thall."
         Women's Missionary Magazine. (May) 573.

SALVATION ARMY
1968   *The Salvation Army Year Book.* Published Annually.
         London, Salvationist Publishing and Supplied,
         Ltd.

SMITH, Daniel
1959   *Bakht Singh of India, A Prophet of God.*
         Washington D.C., International Students Press.

STACEY, Vivienne
1960   *The Islamic Republic.* The B.M.M.F. in West
         Pakistan. Sandbach, Cheshire, Wright's Printers.

1965   *Asian Frontiers.* B.M.M.F. Sandbach, Cheshire,
         Wright's Printers.

1969   *Focus on Pakistan.* B.M.M.F. London, Bradley
         and Sons Ltd.

STEWART, Robert
    1896   *Life and Work in India.* Philadelphia, Pearl
                Publishing Co.

    1899   Second edition.

STOCK, Eugene
    1899-   *The History of the Church Missionary Society.*
    1916   London, Church Missionary Society, Vols. II,
                III, & IV.

STRICKLER, Herbert J.
    1926   "The Religion and Customs of the Chuhra in
                the Punjab Province of India." An unpublished
                M.A. Thesis, University of Kansas.

SYNOD OF THE PUNJAB OF THE UNITED PRESBYTERIAN CHURCH OF
NORTH AMERICA.
    1905-   *Annual Meeting Minutes.* 1905 (English),
    1969   1929 (Urdu), 1969 (Urdu).

TAYLOR, Lechmere
    1906   *In the Land of the Five Rivers,* Edinburgh,
                R. & R. Clark, Ltd.

TIPPETT, Alan R.
    1970   *Church Growth and the Word of God,* Grand
                Rapids, Michigan, William B. Eerdmans
                Publishing Co.

ULLAH, Barkat
    1957   *Eminent Christians No. 2. The Pioneer
                Missionaries of the Punjab.* Lahore,
                Punjab Religious Book Society. (Written in
                Urdu).

    1959   *Ihsan Ullah, Master Builder of the Punjab
                Church.* Lahore, Punjab Religious Book
                Society. (Written in Urdu).

UNITED PRESBYTERIAN CHURCH OF NORTH AMERICA

1856–   *Annual Minutes of the Sialkot Mission.*
1967   (m/f 4 rolls) 1856–1961, 1962, 1963, 1967.

1856   The Session Book of the Congregation of the
         Associate Church of Sialkot 1856–83. (Hand-
         written)

1868–   *Minutes of the General Assembly of the United*
1960   *Presbyterian Church of North America.* 1868–
         1960. (See Presbyterian Mission for 1961 ff.)

1882–   *Annual Reports of the American United Presby-*
1913   *terian Mission in India of the U.P. Church*
         of America. 1882–1885, 1898, 1900, 1903, 1905,
         1912, 1913.

1895–   *Annual Report of the Board of Foreign Missions*
1959   *Presented to the General Assembly of the U.P.*
         Church of North America. 1895, 1915, 1935–37,
         1939, 1941, 1944, 1945, 1947, 1955, 1957, By
         C.O.E.M.A.R. in 1959.

1910–   *Foreign Mission Handbook.* United Presbyterian
1953   Church of North America. 1910, 1912–26, 1941
         1947, 1953.

1916   *After Sixty Years.* Produced by the Indian
         Mission of the United Presbyterian Church of
         North America.

1919–   *Triennial Reports of the Foreign Mission of*
1930   *the U.P. Church of North America,* 1919–1930.

1920   *The Five Years' Program for Foreign Missions*
         of the United Presbyterian Church of North
         America. (no place), Board of Foreign Missions
         of the U.P. Church of N.A.

1923   *Findings Report.   Mission and Board Secretaries'*
         Conference 1923. Lahore, Civil and Military
         Gazette Press.

UNITED PRESBYTERIAN CHURCH OF NORTH AMERICA (continued)
1924   *Report of the Deputation to the Field in*
            1923-24 to the Board of Foreign Missions.
            Philadelphia, Board of Foreign Missions of
            the U.P. Church of N.A.

1931-   *Annual Reports of the Foreign Mission of the*
1941   *U.P. Church of North America, 1931-1933, 1941.*

VAN MILTENBURG, Alcuin
1947   *In the Land of the Sindhi and the Baluchi,*
            Karachi, Rotti Press.

VELTE, H.C.
1929   *Survey of the Evangelistic Work of the Punjab*
            Mission of the Presbyterian Church in the
            U.S.A. Lucknow, India, Methodist Publishing
            House.

VEMMELUND, Laurits
1972   *The Christian Minority in the Northwest*
            Frontier Province. Rawalpindi, Pakistan,
            Ferozsons.

WAGNER, Peter
1971   *Frontiers in Missionary Strategy.* Chicago,
            Moody Press.

WALTON, Sir John Charles
1962   "Pakistan." *Encyclopedia Britannica, Vol. 17,*
            Chicago, Encyclopedia Britannica Inc.

WATSON, Charles
1905   *In the King's Service.* Philadelphia, Board of
            Foreign Missions of the United Presbyterian
            Church of North America.

WHITEHEAD, Henry, ed.
1927   *C.M.S. Mass Movement Surveys, India.*
            Paugbourne, India. (no publisher)

YOUNG, William G.
    1971   "The Life and History of the Church in Pakistan."
                Al Mushir (The Counselor). Vol. XIII, No.
                9-10, Sept.-Oct., pp. 1-14. Rawalpindi,
                Pakistan, Ferozsons Press.

    n.d.   *Writers and Translators of the Hymns of the*
    c.1973   *Sialkot Convention Hymn Book*. Lahore, M.I.K.
                Press. (in Urdu).

YOUNGSON, John F.
    1896   *Forty Years of the Punjab Mission of the*
                Church of Scotland. Edinburgh, R. & R. Clark
                Ltd.

    1930   "Chuhras," *Encyclopedia of Religion and*
                Ethics.   Vol. III, Edinburgh, T. & T. Clark.

Index

The Stock Family in Kutchi Kohli dress. Back: Fred, Paul, Sara, Dale. Front: Ruth, Lois, Margaret.

The Rev. Frederick E. Stock received the B.S. degree from the University of California at Berkeley, the Bachelor of Sacred Theology from Biblical Seminary, the Masters of Theology from Princeton Theological Seminary, and the M.A. in Missiology from Fuller Seminary School of World Mission.

Margaret A. Stock is a third generation missionary, daughter of Dr. and Mrs. J. Lowrie Anderson who served 46 years in the Sudan, Lebanon, and Kenya. She received the B.S. at West-minster, New Wilmington, and the Masters of Religious Educa-tion from Biblical Seminary.

Until 1970 the Stocks were located in the Punjab at Sargodha developing the ministry through Bible Institutes, youth work, stewardship programs, and literacy classes. They then moved to Hyderabad, Sindh, in order to survey evangelistic oppor-tunities among Scheduled Caste tribal people. The couple is presently developing more effective means of evangelism and church growth among these responsive people.